D1568775

Gun Women

Gun Women

Firearms and Feminism in Contemporary America

MARY ZEISS STANGE AND CAROL K. OYSTER

NEW YORK UNIVERSITY PRESS

New York and London

NEW YORK UNIVERSITY PRESS
New York and London

Library of Congress Cataloging-in-Publication Data
Stange, Mary Zeiss.
Gun women : firearms and feminism in contemporary America /
Mary Zeiss Stange and Carol K. Oyster.
p. cm.
Includes bibliographical references and index.
ISBN 0-8147-9760-1 (acid-free)
1. Gun control—United States—Public opinion. 2. Women—United States—
Attitudes. 3. Firearm owners—United States. 4. Women hunters—United
States. 5. Public opinion—United States.   I. Oyster, Carol K. II. Title.
HV7436 .S73 2000
363.3'3'0820973—dc21   00-009690

New York University Press books are printed on acid-free paper,
and their binding materials are chosen for strength and durability.

Manufactured in the United States of America
10 9 8 7 6 5 4 3 2 1

for Doug
always, and in all ways

and

for Katherine,
my daughter,
an aspiring gun woman

Contents

All illustrations appear as a group following p. 110.

Acknowledgments

Gun Women, in one sense, is the product of a two-year collaboration between its authors. Yet, in another and broader way, it is the result of a decade's worth of critical conversation about women, guns, and feminism. We thank Don B. Kates, Jr., for initially involving each of us in that conversation, for serving over the years as a near-inexhaustible source of information on gun-related issues, and especially for introducing us to each other in 1997 on the hunch that we might hit it off, and setting the stage for this collaboration. Others who have helped shape our thinking about women and firearms, and without whose insights or scholarship this book could not have happened, include Mark Benenson, Kitty Beuchert, Paul Blackman, Robert Cottrol, Jan Dizard, Frances Haga, C. B. Kates, Gary Kleck, David Kopel, Nicholas Johnson, Alan Lizotte, John Lott, Gary Mauser, Joseph Olson, and Penelope Ploughman. We also must thank Martha McCaughey, both for her scholarship and for the faith she gives us that Third Wave feminism indeed has a future!

Our special gratitude goes to the women who contributed the personal narratives that precede each chapter—Susan Ewing, Jennifer Gwyn, Abigail Kohn, Vivian Lord, and Peggy Tartaro—as well as those who are the subjects of Nancy Floyd's photographs. Their voices, along with those of the many women we interviewed and surveyed for chapters 2, 3, 4, and 5, added untold richness and depth to our thinking and our writing. This book is, ultimately, theirs.

Additionally, Mary Stange wishes especially to acknowledge the following: Shari LeGate of the Women's Shooting Sports Foundation, Diane Lueck of the "Becoming an Outdoors-Woman" Program, and

Peggy Tartaro of *Women & Guns* magazine for information they provided along the way; Sandra Froman and Edie Reynolds for getting questionnaires into the e-mail boxes of gun women across the country; and Eva Hatenboer and Rebecca Burnham of the Philosophy and Religion Department of Skidmore College for providing research assistance and clerical support.

Carol Oyster is especially grateful to Paul Petterson for providing me with contacts such as Aaron Zellman and the important work on police responsibility, Joe Roberts of the National Rifle Association for searching the archives to provide me with historical references and contacts, and Special Agent Roger Trotter of the Federal Bureau of Investigation for facilitating my access to the remarkable women of the FBI. Thanks, too, to Gary Kleck and Gary Mauser for helping sort out the literature on defensive gun uses.

We are deeply grateful to Niko Pfund at New York University Press for his patience, humor, and editorial guidance that improved the book while keeping it true to our original intent, and preserving our voices as authors. Thanks, too, to NYU Press's managing editor Despina Papazoglou Gimbel for the care with which she guided the manuscript through publication. We are indebted to Douglas C. Stange, for coming up with the book's title, as well as with the idea on which the cover design is based.

Portions of chapter 1 originally appeared, in different form, in "Arms and the Woman: A Feminist Reappraisal," in David B. Kopel, ed., *Guns: Who Should Have Them?* (Amherst, New York: Prometheus Books, 1995).

Introduction

Pro-Firearms, Pro-Feminist

This book's authors are gun women. We own and use firearms for a variety of good reasons. We know many other women who do, too. Like most of those women, we are concerned about knee-jerk anti-gun rhetoric, and the tendency for the debate over guns and gun control to degenerate into name-calling between "bleeding-heart liberals" and "gun nuts." Like other gun women, we are also concerned about the potential erosion of our right to keep and bear arms. This does not mean we are opposed to reasonable gun control. Indeed, quite the opposite. Like most gun owners—the law-abiding majority, at any rate—we accept and affirm that reasonable forms of firearms regulation are necessary and important. However, the arguments for and against specific forms of gun control fall outside the scope of this book. Somewhere between eleven and seventeen million American women currently own guns.[1] We are interested in the positive impact of firearms on the lives of these women.

The book is also unashamedly feminist. Some of our sister gun women call themselves feminist; many do not. These days, the decision whether or not to apply the "F-word" to oneself seems, almost inevitably, to depend upon where a woman wants to stake her claim in the political landscape. And, thanks largely to the media's drive to oversimplify any and every issue for the sake of its speedy presentation, that terrain tends to appear flatter, to the casual onlooker, than it really is. It is, in fact, possible to be politically progressive and vigorously pro-gun, just as it is possible to be politically conservative and determinedly pro-choice. Yet most people, whether scholars or laypersons, like to equate gun owning with conservatism, and feminism with liberalism. The realities are far more complex. Gun owners, male and female, represent an array of political and social perspectives. So, of course, do feminists.

These days, more people get more of what they know, or think they know, about guns from soundbites than from sound reasoning. Unfortunately, this seems especially true for the majority of feminists who equate feminism with being anti-gun. Indeed, given the prevailingly anti-gun climate in most feminist circles, it is remarkable that many gun women nevertheless do draw a direct relationship between their feminism and their firearms. It's hard, after all, to proclaim solidarity with a movement that has, by and large, rejected you. Whether gun-owning women should identify with feminism is, in our view, ultimately a matter of choice for them. Far more to the point of this book we contend that feminists should pay serious, constructive attention to the fact that millions of women are not only armed, but also derive immense satisfaction and empowerment from owning and using guns.

Feminist scholars, journalists, jurists, and activists have devoted thousands of pages to arguing the evils of firearms, especially in relation to women. It is time we looked at the ways in which guns can be good for women. This book intends to open up the conversation about women and guns in America. We make no claim for its being the last word on the subject of feminism and firearms. Indeed, it is virtually the first word. Very few feminist writers have seen women's gun use as a positive thing; they are cited in the chapters that follow. This relative handful have either written short articles on the subject or mentioned it in the course of developing other, larger themes. *Gun Women* is the first book-length study devoted to exploring the positive feminist implications of women's gun use and ownership.

Aside from its pro-firearms/pro-feminist orientation, two other characteristics distinguish this book from other works on the subject of women and guns. The first is that we do not intend to "preach to the choir" about the advantages of women's gun ownership. We trust, of course, that gun owners and enthusiasts, both female and male, will find much to like and to agree with here. They will probably also find things they don't like so much, and that's as it should be. Books like Paxton Quigley's *Armed and Female* and Tanya Metaksa's *Safe, Not Sorry,* which argue, fairly and persuasively, for women's gun ownership, already exist. But one was written by a spokesperson for a firearms manufacturer, the other by an official of the National Rifle Association. We do not intend to advance the agenda of any special interest group, regardless of our personal affiliations and individual interests.[2]

In fact, we are equally alarmed by the excesses displayed by advocates at either end of the political spectrum when it comes to guns and gun control. In our experience, both as scholars and as gun women, the truth lies less between than beyond the extremes of a discourse about guns which too often, on both sides, degenerates into ranting and name calling. However, it is undeniably the case that the American news media have by and large aided and abetted the anti-gun side of the argument. As constitutional scholar Don B. Kates, Jr., remarks:

In general, American news media do not air indiscriminate stereotypical condemnations of entire groups. But to this general rule there is one exception. As a class, gun owners are routinely reviled by editorials, columns, and cartoons characterizing them as "gun lunatics who silence the sounds of civilization," "gun nuts," "gun fetishists," "traitors, enemies of their own patriae*," "anticitizens," "terrorists," sexually warped "bulletbrains," Klansmen, thugs, and vigilantes who represent "the worst instincts in the human character."*[3]

It's hard not to take this sort of invective personally, which may help to account for the fact that the debate over guns tends to be so polarized. And the popular media seem to thrive on fostering this polarization. A study recently released by the Media Research Center reported that between June 1997 and June 1999, the major television networks aired 653 stories dealing in one way or another with gun policy. According to the report, 393 of these stories—well over half— could be characterized less as straight reporting than as advocacy, and of these stories nine out of ten presented an anti-gun perspective.[4]

Meanwhile, Brian Patrick of the University of Michigan surveyed the way five national newspapers (*New York Times, Washington Post, Wall Street Journal, Los Angeles Times,* and *Christian Science Monitor*) handled stories about five special interest lobbies: American Association of Retired Persons (AARP), the American Civil Liberties Union (ACLU), the National Association for the Advancement of Colored People (NAACP), Handgun Control, Inc. (HCI), and the National Rifle Association (NRA). In the 1,500 articles, columns, editorials, and letters to the editor that Patrick collected between 1990 and 1998, he found the NRA was referred to in terms that were consistently, and tellingly, different from those applied to the other groups. For example, the NAACP was accorded the status of "venerable civil rights organization" and "national civil rights group." The ACLU was typically referred to as "a leading champion" of civil liberties or an "abortion rights group." HCI was labeled a "citizens' lobby," a "non-profit organization" or "public interest group." Yet the NRA, also non-profit and also a citizens' lobby, was more likely to receive such labels as "powerful gun lobby," "strident lobby for the nation's gun manufacturers," "most feared lobby," "intimidating lobby of weapons peddlers," "the Beltway's loudest lobby," "a rich and paranoid organization," a "gun lobby consisting of everything from neo-Nazis to nature-loving hunters."

Press accounts similarly accord different weight to these lobbying groups as sources of information. When the AARP provides information about senior citizens for a story, we are told the organization "concludes" or "documents" or "reports." When the NAACP is the source on race-related issues, its facts are "declared" or "announced." But when the NRA provides information about guns and gun use, the organization "claims," "contends," "likes to portray," or "alleges."[5] There is more than a little irony in all this. HCI commandeered the public-informational high ground only fairly recently, in the early nineteen-nineties, on the basis of a number of federally funded studies that achieved results showing guns (particularly handguns) to be a menace to the public health in general, and to women's health in particular.[6] Before then, print media and broadcast networks seeking factual and demographic information on firearms and their use customarily looked to the NRA for that information and repeated it uncritically, even in the context of features with an anti-firearms thrust. This stood to reason. As the nation's largest and oldest organization devoted to firearms use and ownership (the nearly three-million-member NRA was founded in 1871), the National Rifle Association had the best and most extensive records on the subject.[7] The press called into question the reliability of the NRA's data only when another "citizens' lobby" stepped forward with information that appeared to conflict with it.

Now, our point here is not necessarily to uphold the reliability of the NRA's information over that of its ideological opposite number, although, as we shall argue below, there are some good reasons why HCI's information may indeed be less trustworthy. Those reasons have less, however, to do with the numbers reported than with the ideological bent of the persons manipulating them. And given the ideologically freighted way in which an ostensibly impartial press tends to portray guns and gun-related issues, it is no wonder that many people view gun use less as a pastime than as a pathology.[8] A further bit of irony emerges here: the same anti-gun studies that provide grist for the media's mill rely in turn on anti-gun press reports as *their* sources regarding the nature and extent of gun-related violence in America.[9]

What one loses sight of in all of this are the facts that approximately half of all American households have one or more firearms present, and most of these firearms are legally owned and used by normal, well-balanced adults, a growing number of whom appear to be female. And so the second factor that sets this book apart from other works about women and guns has to do with our approach to the facts available to us. We aim to tell the truth about women and guns. However, we recognize that getting at that truth means wading through statistics that are often skewed; weighing statements about "facts" that are actually matters of opinion—albeit frequently heartfelt opinion; and confronting other aspects of guns and gun ownership that are indeed matters of fact, but can be understood only in their appropriate contexts. Throughout this book, we are frank with the reader about the nature and limits of the numerical and other resources to which scholars and activists equally appeal to build their cases for or against firearms. There are no gospel truths, no self-evident facts when it comes to guns. We have come to believe that those who suggest there are, are the least dependable commentators on the subject.

Very early on in researching this book, we discovered that we had an additional problem to confront. We were intending to document the experiences of invisible women. Not only is it impossible to ascertain the precise number of women who own or have access to or regularly use firearms, the extensive social-scientific literature on guns and their use almost invariably fails to take gender into account. Thus, most of the conclusions extrapolated from that literature arise from and support a masculine perspective on guns and gun use—since conventionally, most gun owners and users have been males, as have most victims of gun-related violence. How, we wondered, might the numbers look different if we recognized that a small, but nevertheless significant, proportion of guns are in women's hands? How might the debate about guns and gun control change if female gun owners were taken into account? And how might our cultural conversation about guns and violence be deepened, enhanced, and, yes, further complicated, if we were to put firearms and feminism into the same conceptual framework?

In what follows, our concern is more to raise than to answer questions like these. American gun women need first to be brought into the light of day, their voices to be heard. This will mean challenging some conventional ideas about women's capacity for taking instruments of power into their own hands, ideas with which feminists and anti-feminists have often been equally comfortable. It will mean shattering some stereotypes and reevaluating some truths about female weakness, fear, vulnerability, and nonaggressiveness. And it may just mean that men will have to alter the way they look at themselves as well as at women. In short, we have written this book because we believe that American gun women, invisible and silent no longer, can make an enormous difference in the way we understand ourselves, our culture, and the problems we as a society are confronting today. We hope you, the reader, will agree.

A Note to the Reader

In the chapters that follow, if citations to other sources are not provided, statements quoted from or attributed to individual gun women derive from interviews conducted by the authors or correspondence with them.

Snapshot

Mary Zeiss Stange, *Trajectories*

I.

"So, you want to go out back and do some plinking?"

Plinking? What on earth was he talking about? I was visiting relatives in Connecticut. My cousin Bobby, the family cutup, was bored. He figured a little shooting would help pass the time.

"It's a lot of fun, really," he urged me, in the face of what must have been my most studied and incredulous stare. "We take my .22 and a few empty cans down to the end of the yard, where the woods start. Set the cans up along the fence and blast. It's easy. Don't worry, we won't keep score or anything. We'll just shoot for fun."

As part of my mind tried to wrap itself around the notion that my goofily lovable sixteen-year-old cousin owned and actually shot a real gun, the other part struggled to frame a response to his invitation. "Uh, no, thanks," I smiled.

"Why not?" he teased. "You're not scared of guns, are you?"

"Oh, no. I'm just afraid I might enjoy it."

"Suit yourself." He shrugged—after all, he was just trying to be a good host—and grabbed a box of ammo and his gun. For the next hour or so, conversation around the kitchen table was punctuated by the popping of Bobby's rifle. His parents seemed to find this the most natural thing in the world. Amazing, I thought, the things we don't know about our relatives.

To plink, or not to plink. That had been the seemingly innocuous question. I was a grown woman, in my mid-twenties. Finishing my doctoral course work and embarking on a college teaching career. Flirting with Second Wave feminism. Doing serious scholarship. And stopped dead in my tracks by a good-natured invitation to pick up a gun and shoot it.

"I'm afraid I might enjoy it." The words had startled me, even as I spoke them. At the time, I rationalized my response: no point in taking up an activity I wouldn't be able to pursue. Besides, I didn't need to know anything about guns. Besides, I was a pacifist. Besides, guns were all about masculinity. Besides . . .

But I knew, of course. I had felt it deep down, buried so snugly that I could scarcely acknowledge its presence. The sense of thrill, of forbidden fruit. What exactly was I afraid of? Not the gun, oddly enough, but the enjoyment of it. I tucked that brainteaser neatly away, before the issues it raised could become too nettlesome. It nestled in my memory, somewhere in the neighborhood of my girlhood fantasies of trick riding with Annie Oakley, armed with my pearl-handled Dale Evans six-shooters, the ones that had come complete with a "silver"-tooled cartridge belt and a supply of red plastic bullets.

Aside from those toy pistols, guns had not been a factor one way or the other in my growing-up. An only child, I'd had indulgent parents who gave me pretty much whatever I wanted and led me to believe I could be pretty much whatever I wanted to be. A member of the first TV generation, my action fantasies were shaped by Davey Crockett and Daniel Boone, *Wagon Train* and life on the Ponderosa. I also read a lot. My tastes ran less to *Little Women* than to *Treasure Island*. I enjoyed the classic Nancy Drew books: the ones where our teenage sleuth drove a roadster and carried a pistol. When we played "Clue," I liked it best when Miss Scarlett used the gun in the library.

But if guns were as natural a part of my girlhood fantasies as horses or sporty cars, they were just as "naturally" foreign to the suburban New Jersey world in which I actually lived. I knew our next-door neighbors had guns; their two boys were scouts and went camping and hunting. On my sixth birthday, the older boy had used the balloons strung up in our backyard for target practice with his BB gun. Of course, in my pink-ruffled party dress, I didn't think this was at all funny. I remember my parents, and his, trying awfully hard to suppress their chuckles as they read him the riot act over it.

Twenty-five years would have to pass before I would come to understand how irresistible those targets must have looked to him.

II.

In 1982 I fell in love with the man I would marry the following year. Doug was a teaching colleague of mine, a social and political progressive, with two doctoral degrees. He was proud to say he was a feminist, before that was fashionable for men. He was also a lifelong hunter, and self-described "gun nut." We agreed that since there were going to be firearms in the house, I would have to familiarize myself, at the very least, with the basics of their safe handling. One afternoon during our courtship, he said, "Let me introduce you to one of my guns." He withdrew from its case a Colt-Sauer bolt-action rifle.

"How, um, high-powered is it?" I asked, hoping not to sound as ignorant as we both knew perfectly well I was.

"It's a .270 Winchester—a good all-round big-game caliber. Flat-shooting. This gun's a real tack driver."

"Winchester? I thought you said it was a Colt-Sauer?"

"That's the ammo. They call it that because Winchester developed it. Actually, the .270 is necked down from the .30-06 Springfield." And so on. For the next ten minutes or so, he might as well have been speaking Chinese, for all I comprehended about bullets, calibers, and cartridges. But one thing was clear to me: the rifle that I held, gingerly, across my lap was a beautiful piece of craftsmanship, its dark wood gorgeously grained and highly polished, the blued metal agleam from a recent oiling. The gun's weight surprised me; with the scope, it must have been close to nine pounds. It never occurred to me to even try shouldering it. Instead, I found myself stroking it like a cat.

The following fall, by which time I had been similarly "introduced" to several rifles and shotguns, I asked Doug if I could go hunting with him sometime. "Oh, I don't know, Mare. You're the satin-sheets type. You won't like it," he demurred. But I kept pressing, and eventually he relented. We would just take a day trip, and I would essentially just tag along.

The habitat was pretty poor at the public hunting area we went to, and the few deer we saw were small and undernourished. Doug decided to pass on them. But it was a bracing November day and we were both in high spirits. I cannot now recall what we were talking about, or what impelled me to ask, but I sort of slid the conversation around to what had become, for me, a suddenly obvious question: "Do you suppose now would be a good time for me to maybe try to shoot?" The rifle Doug carried that day was a .308 Browning Lever-Action. (I recognized it as the same sort of gun Chuck Connors used in *The Rifleman.*) He looked at it, at me, said, "Sure. Why not?"

Doug set up a shooting range for me: an old rusty enameled

bucket was my target, poised against a hillside about a hundred yards away from the fallen log that made a steady rest for the gun. He showed me how to hold the rifle, how to adjust to the scope's eye relief. "Just put the crosshairs on the bucket, and when you're ready, pull the trigger."

Steadying my breathing, I did as he said. BOOM! The bucket sat motionless.

He showed me how to work the lever, chambering another round. "Try again."

I did. Same thing happened: the bucket didn't budge.

"Maybe you're shooting high," he ventured. "Aim lower this time."

I fired, and a cloudburst of dust exploded in front of the bucket.

"Hmm. Too low, I guess. I'm not sure what you're doing wrong. Let's go and see if we can figure out where your other two bullets went." I carefully put the gun down, and we jogged over to the bucket. There were two bullet holes, dead center. The bucket hadn't moved because I'd hit it squarely. "Can't argue with that," he smiled. And I thought, hey, I might enjoy this.

Over the course of the next year, I began to take riflery seriously. I wasn't put off by the shoulder-pounding that firing a large-bore rifle entails, but I didn't especially care for the lever-action. I trained, shooting paper targets with a Browning semi-automatic ("BAR") .30-06, and cans with a Sako .220 Swift (Bobby had been so right about plinking!). Late in the summer, we drove up into the Lewis and Clark National Forest near our home in Helena, Montana, to sight-in Doug's rifles for hunting season. I shot well with BAR. Doug handed me the Colt-Sauer. Kneeling, with a rest, I shot a pretty good group of three bullets at a hundred yards. "You've never shot from the prone position. You should try it," he said, and showed me the right posture.

Lying on my belly, my elbows firmly planted and the rifle's forearm resting on a couple of sandbags, I centered the target in the crosshairs and squeezed the trigger. BAM! The big, heavy gun jumped up, the scope whacking me in the forehead. "Wow," Doug whistled. "I've heard about that, but never seen it happen!"

"What are you talking about?" I yelped. I was rather badly shaken, and the blood running down my face got Doug's attention. Once he had established that all I had sustained was a rather nasty cut and a blossoming bruise over my right eye, and once he had calmed me down enough to assure me that I would not be disfigured for life, Doug explained: "Recoil. Your upper body absorbs it, but firing in the prone position your body can't move, so the gun does. You have to be sure you have a firm grip on the gun's forearm."

"So why didn't you tell me that before I shot?" I was leaning somewhat woozily against the pickup, bandana pressed to my now-aching head to stanch the bleeding. Doug was quickly collecting our gear, so we could drive back home and get some ice and a butterfly bandage on my wound.

"It didn't occur to me. Sorry. You were doing so well on your own. . . . Hey, look," he strode back, grinning, with the paper target. "You hit it well, anyway!"

III.

I didn't tag along on Doug's hunting trips for long. He found me to be a surprisingly agreeable hunting partner, after all, and I discovered that something in me—the carnivore, perhaps—needed to be more than a bystander. I had heard hunting described as "an intellectually honest way of being a meat eater" and found that argument compelling. I began hunting large game with a rifle; shotgunning for upland birds and waterfowl would come later. The first few seasons, I used Doug's BAR .30-06. When it came time to select a rifle of my own, however, I decided on a bolt-action Sako Hunter, chambered to .270 Winchester.

Several things attracted me to this particular gun. It was beautiful, for a start, its brunette walnut "Monte Carlo"-style stock subtly grained, with a tiger-stripe pattern on the forearm. Made in Finland, Sako rifles are noted for their exceptionally high quality-control standards. That impressed me, as did the fact that a large percentage of Sako employees are women; indeed, before each gun leaves the factory it is test fired for accuracy by a female sharpshooter. I suppose I liked the idea that another woman had given her blessing to the gun I would be using.

However, this is not a "lady's gun." It is heavier than many rifles, though somewhat lighter and more slender than the Colt-Sauer, the memory of which lingers in a crescent-shaped scar (shooters call it a "scope bite") over my right eyebrow. Nor is it a "lady's" caliber. Only recently have shooting experts ceased warning women away from larger calibers like the .270 in favor of more "feminine," but in some conditions less adequate, smaller calibers like the .243. When I picked out my rifle in the mid-eighties, the general consensus was that even if a .270 wasn't "too much gun" for a small-statured woman like myself, it was certainly more gun than any woman really needed. But I was less concerned with the gender politics of ballistics than with the Montana conditions under which I customarily hunted: conditions in which a two- or even three-hundred-yard shot was not out of the question and for which the .270 had been developed in the first place.

I have, by now, killed dozens of deer and antelope with my Sako. Some were shot from long range, though I prefer getting within 150 yards or less when I can. I would like to say that all of them were instant, one-shot kills. But no hunter who spends much time in the field, and who is being honest about it, can make such a claim. There were occasions, especially in my earlier hunting years, when I did not shoot as accurately or as quickly as I might have wished. But it always felt to me as if I let my rifle down, not the other way around.

Non-shooters may find hard to understand the extent to which over time a gun becomes less like a tool and more like an extension of one's self, or like a companion in the field. My .270 and I have spent countless hours together, in all sorts of weather. I have carried that rifle on treks long enough that my shoulder grew numb from its weight, and worked up a sweat stalking antelope with it, shinnying crablike along the ground on my elbows and knees. I've sat shivering in the predawn chill of a favorite deer stand, cradling the gun in my arms and watching frost gather along its barrel. On most of the hundreds of days I have spent hunting, I did not fire a single shot. That's the way hunting, good hunting, is.

IV.

I had very good hunting this past deer season, the fall of 1999, in Montana. I fired my rifle twice. The first shot was a mule deer buck. He was about 150 yards off in the early morning stillness—quartering away from me, casually grazing. I was able to ease into shooting position, with plenty of time to place my shot, low behind his shoulder. I fired, and the buck fell instantly. When I field-dressed him, he had a stomach full of sweet grass. The rut was on; he had probably spent the night mating with a doe.

My second kill was a small mule deer doe, a few days later. She had been making her way across a snow-covered field with another doe. They were well over three hundred yards away, but the wind was calm and I was confident. The deer were aware, not exactly of me, but of the fact that something was amiss in the field they traversed each morning and evening: two shapes—Doug and myself—that weren't usually there, on that hillside. Sniffing the air, the does began shuffling from one forefoot to the other, preparing to bolt. This time, I didn't have much time. I dropped to a sitting position in the snow, rested the Sako on my knee, clicked off the safety, and fired. The doe jumped, and fell about twenty feet from where she had been standing. That was a reflex action. The bullet had stopped her heart. She was dead before she hit the ground. Her companion bounded off toward the security of the nearby pine forest.

It's something of a cliché in hunting literature, to say the animals "never knew what hit them." But in the actual experience of hunting, this is anything but a cliché—it is what all hunters wish for. When conditions are right, the gun provides the means of fulfilling that wish, and it is in this sense truly an extension of the hunter's self. The bullet's trajectory traces the hunter's profoundly good intention. For a beautiful living, breathing animal is not—cannot be—a "target" in the same way as a piece of paper or a pop can. I can only take the deer's life because its meat will nourish my own. I cannot afford to forget the responsibility I bear toward the animals who help keep me alive. In the best of circumstances, as last fall, they will not know what hit them. But *I* will, I must, always.

Snapshot

Carol K. Oyster, *Rings on Her Fingers, Shells in Her Gun*

Firearms didn't play an important role in my childhood, although I knew my father kept a revolver in his dresser drawer. Somehow it made me feel safer to know it was there, but it wasn't until I felt threatened that I realized how much I depended on its presence.

I was in my late teens, babysitting for my much younger brother. As I tucked him into bed, I glanced up at the window above the headboard and saw a man staring in at me. I screamed at him to leave but he just stood there, smiling oddly. Finally, I shouted I was going to wipe the smile off his face, ran across the hall, and pulled the revolver from my father's drawer. He was still there when I raced back into my brother's room, brandishing the gun. I was still screaming as I pointed the gun at the window. He left. Quickly. To this day I don't know whether the gun was loaded.

It was thirty years later that I next encountered a firearm. The man I was dating was a firearms instructor and more than anxious to share his knowledge. He taught me to shoot a wide variety of handguns and I discovered I was good at it. And it was fun! The engagement was sealed not with a ring, but with my own first handgun. There is a photo in my wedding album, from the reception, of me in my wedding dress proudly showing off a target.

We moved on to rifles and shotguns. Having almost unlimited access to a shooting range, I got a lot of practice. With a lot of different firearms. I shot with military and police officers. We shot standard issue police and military handguns, exotic handguns; various calibers of rifles (including now-illegal "assault rifles" with their bayonet lugs, and their currently legal identical twins without the lugs), and multiple shotguns. I shot Glock handguns with a company representative, was coached on shooting skeet with Beretta shotguns by a Beretta company instructor, and shot Heckler & Koch rifles with the company representative at the NRA headquarters range. I shot semi-automatic and full automatic weapons (also known as machine guns). I found I preferred situations that require finesse and accurate aim to chewing up either a bermed embankment or a target with a submachine gun. I kept raising the bar: smaller targets, longer distances, different shooting positions.

Each time I shot with a new group of men, however, there was an implicit challenge to my ability. An empty gun would be placed in front of me along with an empty magazine and a box of bullets. Then there was the pregnant pause before I began to load the magazine, then the gun. Because I talk with my hands a great deal when I teach, I keep my nails long and manicured and wear multiple rings. The assumption seemed to hover in the air that such a woman couldn't possibly handle this situation. Once I had slapped the loaded magazine into the gun, everyone else resumed breathing and waited for me to shoot. After a comment such as, "Gee, you must have done this before," I was left alone to continue practicing. I found that the men on the range were a lot more respectful when they realized I not only knew what I was doing, but that in many cases I could outshoot them.

It felt inevitable that I would want to continue to test my skills by moving into hunting. Not only was I further raising the stakes, I would be directly providing food for my family if successful. I hunted deer for two seasons, and each season I filled the freezer with venison. I discovered almost accidentally that a number of my academic colleagues (all male) hunt. And a group of them teach a hunter education course. They'd been looking for a woman to add to the team. By the time you read this, I'll have finished my training and joined them. Each successive class has attracted more women and girls, and we're hoping a woman on the team will help attract even more. Or make the men who bring their sons to the class stop to think for a moment about their wives and daughters as potential hunting buddies.

Now that I'm divorced I once again find comfort in the fact that there are firearms in the house to provide protection for me and my family. I've come full circle, it seems. Except now I know when and whether the gun is loaded.

1 "High Noon at the Gender Gap"

Feminism and the Firearms Debate

Picture a gunman. What do you see? Probably someone on the dangerous, sinister side. A terrorist in a ski mask, perhaps, or a black-hooded sniper. A bank robber. A gangster. A Mafia hit man. Or maybe an outlaw, or a vigilante. A member of the posse. A gunslinger. Shane. The Man Who Shot Liberty Valance. A commando. Rambo. A dark stranger lurking in the shadows ("Your money or your life"). A cowboy. A revolutionary. An assassin. Lee Harvey Oswald, smiling with his Mannlicher-Carcano. David Berkowitz ("Son of Sam"), smiling in the back seat of the patrol car. A criminal. A member of a street gang. Maybe a cop. A member of a SWAT team. A militia man. A desperado. Jesse James. Dillinger. Butch Cassidy and the Sundance Kid . . .

Images abound, don't they? Now, picture a gun*woman*.

It's much more difficult, isn't it? Calamity Jane comes to mind. Belle Starr. And Ma Barker. Bonnie Parker, of "Bonnie and Clyde" fame (but that was really Faye Dunaway, wasn't it?). La Femme Nikita.

Thelma and Louise. Patty Hearst, in her "Tanya" phase with the Symbionese Liberation Army. Perhaps Manson follower Lynnette "Squeaky" Frome, in her bungled assassination attempt against then-President Gerald Ford. And that is about it, when it comes to conventional images of women "armed and dangerous."

Or at least it has been, until fairly recently in American cultural history. We live in a "gun culture," a "gunfighter nation."[1] Firearms have shaped this society, for better, and sometimes for worse. In the popular imagination, these firearms have always been, and belonged, in male hands. If this has been true of the outlaws among us, it is even truer for those whose legitimate gun use forged American democracy: the Minuteman, the lawman, the soldier, the pioneer.

In these male hands, the gun has served a symbolic function that exceeds any practical utility. It has become the symbol par excellence of masculinity: of power, force, aggressiveness, decisiveness, deadly accuracy, cold rationality. These are not things generally believed to be available to, let alone desirable for, women. Annie Oakley, whom Sitting Bull nicknamed "Little Sure Shot" and who managed to project an aura of petite femininity even as she outshot every male opponent who had the guts to take her on, looks, if anything, like the rare female exception that proves the gender rule.

But of course, as Oakley herself knew, gender rules are made to be broken. And, as even a cursory study of American social history bears out, gun use has never been solely the prerogative of men. Here, as elsewhere in the tangled history of gender relations, popular myth flies in the face of historical fact. There have always been gun women: pioneers, hunters, adventurers, defenders of their homes and families. There have been some outlaws, too, although as with their male compatriots, the vast majority of gun women are, and have always been, law-abiding citizens who possess and use firearms for an array of legitimate purposes.

It is true that the number of female firearms users has always been smaller than the number of men. It is equally true, however, that women have been an increasingly visible component of the gun-owning population since the 1980s. If, as conventional wisdom has it, women and guns don't mix, then how can we account for the fact that today in America, one in four guns is being purchased by a woman?[2]

The Decade of the Gun Woman

The 1990s were the decade in which the American gun woman began to assert herself as a cultural force. Women and guns became big news. Several gun manufacturers had, in the 1980s, brought out handguns specifically designed for women. The guns proved popular, and one of them, Smith & Wesson's LadySmith revolver, was a spectacular success. The firearms industry at large was aggressively targeting a female market that had more disposable income than ever before. The National Rifle Association (NRA), eager to increase its female membership, established a Women's Issues and Information Office and developed a women's self-defense seminar series called "Refuse to Be a Victim." The National Shooting Sports Foundation (NSSF), a marketing group, underwrote the creation of the Women's Shooting Sports Foundation (WSSF). Hit films *Thelma and Louise* and *Terminator 2: Judgment Day* (both 1991) featured strong, gun-toting women and spawned a succession of "bad girl" movies. An action film noire, *La Femme Nikita* (1990), became the basis for a popular cable TV series about a female hired gun. The magazine *Women & Guns* hit the newsstands. A revival of the musical *Annie, Get Your Gun* was a smash hit on Broadway.

Meanwhile, anti-gun groups like Handgun Control, Inc., and the Coalition to Stop Gun Violence gained national prominence. From the late 1980s through the mid-1990s, a number of anti-gun public health studies, authored by Arthur Kellermann and colleagues, were published by the *New England Journal of Medicine*. Public concerns about gun proliferation were exacerbated by the standoff between federal law officers and the Randy Weaver family in Ruby Ridge, Idaho, and the tragic outcome of the siege at the Branch Davidian complex in Waco, Texas. In both cases, women and children figured prominently as victims. In 1993, Colin Ferguson shot twenty-three people, killing five, on a Long Island Railroad commuter train. Carolyn McCarthy, whose husband was murdered and whose son was permanently disabled in the attack, was subsequently elected to Congress on a gun control platform. The Brady Act, mandating a background check and five-day waiting period for the purchase of a handgun, was signed into law in 1993. It was followed by the federal "assault weapon" ban, outlawing certain semi-automatic rifles and large-capacity ammunition clips, in 1994. The 1996 massacre of a kindergarten class and their teacher in Dunblane, Scotland, led to a ban on handguns in the United Kingdom. A rash of school shootings in the late nineties led anti-gun activists to call for a similar ban in the United States.

A Harris Poll published in 1993 predicted that gun control might well become "the next great women's issue in the country."[3] That statement proved prophetic, though in ways not necessarily envisioned by the pollsters. While many women were asking "Why guns?" for many others the big question had become "Why not?" The number of women hunters jumped dramatically, from approximately 3 percent to more than 10 percent of the total hunting population. Recreational and competitive shooting rapidly grew in popularity among women. So did classes in women's lethal-force self-defense.

Analysts hotly debated whether the number or proportion of women gun owners was actually growing or merely seemed to be (a question of statistical sleight-of-hand to which we will return in the next chapter). But whatever the numerical realities, by the early nineties it was, quite simply, no longer possible to ignore the fact that millions of American women were buying and using firearms. Virtually every major newspaper, broadcast network, and news magazine routinely carried stories by turns celebrating and condemning the new trend toward female gun ownership.

Most of these stories treated women's gun use as at best a mixed blessing, at worst a disaster waiting to happen. "Should you own a gun?" asked a typical news item in *Glamour* magazine. "The answer is probably no," the piece began, and went on to enumerate several implicit disincentives to gun ownership, among them "Are you willing to kill someone?" and "Have you considered the likelihood of a tragic accident—for example, suppose you shot a so-called intruder who turned out to be a family member come home unexpectedly?"[4] An article entitled "What You Know about Guns Can Kill You" in *Vogue* even more flatly ruled out firearms possession as a reasonable option for women: "The familiar argument says guns don't kill, people do. But scientists now see violence as a disease, guns as dangerous in themselves—and women as especially vulnerable."[5] An editorial in *USA Today* put the case even more baldly. It read, in part:

Women of America: Watch out. The National Rifle Association is increasing its focus on you as gun owners. More of you and your children are going to die. . . . [A]n accessible, loaded firearm in the home is a prescription for tragedy that is regularly filled. . . . They [the NRA, in its "Refuse to Be a Victim" self-defense program] merely encourage women to add to their daily peril. That's a sure path to more gun violence, more spattered blood, and more pointless death.[6]

Handgun Control, Inc., chairwoman Sarah Brady told the *New York Times,* regarding the NRA's "Refuse to Be A Victim" program,

"They prey on fear, they prey on guilt. The newest twist is 'Be assertive; do what the men are doing.' Well, no thank you"[7] Columnist Ellen Goodman argued that "women . . . have come to one of those forks in the road. Either they will work to disarm others, or more and more will arm themselves." She concluded against the latter option: "It's more powerful to flex our muscle collectively than to buy one more .38 caliber piece of 'personal protection.'"[8] Writing in *The New Republic,* Karen Lehrman flatly rejected even the implication that gun use might be a matter of choice for women: "All this women's lib stuff . . . can't obscure the gun lobby's real agenda—exploiting women's fears of rape. . . . The anti-date rape crowd couldn't have said it any better."[9]

The prevailing image that emerged from popular media depictions of the armed woman could be summed up as follows:

- She is driven by fear that, even if well-placed, is not a good reason to consider arming herself.
- She is being manipulated by advertising calculated to heighten her fears and exploit them.
- She is very likely incapable of comprehending the possible consequences of her actions.
- She is potentially dangerous to others and therefore needs to be protected from herself.
- She is trying to buy a false sense of security and personal autonomy.
- Her decision may well end in tragedy.

Or, as Peggy Tartaro, editor of *Women & Guns* magazine stated it: in the popular perception, any armed woman is automatically both Thelma and Louise on a very bad day, and dangerous to everyone within a 50-mile radius.

The negative popular image of the gun-armed woman was reinforced in the academic and professional literature. Most notable were the Kellermann studies, which provided much of the pseudofactual grist for the anti-gun mill.[10] Among the findings of these studies were such now-familiar factoids as these: that a gun in the house is forty-three times more likely to be used against a friend or family member than a stranger; that the very presence of a firearm increases the likelihood of its lethal use; that firearms are very seldom used effectively in self-defense; that there is a direct correlation between strict gun regulation and low incidence of gun-related violence; that guns pose an especially great danger to women and children. These "findings" have been challenged by a host of well-credentialed critics. They have never been duplicated—indeed, they cannot be, since the authors of these studies refuse to share their data with independent researchers. Nonetheless, they have appeared so often both in news accounts and in anti-gun fund-raising solicitations that they have achieved the status of established fact.

Playing on Fear

By far the most common criticism leveled at the firearms industry, with regard to its increased marketing to women, is that gun makers are cashing in on women's very legitimate fears for their own safety. Indeed, what sociologists Margaret Gordon and Stephanie Riger have called "the female fear"[11]—women's pervasive and ever-present awareness of the potential of sexual assault and the negative social and economic consequences of this awareness—certainly helps to explain why women might opt for firearms ownership. And just as certainly, some of the advertisements often singled out for criticism are clearly designed to frame women's gun ownership in the context of fear of (presumably sexual) assault.

However, contrary to what the media and anti-gun organizations

routinely assert, while fear may be one among several factors predis-
posing a woman toward gun ownership, it appears to play a subordi-
nate role in most cases. The results of numerous studies, regarding the
precise role that fear of victimization plays in the procurement of
firearms, are at best inconclusive. A widely cited 1994 study from the
National Opinion Research Center (NORC) in Chicago, focusing on
women gun owners, established that they are not more likely to have
been victims of violent crime, and are only slightly more likely to
live in "fearful" neighborhoods.[12] We will return to this subject in
the next chapter, but it bears remarking now that, as criminologist
Gary Kleck points out, "gun acquisition, even for protective reasons,
may be a fairly unemotional act of prudence and planning for the
future."[13]

This is important because, in our culture, women have always
been defined more in terms of emotion than rationality. Critics of female gun use are generally more comfortable seeing women in the
light of conventional stereotypes. So, too, are many defenders of
women's right to keep and bear arms. Hence the depiction, in both
the popular and the academic press, of women driven by fear—and
often against their feminine inclinations—to procure guns. The general impression is that, as British scholar Susie McKellar concluded in
her study of firearms advertising directed at American women,

the majority of American women who are arming themselves for self-defence,
are scared, and are doing so reluctantly. Gun ownership amongst women is
not considered an American birthright as it is for men and, consequently, does
not hold the same significance that it does for men. . . . The main way gun
manufacturers appeal to women is through emotive, stereotyped images of
women as child-bearers, nurturers and carers and the handgun control lobby-
ists are likewise appealing to their sense of responsibility by using the same vi-
sual language.[14]

McKellar arrived at her conclusion via consideration of ads that clearly played on, or sometimes against, images of conventional femininity. One, for Colt's compact semi-automatic pistols, depicted a mother tucking her child into bed, under the legend "Self-protection is more than your right . . . it's your responsibility," and likened a gun to a home fire extinguisher. Another pictured a nightstand with a photo of a mother and her two daughters, beside which rests a Beretta pistol. Noting "it's a different world today, than when you grew up," an ad for Smith & Wesson's LadySmith revolver pictured a young woman at a shooting range, and asked, "What Would Mom Think Now?" An ad for a company marketing concealed-carry pocketbooks showed a lone woman crossing a darkened parking lot to her isolated car and asked, "Now that you've purchased a gun, shouldn't you have it with you?"

Advertisements like these clearly can be read as attempts to exploit women's legitimate concerns. But do they turn women into unwilling gun owners? In 1995, marketing professors Elizabeth Blair and Eva Hyatt set out to prove they did, but wound up finding the opposite. In a study of the marketing of guns to women,[15] Blair and Hyatt found that attitudes toward guns varied predictably along gender lines: men were generally more pro-gun, women generally less so. But "for both men and women, respondents exposed to the advertisements are not significantly more pro-gun than those who were not exposed." Indeed, the only statistically significant difference in attitudes they recorded was that women who saw the NRA's "You Can Choose to Refuse to Be a Victim" advertisements were more likely to think of the NRA as "very concerned about women's safety." Despite criticism to the contrary—criticism with which both researchers admitted they had originally concurred—they could only conclude that "advertisements for guns and gun-related products are not likely to make a woman significantly more pro-gun."

Could advertisements make women anti-gun? The gun control lobby surely thinks so, and has used "the female fear" in roughly the same way as have some firearms manufacturers' ads. Take, for example, a fund-solicitation letter like the following from the Coalition to Stop Gun Violence. The letter begins:

Like most people, Pam thought gun violence always happened to someone else. So she was caught off guard when she was held up at gunpoint.
And even when she gave up her purse and ran to her car, the gunmen followed and shot her dead.
Dear Mary Stange,
You could be next [16]

The most ambitious, and influential, study to date of the firearms industry's manipulation of women's fears was a report issued in 1994 by the Violence Policy Center, an anti-gun think tank in Washington, D.C. *Female Persuasion: A Study of How the Firearms Industry Markets to Women and the Reality of Women and Guns* depicted women as the hapless victims of a callously scheming firearms industry. In the (approving) words of *New York Times* columnist Bob Herbert, the report demonstrated that "the good old boys of the gun industry—those pernicious purveyors of bloodshed, mayhem and grief—don't give a rat's tail about the safety of women."[17] The report relies heavily on Kellermann's questionable research findings. It asserts as fact such preposterous statistics as the finding that ninety percent of homicides are *not* crime related (implying that they are, rather, "tragic accidents" facilitated by the mere presence of a gun), or that for each time a woman uses a gun to kill an attacker, 239 women die in homicides (neglecting to mention that the defensive "use" of firearms seldom involves killing). At the same time, the report dismisses virtually all information provided by the NRA and the firearms manufacturers as merely anecdotal. It castigates the industry for "enticing" women into firearms use that will almost inevitably turn tragic for them.[18]

Using fundamentally the same logic, two legal scholars argued in 1991 that gun advertising directed at women ought to be highly regulated, if not outright prohibited. Debra Dobray and Arthur Waldrop did not make the same argument about advertising directed at men. In their reasoning, men can be counted on to know how to use guns, and would not therefore be deceived, or shall we say "enticed," by the ads. Women are another story:

Since women may be less aware of the correct usage of guns and less familiar with the handling of concealed weapons, arguably the "reasonable woman" standard for deception might be less stringent than the reasonable person standard, and deception may be more easily found. . . . Lawsuits may be anticipated to be filed by women who injure themselves or others because they were not warned regarding proper usage, or the need for training, with respect to handguns designed especially for them.

In other words, they argue, advertising guns to women is irresponsible, to the extent that women are not truly capable of understanding the responsibilities and consequences of gun ownership. In addition, they claim that women would not even *want* guns, were it not for advertisements preying on their fears—ads the article characterizes as "immoral, unethical, oppressive, or unscrupulous." To drive home their point, the authors cite a Michigan case in which a slingshot manufacturer was found liable for injuries caused by slingshots sold through advertising directed at children: "If the analogy can be made between indulging young children's impulse for buying and playing on the fears of women, then it would seem that the manner of distributing women's handguns constitutes an actionable defect."[19] The analogy speaks volumes.

Reasoning along similar lines, attorney Alana Bassin argued in a 1997 article about "Why Packing a Pistol Perpetuates Patriarchy,"[20] that pro-gun women are "victims of the NRA and gun industry marketing campaigns exploiting our nation's violence," and further, that "women advocating gun use have misdiagnosed societal violence." What is Bassin's diagnosis? "Guns are a source of male domination." The male-run firearms industry, by craftily duping women into believing "everybody is doing it—you should too," makes women willing participants in their own victimization, rather like victims of Stockholm Syndrome (whereby hostages come to identify and sympathize with their captors). Women may think guns are an "equalizer," they may feel more secure, but they are deluded. Bassin relies on the Kellermann studies to support her argument. But then she also cites something called *The How and Why Wonder Book of Guns,* leaving a reader uncertain about the depth both of her research and of her knowledge about firearms. Bassin shares with most other knee-jerk critics of guns and gun culture an apparent disinclination to really grapple with the complex issues the gun control debate necessarily raises. But in this regard, too little knowledge can be a dangerous thing.

Playing with Fire

It is of no small interest that Bassin, in presenting an ostensibly feminist argument for bringing an end to patriarchy by "unpacking" women's pistols, paints a portrait of gun-owning women that looks vaguely like the Stepford Wives. Yet throughout the 1990s, evidence was building that indicates precisely the opposite of woman-as-victim/child to be the case.

Women are far more likely than men to educate themselves about firearms ownership and use; they are far more likely to seek instruction, and every firearms safety instructor will attest that they make better students than men or boys do. They are responsible for proportionally far fewer gun-related accidents (or gun-related crimes) than men or boys are. And gun-armed women are far more likely to succeed in defending themselves against violent assault—either by threatening an assailant with a gun or, in fewer instances, by actually firing the gun—than are unarmed women.

For some commentators these facts represented a healthy reversal of the popular stereotype of woman-as-victim. For example, in *Fire with Fire,* her 1993 book about "the new female power and how it will change the 21st century," feminist writer Naomi Wolf declared:

The premise that women are helpless victims, unable to defend themselves, was entirely ignored by twelve million women who did something highly unvictimlike throughout the 1980s: They bought handguns. As violence against women reached epidemic proportions, women were not just sitting around. Quietly, carefully, with thorough training and in unprecedented numbers, while they looked after their families and tended their marriages, they were also teaching themselves to blow away potential assailants. By 1992, women had become the fastest-growing segment of the firearms-buying public. One woman in nine was legally packing.[21]

Other writers took sharp issue with Wolf. *Newsweek* book reviewer Laura Shapiro castigated Wolf at some length for even suggesting that it might be a good thing for women to arm themselves.[22] In *Ms.* magazine, Ann Jones, author of several books about violence against women, lamented the fact that we live in "a world where popular, state-of-the-art, so-called feminist Naomi Wolf cites pistol-packin' mamas in NRA publications as splendid examples of 'pioneer feminism.'"[23] This dismissal of Wolf as a "so-called" feminist was particularly striking, given the fact that a mere three issues earlier, *Ms.*

had featured her in its cover story celebrating diversity in feminist thought.[24]

This reaction against Wolf was characteristic of the anti-gun tenor of Second Wave feminism. While feminists praise diversity in principle, in practice there have been certain issues—abortion rights and pornography come to mind—in regard to which diversity of thought does not necessarily apply, at least among those concerned about feminist "orthodoxy." Indeed, issues like these have tended to be touchstones: with-us-or-against-us matters of ideological purity. It is only in the context of such polarization that Wolf could, on the basis of one approving mention of women's armed self-defense, fall so decisively from feminist grace.

Anti-gun feminists often cite, as if it's a rationale for their position, the late poet Audre Lorde's statement that the Master's house will never be dismantled using the Master's tools.[25] They argue against resorting to male-identified instruments of power, guns chief among them. However, this argument gets called into question when one sees the same feminists cheering wildly at a screening of *Thelma and Louise*. In response to that 1991 film's tremendous popularity among women, and especially among feminists, screenwriter Callie Khouri quipped: "People tell me Thelma and Louise are terrible role models . . . I say, 'I know. Don't try this at home!' Movies are meant to take you places that you *can't* go physically, but you *can* go emotionally."[26] The message seems to be: Look, but don't touch. Guns are fine for women in feminist fantasy, but not in fact.

"Fantasies of female power and revenge may be seductive," Letty Cottin Pogrebin wrote for *The Nation* in 1989, but women should resist them, for their own good. In an article entitled "Neither Pink nor Cute: Pistols for the Women of America," Pogrebin attacked Smith & Wesson's advertising campaign for its LadySmith revolver.[27] She questioned the firearms manufacturer's motives for producing a gun designed specifically for women. "They are arming women with deadly seriousness," she objected, "as if it was high noon at the gender gap." Pogrebin, a cofounder of *Ms.* magazine, was of course hardly blind to the fact that we do indeed live in a society in which violence against women has reached epidemic proportions. She had to acknowledge that if Smith & Wesson was playing off women's fears in its ad campaign, those fears themselves were nonetheless legitimate.

Interestingly, Pogrebin reported being "surprised" by her own reaction to the very idea of the LadySmith: "I'm for gun control and nonviolent conflict resolution, yet suddenly I imagined every woman armed, powerful and instantly equalized . . . POW—one less pervert; BANG—another rapist blown away . . . pistol-packin' mamas will fight back: ZAP—victims no more." But her righteous fantasies of women taking control for their own safety were quickly "eclipsed by more likely scenarios":

> *They shoot a lover or spouse in the heat of a quarrel, or are shot themselves.*
> *They are overwhelmed by a stronger assailant who turns the gun against them.*
> *Their child finds the gun and thinks it is a toy.*
> *They hear noises, panic, forget all safety instructions and shoot someone who is not an intruder.*
> *They overreact and shoot someone who could have been verbally restrained or pacified.*
> *They shoot when they could have chosen to escape.*
> *They shoot and harm an innocent bystander.*
> *Their gun discharges accidentally, or misfires.*
> *They get depressed and shoot themselves.*

That the above reads like a checklist from the Coalition to Stop Gun Violence is not especially noteworthy in itself—it is, after all, the "conventional wisdom" constantly reiterated in the press. What is striking, though, is the degree to which one of the major voices of Second Wave feminism is here willing to accept an image of women that stresses their instability and ineptitude, the likelihood that they will "panic" or "overreact," and make some sort of tragically stupid mistake. Never mind that, when Pogrebin was writing as now, women had a far better track record of firearms safety than men.

The relationship between women and guns—and between *feminism* and guns—is far more complex than most feminists have wanted to acknowledge. It seems the very seductiveness of images of female kick-ass, shoot-to-kill power throws up some sort of warning sign: We don't want to go there. It may reveal something disquieting about ourselves. It is in some ways much easier to regard guns as instruments of male domination, and let men "own" all that aggressive power, than to recognize that women, too, can—even *should*—have access to that kind of flat-out, hands-on force. Fantasies are one thing, as Pogrebin wrote, realities another.

The problem is that, too often, the feminist fantasy about guns has produced some less-than-ideal responses to real-world realities. A classic example is an essay written in 1989 by Wendy Brown, a women's studies professor at the University of California, Santa Cruz.[28] Brown recounted the dismay she and some friends felt when they returned from a week of backpacking in the High Sierras to find that her car would not start. Stranded at a remote trailhead, they were understandably relieved to discover another vehicle parked nearby. Seeking assistance, Brown encountered in it "a California sportsman making his way through a case of beer, flipping through the pages of a porn magazine and preparing to survey the area for his hunting club in anticipation of the opening of deer season." He was wearing an "NRA freedom" cap that told her that he and she were "at opposite ends of the political and cultural universe." But, Brown says, "Not feeling particularly discriminating, I enlisted his aid." After two hours of concentrated labor, the man managed to get Brown's auto running, and she and her friends were on their way.

Afterward, Brown reflected that her rescuer and she were indeed opposite numbers. He had come to the high country "preparing to shoot the wildlife I came to revere, he living out of his satellite-dished Winnebago and me out of my dusty backpack, he sustained by his guns and beer, me by my Nietzsche and trail mix." His gun—or rather, his NRA cap, since there is no evidence that he was in fact armed on this occasion—was, however, the decisive factor separating them.

It occurred to me then, and now, that if I had run into him in those woods without my friends or a common project for us to work on, I would have been seized with one great and appropriate fear: rape. During the hours I spent with him, I had no reason to conclude that his respect for women's personhood ran any deeper than his respect for the lives of Sierra deer, and his gun could well have made the difference between an assault that my hard-won skills in self-defense could have fended off and one against which they were useless.

Now, Brown was probably right about the limits of her self-defense training; numerous studies have shown that for aggressive resistance to succeed against sexual assault, the level of resistance must be equivalent to the level of force employed by the attacker. The option of arming herself to forestall the sort of assault in the circumstances she imagines here obviously never occurred to her.

But nothing in Brown's own recounting of this tale suggested that the man had in any way threatened her. In fact, he didn't need to; her fantasy, based solely upon his wearing an "NRA Freedom" baseball cap, was more than enough threat for her. Indeed, for Brown this fact was the heart of the matter, because of the way it pointed to "the differences between the social positioning and experiences of men and women in our culture." Men (especially perhaps gun-wielding sportsmen) are potential rapists, women (especially left-leaning feminists?) potential victims. Feminist analysis was in this case reduced to the facile application of an unflattering stereotype, with utter disregard for any factual evidence that might challenge its validity.

In fact, there is no substantial evidence to suggest that sportsmen or gun enthusiasts are any more prone to rape than the rest of the male population. Studies aiming to find a significant correlation between hunting and incidences of rape have found either no correlation or a negative one.[29] And when it comes to the question of "social positioning," Brown's story raises some disturbing issues of class. Legal scholar Douglas Laycock has remarked how differently this story would have been told, had Brown's car broken down in Harlem, and her Good Samaritan been a young black male carrying "a gun, a beer, a porn magazine, and a boombox":

Either her fear of rape would not have appeared in a respectable journal, or it would have appeared in a confessional tone and emphasized a very different moral. The point would have been: "He came only to help me, and I was afraid to let him; see how fear and racism distorts our whole society." The point would not have been: "I was forced to ask him for help, and it is a good thing I was not alone or he might have raped me."[30]

Like other knee-jerk anti-gun feminists, in positing a world in which men with guns and women without them "live at opposite ends of the political and cultural universe," Brown was perpetuating what science writer Natalie Angier, in a play on baby talk and its infantilizing effect, has more recently dubbed "the myth of the goo-girl." According to this dominant myth in American culture, girls and women are not really capable of genuine, hands-on aggression. From infancy, physical aggression is discouraged in girls: "Not only are they instructed against offensive fighting; they are rarely instructed in defensive fighting. Girls don't learn how to throw a punch."[31] Psychologist/criminologist Anne Campbell makes a kindred point: "The very use of violence clearly casts a woman in the role of villain. Boys recognize bad guys by their refusal to follow the rules of fighting. Girls recognize bad women by their use of aggression at all. Good girls don't fight."[32] And, ipso facto, they don't fight back.

Can Feminists Fight Back?

What, then, are women supposed to do, when faced with the threat of real (not fantasy) attack, in this bad guy/good girl world?

One feminist who has devoted a career to researching this question is Ann Jones, who knows a lot about women and violence. When *Ms.* Magazine decided to devote its May/June 1994 issue to the subject of women and guns—the striking cover of which sported a Smith & Wesson semi-automatic pistol, casting a hot-pink shadow, with the banner: "Is This Power Feminism? The Push to Get Women Hooked on Guns"—the editors asked Jones, author of *Women Who Kill* and *Next Time She'll Be Dead,* to provide the feature article. Her article, provocatively titled "Living with Guns, Playing with Fire," presented a problematic picture, to say the least, of women's relationship to firearms. Following the familiar pattern, Jones portrayed the NRA as a demonic force, seeking for its own nefarious reasons to lure women into firearms ownership. But unlike some other anti-gun feminists, while she questioned the NRA's motives and its use of the rhetoric of choice ("You can choose to refuse to be a victim"), she did at least acknowledge that the question of armed self-defense might indeed occur to a reasonable woman faced with life in a violently antifeminist society: "Women are fearful, yes. With good reason. But we're also beyond fear. We're fed up. . . . Women's interest in guns—such as it is—isn't just about fear. It's about fighting back."[33]

This is an important insight. Jones saw some women's decisions to arm themselves as a reflection of a widespread "mother lode of anger" among women, "a vast buildup of unrequited insults and injuries." Significantly, Jones goes on to disclose that "I know something about fighting back myself—and about the consolations of a gun." A former gun owner, Jones was prompted by the assassination of the Reverend Martin Luther King, Jr., to forswear guns and the violence they represented to her. "The threat of violence, if it makes you play by its rules, is just as deadly to the spirit," she realized, "as violence itself. It wasn't a gun I needed. It was courage."

Jones writes that it saddens her now to read stories of women purchasing guns "to gain a sense of power and control," and recounts, evidently by way of illustration, the story of April LaSalata. In 1988, this Long Island woman was viciously assaulted by her ex-husband, Anthony. He was charged with attempted murder as a result. When he was released on bond and the judge refused the prosecutor's request to increase bail to keep the man in jail, April LaSalata applied for a permit to carry a gun for self-protection. Her permit was denied. Within a year she was dead at the age of thirty-four, shot twice in the head on her own doorstep, by her ex-husband.

Jones asks: "If April LaSalata had been granted that gun permit, could she have saved herself? Maybe so. Maybe not." She immediately follows this equivocation by remarking, "As a practical matter, leaving the human drama aside and looking at the studies and the numbers, it doesn't make much sense to own a gun." With this rather cavalier dismissal of April LaSalata's "human drama," the reader can only infer that it wasn't a gun the unfortunate woman lacked, it was courage.

For Jones, as for a number of her sister feminists, it is up to the law to protect women from domestic and other forms of abuse, and achieving women's safety through legal means is a job for women and men collectively. Fine. But why rule out aggressive self-defensive action on the part of individuals? Because, Jones says condescendingly, it is not "a job to be done piecemeal by lone women, armed with pearl-handled pistols, picking off batterers and rapists one by one."

In a subsequent issue of *Ms.*, Jones was interviewed about reader response to her anti-gun article. Her replies suggested a deplorable level of white middle-class insulation from the facts of many other women's lives. Asked, "What do we tell women who feel the police won't help them?" Jones responded: "That's a good question. The alternative may be to go underground, and many women do that. . . . I got letters, too, from women who said that they managed to save themselves with a gun, and I think it's a terrible commentary on how we live now. I would suggest that women go underground, but I understand why many women don't."[34]

One has to ask, are these the *only* alternatives a feminist can imagine? Either going "underground," whatever exactly that means, or engaging in hand-wringing about the terrible state of things? Jones's desire to imagine a better world, a world in which women could live in freedom from fear, is laudable enough. But what are women at risk—most of them non-white and/or underprivileged—to do in the meantime, while she and feminists of like persuasion debate nonviolent strategies for building that world? As legal scholars Carol Silver and Don Kates have remarked, "musings about better solutions are of very little aid to a woman who is being strangled or beaten to death."[35] Or, we might add, to a woman who has come to the well-reasoned decision that she would be safer with a gun.

It is precisely on the issue of fighting back that feminists like Pogrebin, Brown, and Jones have drawn the accusation that they would rather wallow in their "victimhood" as women than confront the implications, for men and for women, of what it might really mean for women to claim their equality. Naomi Wolf drew a considerable amount of criticism when she suggested in *Fire with Fire* that the main stumbling block in contemporary feminist thinking was its tendency toward what she and others have termed "victim feminism," with its reinforcement of the by now all-too-familiar idea that "good girls" are not only nonviolent, they are incapable of genuine aggression. Wolf had dared to spin a different sort of feminist fantasy:

I don't want to carry a gun or endorse gun proliferation. But I am happy to benefit from publicizing the fact that an attacker's prospective victim has a good chance of being armed. . . . Our cities and towns can be plastered with announcements that read, "A hundred women in this town are trained in combat. They may be nurses, students, housewives, prostitutes, mothers. The next woman to be assaulted might be one of these."[36]

The critics who, like Jones, castigated her over this remark missed the significant, and subtle, point that Wolf was making. She was talking about the power of *the threat* of violent retaliation—and about the fact that until men *and women* take seriously women's potential for aggressive self-defense (we would argue, for aggressive action in general), all of our talk about nonviolent strategies to combat violence against women is meaningless.

Women are often their own worst enemies in this regard. A female self-defense instructor remarks: "In my classes, women always ask, terrified, 'Well, what if the rapist has a knife?' I think it's long past time that *rapists* start worrying about whether or not a woman has a gun—or at the very least, about a woman's willingness and ability to do some serious damage to any man who fucks with her space."[37] Significantly, this remark appeared in an article with the wonderful title, "There Are Other Ways of Taking Care of Bret Easton Ellis [author of the repulsively misogynistic novel *American Psycho*] than Just Censoring Him," which the authors, Tara Baxter and Nikki Craft, found impossible to place in any feminist journal, because—as editor after editor informed them—it "focused on the imagery and advocacy of violence by women against men" and "printing it might only 'escalate the violence' pandemic among us."[38] What it "focused on," actually, was the idea that women can, and should, take an aggressive role in their own self-protection.

We live in a violence-saturated culture, it is true. It is also true that males are the prime offenders, women and children far too often the victims. But it hardly follows that if women take an active role in protecting themselves, they are "escalating" the violence. This idea is bizarre. In the best of possible worlds, we like to think we could just make all the violence stop. But we do not live in that world, and no amount of fretting about the sorry state of human affairs is going to get us there.

This does not necessarily bode well for women who believe their best bet is nonviolence. Radical feminist D. A. Clarke makes the following point about females fighting back:

Historically, the prospect for peoples and cultures which avoid violence is not good. They tend to lose territory, property, freedom, and finally life itself as soon as less pleasant neighbors show up with better armaments and bigger ambitions. It's hard to survive as a pacifist when the folks next door are club-waving, rock-hurling imperialists: you end up enslaved or dead, or you learn to be like them in order to fight them. The greatest challenge to nonviolence is that to fulfill its promise it must be able to prevent *violence. The image of the nonviolent activist righteously renouncing the use of force—while watching armed thugs drag away their struggling victims—is less than pleasing.*[39]

Clarke's stone-age imagery is particularly apt here. Feminist archaeologists have begun to suggest, and cross-cultural ethnographic evidence bears out, that from the Upper Paleolithic period forward, those tools that have been defined as male tools, access to and the manufacture of which is denied to women, all fall into the category of tools that also function as weapons.[40] This fact has implications beyond the gendered division of labor; it also accounts for males' ability to keep females in their place. Women's literal disempowerment plays a crucial role in a psychological disabling that in many ways continues to be self-imposed.

The gun is only the symbol of male power to the extent we let it be. And as some feminists are finally beginning to realize, it can function as a particularly potent symbol of female resistance to male aggression. Baxter and Craft have begun marketing buttons with messages like "So Many Men, So Little Ammunition," "Men and Women Were Created Equal, and Smith and Wesson Make Damn Sure It Stays That Way," "The Best Way to a Man's Heart Is through His Chest," "Feminine Protection" (accompanied by a picture of a gun), and "How Dare You Assume I'm Non-Violent."[41] This isn't just wordplay. It points directly to the fact that more and more women are refusing to play the "goo-girl" role. And isn't this just what feminism is supposed to be all about? It all comes down to ideas about women and power.

Taking Power Literally

You might say a symbol can only truly function to the extent that it can be taken literally. This has been the problem with so much feminist advocacy of nonviolent "resistance": so long as women are perceived—and *perceive themselves*—as incapable of genuine aggressive action, nonviolence is not a strategy. It is merely the role culturally assigned to women. However, as Clarke astutely observes,

if the risk involved in attacking a woman were greater, there might be fewer attacks. If women defended themselves violently, the amount of damage they

were willing to do to would-be assailants would be the measure of their seri-
ousness about the limits beyond which they would not be pushed. If more
women killed husbands and boyfriends who abused them or their children,
perhaps there would be less abuse. A large number of women refusing to be
pushed any further would erode, however slowly, the myth of the masochistic
female which threatens all our lives.[42]

Researchers Gary Kleck and John Lott have convincingly shown
that the primary defensive use of a firearm lies in the threat of its actually being fired.[43] But there are powerful, culturally rooted disincentives to viewing women as capable of being threatening in precisely the same ways men are, especially where guns are involved. Psychologist Nyla Branscombe has conducted studies of attitudes toward
female crime victims, in which she found that in cases of date and
stranger rape, "women who behaved most inconsistently with the female stereotype, i.e. by resisting their assailant both verbally and
physically, were perceived as having been *more* guilty of precipitating
the attack." Meanwhile, "women who competently shot a burglar
were blamed more than women who wielded the gun incompetently
and made a lucky hit. The reverse was true for male homeowners who
shot burglars."[44] Branscombe concluded that not only are women not
supposed to be responsible for their own self-defense; if they do have
to take responsibility for it, it's apparently better if they are not particularly good at it:

[A] woman is less likely to be penalized for using a handgun to defend herself
against an intruder in her home when there is a simultaneous display of in-
competence in its use; she fires the weapon but misses the target completely.
When, however, a woman successfully uses a weapon in a competent fash-
ion—theoretically a greater violation of expectations concerning women's
abilities—then she is more likely to be perceived as guilty of a crime herself
and to be held more accountable for the outcome.[45]

Branscombe's work recalls sociologist Frances Haga's finding, in her "Images of Fear" study of people's perceptions of gun-armed women in situations of clear and present danger, that "people seemed to have already developed intensely held answers to the question of *whether or not women should be defending themselves at all,* and nobody seemed to be wondering who women might be arming themselves against, and with what?"[46] Ambivalence about women's armed self-defense arises both from men's and women's subjective impressions about what is appropriate female behavior, and from commonly held cultural views about women's relationship to violence.

In a subsequent study, Haga and several associates sought to answer the question: "What's a woman to do to defend herself, and why does whatever she actually does in her own physical defense upset people enough to seem to be always telling her she should have done something else?"[47] Utilizing a telephone survey of nearly ten thousand respondents, the researchers verified what will come as no surprise to any woman: the perception of what constitutes violent crime against a person, and that person's appropriate level of response, depends very much upon whether the perpetrator of the violence is a stranger or an acquaintance. When the attacker is a stranger, "we can envision ourselves responding with sufficient unmitigated violence to end the attack." Hence, notwithstanding the conventional prescription of nonviolent resistance, there tends to be fairly unified social support for a woman who does manage to exercise lethal force against an unknown assailant (the so-called Dark Stranger in sociological literature). Even Arthur Kellermann, whose anti-gun public health studies are the primary resources for those urging strict regulation or outright banning of firearms, admitted to an interviewer: "If you've got to resist, your chances of being hurt are less the more lethal your weapon. . . . If that were my wife, would I want her to have a thirty-eight special in her hand? . . . Yeah."[48]

Of course, gun advertising and gun-control fundraising literature notwithstanding, the great majority of attacks against women are not stranger rapes or random predatory violence. But the woman who seeks to use forceful self-defense at home generally fails to garner the public approbation that would come her way if she had exerted the same level of resistance against a stranger. The perceptual problem seems to reside in patriarchal domestic arrangements; women continue to fear assault primarily from strangers, when more frequently the real danger to them is closer to, or in, the home.

The "blame the victim" reflex is alive and well in the popular mind, though in the wake of the women's movement it now takes the form less of saying the woman "brought on" the attack than of asking what she could have done—nonforcefully, of course—to avoid it. As Haga puts it:

Intuitively, women appear to understand that half the battle of surviving physical/sexual assault is to have conducted themselves "with common sense" for so long, with so many public witnesses and personal friends of irreproachable character that if any criminal predator crashes through the fences of common sense everyone will know that she always locked every door and it wasn't her fault. If as much energy were directed into repelling assailants as is expended in avoiding blame for being in the wrong place at the wrong time, women could be even more successful in defending themselves against predatory attack.

We will be returning to the specific facts and fallacies about women's armed self-defense in the next chapter. The question at hand is: What are women to do, who are sick and tired of being typecast as hapless, childlike victims? Women, that is, who no longer want to live with "the female fear."

Getting Mean and Meaning It

Two women, feminists both, have written with particular power about their conscious decisions to arm themselves against the potential of male violence. Both hail from parts of the country where the "gun culture" is indigenous—Linda Hasselstrom from South Dakota cattle country, Leslie Marmon Silko from the Laguna Pueblo lands in New Mexico. Their backgrounds may help explain why they saw firearms ownership as a valid choice for themselves in the first place. But each is nevertheless sensitive to the fact that in carrying a handgun she has crossed a clearly drawn gender line and, simultaneously, asserted a sense of personal power that women—the good girls among us, anyway—simply aren't supposed to possess.

Both women describe emotional and intellectual odysseys. Hasselstrom, a diminutive, soft-spoken Midwesterner, describes herself as a "peace-loving woman." Nevertheless, she decided several years ago that she would be safer if she carried a pistol. Her reasons were several: she lived on a ranch in a remote part of South Dakota, many miles from the nearest town, and she often found herself alone at home, or on the mostly deserted roads. A professional writer, she traveled frequently.

A woman who travels alone is advised, usually by men, to protect herself by avoiding bars and other "dangerous situations," by approaching her car like an Indian scout, by locking doors and windows. But these precautions aren't always enough. I spent years following them and still found myself in dangerous situations. I began to resent the idea that just because I am female, I have to be extra careful.[49]

A woman doesn't need to experience the isolation of a South Dakota farm to relate to the feelings Hasselstrom describes here. Or to the sense of fear she and a female friend felt when they were harassed by drunken neighbors at a national park campground, and park rangers to whom they complained laughed off the threats. There were other, all-too-familiar incidents, too: being followed on a dark road and realizing she couldn't head for home, because nobody was there; coming home to an empty house late at night, discovering evidence of trespassing in the yard and a light burning in the house that she didn't remember leaving on, and feeling "too embarrassed" to wake up a neighbor; feeling vulnerable in her own home, when the lights were out. This is the stuff the "female fear" is made of.

Hasselstrom took some martial arts training. Kung fu helped, but stories written by several women whose advanced training had not prevented their being raped or beaten convinced her that her more limited self-defense skills would not be enough to fend off a large at-tacker. She wondered whether there was something in her psycho-logical makeup that doomed her to victimhood: "I thought back over the times in my life when I had been attacked or threatened and tried to be realistic about my own behavior, searching for anything that had allowed me to become a victim. Overall, I was convinced that I had not been at fault. I don't believe myself to be either paranoid or a risk-taker, but I wanted more protection."

For that protection she bought herself a pistol. She also learned what she needed to know about herself—and this had to do with more, as she describes it, than whether or not she could shoot. That part was easy enough; she got instruction, she practiced. But she also needed to know, much more significantly, that she could, if need be, *shoot a person*. The psychological practice of imagining herself in situations requiring lethal-force self-defense was, ulti-mately, far more important—and for a female, perhaps more daunt-ing—than the physical training of hand and mind: "People who have not grown up with the idea that they are capable of protecting themselves—in other words, most women—might have to work hard to convince themselves of their ability, and of the necessity. Handgun ownership need not turn us into gun-slingers, but it can be part of believing in, and relying on, *ourselves* for protection. The pistol only adds an extra edge, an attention-getter."

It was an "attention-getter," to be sure, when one day she arrived home to discover a vehicle parked on the road from the mailbox to her house. The several men relieving themselves alongside it had clearly been drinking. Hasselstrom slowed her small foreign car to a stop, rolled the window partway down, told them they were on private land, and cordially asked them to pick up their beer cans and take off. The men circled her car; one began verbally berating her, as others slowly rocked the car and thumped on the roof. "I felt," she says, "very small and very trapped and they knew it." The men began joking about what a good time they planned to have with her.

They stopped laughing when she slipped her pistol from its hiding place on the front seat. In less than a minute, the beer cans were collected and the men were on their way down the road. Hasselstrom's interpretation of the incident shows her to be neither paranoid gunslinger nor self-deluded woman/child:

The men were trespassing and knew it; their judgment may have been impaired by alcohol. Their response to the polite request of a woman alone was to use their size, numbers, and sex to inspire fear. The pistol was a response in the same language. Politeness didn't work; I couldn't match them in size or number. Out of the car, I'd have been more vulnerable. The pistol just changed the balance of power.

Hasselstrom didn't let her guard down once she armed herself. She still practices caution, still remains alert to potential danger, still sees avoidance as the most prudent response to peril. She admits that while she likes the idea that "God made men and women, but Sam Colt made them equal," at the same time "the pacifist inside me will be saddened if the only way women can achieve equality is by carrying a weapon." Undeniably. And what is important to note here is that it *is* possible to be a pacifist and a gun owner at the same time.

For Leslie Silko, pacifism may be less of an issue. In fact, she equates life as a woman to life "in the combat zone." Her choice of metaphor is deliberate, and has to do with what men refuse to understand about being female in American society. "They may notice our reluctance to drive at night to the convenience store alone, but they don't know or want to know the experience of a woman out alone at night. Men who have been in combat know the feeling of being a predator's target, but it is difficult for men to admit that we women live our entire lives in a combat zone."[50]

There was barely a time in her life when Silko was not aware of the existence of firearms, and the need to be careful in their use. Her father took her along on hunting trips when she was a tiny child. Before he let her handle a gun herself, he schooled her in the rules of gun safety and in the difference between real and make-believe:

Guns were not toys. My father did not approve of BB guns because they were classified as toys. I had a .22 rifle when I was seven years old. If I felt like shooting, all I had to do was tell my parents where I was going, take my rifle and a box of .22 shells and go. I was never tempted to shoot at birds or animals because whatever was killed had to be eaten. Now, I realize how odd this must seem; a seven-year-old with a little .22 rifle and a box of ammunition, target shooting alone at the river. But that was how people lived at Laguna when I was growing up; children were given responsibilities at an early age.

Indeed, in her Native American background, girls were given more responsibility than contemporary American society grants its women. Still, Silko grew up in America, and some of the dominant attitude was bound to rub off. Even though her mother carried a snub-nose .22 revolver, and her Grandma Lily "a Beretta as black as her prayer book," even though her father taught his three daughters to shoot and told them they "never had to let a man hit us or terrorize us because no matter how big and strong the man was, a gun in our hand equalized all difference of size and strength," Silko still found that when she moved to a large city (Tucson, Arizona) "sundown" became "lockdown." Not that the daylight hours felt all that much safer. She became aware of the ways the "female fear" were impinging upon her freedom. And she became angry. She began to carry a gun with her, and—like Hasselstrom—she used it on more than one occasion to get the "attention" of men who menaced her. Her rationale? "Only women can put a stop to the 'open season' on women by strangers." As with Hasselstrom, Silko's firearms ownership is not a substitute for courage. To the contrary, it is an expression of true courage: the determination to take charge of her own well-being in a too-often dangerous world.

It isn't height or weight or strength that makes women easy targets; from infancy women are taught to be self-sacrificing, passive victims. I was taught differently. Women have the right to protect themselves from death or bodily harm. By becoming strong and potentially lethal individuals, women destroy the fantasy that we are sitting ducks for predatory strangers.

Silko echoes the sentiments of feminists like Naomi Wolf and De Clarke, who remind us that women are too often their own worst enemies when it comes to rethinking issues of power and aggression. "Women are," she asserts, "TAUGHT to be easy targets by their mothers, aunts, and grandmothers who themselves were taught that 'a woman doesn't kill' or 'a woman doesn't learn how to use a weapon.' Women must learn how to take aggressive action individually, apart from police and the courts." This last remark is especially important because, as we shall see shortly in chapter 2, the police and courts are often not there for women in need of help.

And, in fact, we should not rely on them to be there. Why should we, especially those of us who are feminists, invite the state to be responsible for our personal health and safety? We don't want state interference when it comes to things like reproductive freedom or sexual orientation. If we do not trust the government and its agents with our sexual organs and appetites, why on earth should we trust them with our lives?

Ah, but dependency is still so seductive, perhaps, ironically, even more so in a world where women have made so many apparent strides. (Remember Gloria Steinem's admission in *Revolution from Within* that there were times when all she wanted was to be taken care of by a strong, powerful man?) There is still something appealing, to many women—many socially powerful women, at that—about the image of the little girl who cannot quite fend for herself in a big bad world.

"Trust me," *New York Times* columnist Maureen Dowd writes, "I am not the sort of person who should be able to walk out of a store with a really big gun in half an hour."[51] This was in a column bemoaning the ready availability of firearms, in which Dowd claimed she was shocked to discover that buying a gun is "easier and less expensive than buying a pink cashmere sweater set." She tells of venturing into a sporting goods store in Arlington, Virginia, where she and a female friend were shown a "basic black Mossberg" shotgun. "It was as easy as Thelma and Louise," she fairly giggles. "A driver's license, half an hour for a computerized background check, and the gun would have been ours." Dowd says she was appalled at the prospect that she could actually have purchased a gun, and she certainly was right to be. It is clear in her column, from things like a reference to a "Browning 20-gauge deer rifle," that this woman knows nothing about firearms. She is probably correct, as well, in her assessment that she is not the "sort of person" who should own one. After all, the decision whether or not to have a gun, as Hasselstrom and Silko both forcefully write, has everything to do with self-knowledge.

But why does Dowd choose to appeal to silly, frilly fashion comparisons—the "basic black" gun, the pink sweater set—to make her point, which turns out to be ultimately (and illogically) that all handguns should be banned because she evidently could not be trusted with one? Why does a columnist who just weeks before had won the Pulitzer Prize for scathing political commentary feel an apparent need to play dumb when the subject is guns?

By intriguing coincidence, around the same time Dowd was writing this column, actress Sharon Stone decided to turn her firearms (a shotgun and three handguns) in to the Los Angeles police. In a statement to the press, Stone said her act was a response to the then-recent killings at Columbine High, in Littleton, Colorado. "Our world has changed, and our children are in danger," she said. "I choose to surrender my right to bear arms in exchange for the peace of mind of doing the right thing."[52] Stone urged other gun owners to do likewise. The media, predictably, leapt on the story. After all, here was a woman who in many of her film roles, at least, was not exactly the good girl next door. Her relinquishing of her guns looked almost like a confession of past sins, an attempt at self-reform.

But the story was not quite so simple. In a *Today Show* interview[53] some months after Stone's announcement, Katie Couric questioned her about it, apparently expecting Stone to make a strong anti-gun statement. She did not. Rather, Stone carefully explained several things. She told of how she came from a hunting background in Pennsylvania, had grown up eating game, and in fact identified guns and hunting with family values she continued to hold most dear. However, her wealth secured for her advantages many other people lack, in terms of personal and household security. Strictly speaking, with bodyguards and a household alarm system, Stone did not need a gun to protect herself. But more importantly, she had come to realize that although she had procured firearms for protection, she could not be certain of her ability to use them effectively against an intruder in a panic situation. She talked, in a measured way that comprehended the complexity of the questions involved, about matters of self-knowledge, personal choice, and social responsibility. She did not, refreshingly, talk about pink-sweater-like female weakness. No doubt because of a lifelong familiarity with firearms, Stone recognized what so many knee-jerk critics of gun ownership do not: that the decision to own and use one or more guns is a matter of well-informed choice, in the best feminist sense of that term.

Closing the Gender Gap

In a sense, Letty Pogrebin was right: it is high noon at the gender gap. If, thanks in large part to the women's movement, we can no longer tell ourselves the same old lies about female weakness, then we need to confront some powerful truths about female strength. Up until now, when the subject of "women and guns" has arisen in public discourse, the central question has almost invariably been whether or not women should arm themselves at all. And the answer has, almost as invariably, been no. Women, we have been told time and again, cannot "buy themselves security" with a firearm. It isn't guns that women need, as Ann Jones pontificated, it's courage.

But Jones got it wrong. Women do not appear to purchase guns to supply the courage they lack. It is more reasonable to say they purchase guns as a result of the courage they already possess. In a society still so dominated by traditional categories of appropriate female behavior, it takes courage for a woman take charge of her own safety. It takes courage to defy conventional gender stereotypes. It takes courage to do what "good girls" aren't supposed to want to do, whether it be venturing into a traditionally male-dominated profession like law enforcement or the military, or a pursuit like hunting or competitive shooting.

So, in the chapters that follow, we are less concerned with the question of whether or not women should have guns than with the various reasons so many women *do*. Contrary to the prevailing stereotypes that have so often infected feminist discourse about women and firearms, based upon the best evidence available to us, we work from the following assumptions:

- While the "female fear" is frequently, and legitimately, a factor in women's choice to own and use guns for self-protection, their decision is nevertheless a thoroughly rational one.
- Women as a group are far too intelligent to be "duped" or "manipulated" into something as serious as gun ownership; to believe otherwise is to buy into insidious, antifeminist stereotypes.
- Women are thoroughly capable of comprehending, and living responsibly with, the consequences of gun ownership.
- There are no demonstrable senses in which guns are inherently dangerous to women, or in which gun-armed women are inherently dangerous to themselves or to anyone else.
- There is nothing "false" about the sense of security or personal autonomy that gun ownership can afford women.
- A woman's decision to own a gun may not only avert possible tragedy, it may also open up for her new avenues of

self-awareness, new and more truly empowered ways of relating to other people and the world around her.

For far too long in our history, and in far too many social and political contexts, America's gun women have been invisible. We aim to set the record straight.

Snapshot

Peggy Tartaro, *The Arms of Venus DeMilo*

The dog, a mixed-breed pointer, may have barked and given up. Or maybe he came straight to my room and jumped on the bed, insisting I get up.

The clock reads 2:19, and in my grogginess I still note that it's eight or nine minutes fast, a trick to fool myself that always fails. Still half asleep and registering little except the dog's insistence, I struggle to come to consciousness. Ezra is a good dog, but occasionally needs to go out at odd hours; I pat his head and tell him, "Go back to sleep." But he is not pacified and I finally make contact with other sounds beyond the norm for a city residential street that's almost never silent, thanks in large part to a popular bistro half a block away.

It occurs—or maybe it dawns—at any rate, I realize slowly and then with a sickening mental "whack" that the noise is downstairs,

Peggy Tartaro is the editor of *Women & Guns* magazine.

alien and hostile. This is where time stands still, or seems to. Later, I remember there's even a name for the sensation of time slowing down in situations of great stress.

I get up, and am not at all quiet about it. I reach the phone and call 911. I give my address and add, "That's Buffalo," because somewhere in my head is the newspaper story of the countywide 911 system that mixes up the same street name in different towns. "There's someone breaking down the back door," I say.

"Where are you?" the operator asks.

"Upstairs, we're all upstairs, even the dog," I add, as if asking for congratulations.

I flip on the front hall light and say loudly, "The police are on their way." I honestly don't remember if I say, "I'm armed," or "I have a gun." It was part of my plan to have it, and I do, an autoloading 20-gauge shotgun that is solid and reassuring. I wake my parents and tell them someone's breaking in and the police are coming, and even as I do, I can see them arriving, a couple of cruisers without lights.

More frozen time and a voice says, "It's the police, it's okay." In fact, it's very safe—a lot of police are here. And whoever had gained entry by breaking through a panel on a thick oak door is gone.

Elapsed time: maybe seven or eight minutes, not more than ten. All that action, drama, and emotion, and it would hardly fill an average movie trailer. I know no one would want to see this movie—it's barely interesting to me in the retelling after the first couple of times.

For ten years I've been fielding calls from TV producers and magazine and newspaper writers. Because I'm editor of *Women & Guns* magazine, they almost all want the same thing from me, and in the same order. First, a little business: how many women own guns? They're distrustful when I tell them the number isn't written down anywhere, that they can sidle up to it, but not capture it completely.

Then comes the next request: a pin-up girl for women gun owners. The interviewers are, almost universally, and regardless of sex, interested in the figure they see in their heads: the lead in a "Woman in Jeopardy" made-for-TV movie, beautiful and vulnerable, but at the last minute able to blow the bad guy away. Venus DeMilo with prosthesis by Smith & Wesson.

I tell them that the little movie in their head is not the way it usually happens. My homely story is the way it is for most women gun owners: danger, quickly over, because of thought and careful planning for survival. Perhaps the resolution doesn't involve headlines or, as in my case, even an arrest.

I try to express how satisfying it is to be brave, how important it is to learn that skill. Prior arrangements for survival, I tell them, do not make me a crazy person. Dare I admit that I've practiced my access to my guns, my ammunition, my dash to the phone, even the decision to flip on the hall light?

Still not satisfied, they often wheedle for just one sacrifice to the Cult of the Victim. I see their point. It makes a better story when there's an epiphany and not a laundry list. But I can't make the facts fit their story. Giving one talk-show booker the name of someone who I thought would make herself available, I cautioned that she might not want to travel because she was pregnant. A pause, and then a hopeful, excited inquiry from the booker, "Is she *visibly* pregnant?"

This is the maddening dilemma for women gun owners: not the internal, but the external. We've come a long way, indeed, and on both sides of the gender gap there seems to be recognition, if not acceptance, that women are capable of plenty of things. Could firearms ownership be the sticking point? The place where avowed "feminists" meet the "traditional" men who think strong women are frightening?

Both view Venus DeMilo differently—on the one hand a "victim," and on the other an "ideal." But in both cases, unarmed.

Women who own firearms come in all shapes and sizes, ages, and backgrounds. With the exception of those who grew up in active gun-owning families (either in rural areas where firearms are seen as a tool or where guns are part of the family sports equipment), it takes considerable effort to make the decision to be a gun owner, to acquire a firearm and to learn to use it.

Most of these women tell me that the hard part was not learn to hold the gun, or to load it, fire it, or even clean it, but to *decide* to do all those things. Having made the decision, they are often left bewildered by the images of themselves in popular culture. Just as they are bewildered by the standard media response, the jaw-dropping, "Is she visibly pregnant?"

My own gun ownership seems matter-of-fact to me, as I am sure it does to most women. Do we marvel that we own and operate cars? Blenders? Computers? Roth IRAs? Of course not!

Yet in just this one remaining area, we seem forever caught in another century, one that probably never existed for most of our foremothers—the one where Ms. DeMilo waits for others with arms to be put on her pedestal.

2 Sisters Are Doing It for Themselves

The Question of Women's Armed Self-Defense

In 1994, Betty Friedan called the trend of women's gun ownership a "horrifying, obscene perversion of feminism."[1] Anti-gun feminists, and gun-control advocates of various political stripe and intensity, all seem to agree: women and guns don't mix. And certainly not where self-defense is concerned. An extensive litany of reasons against women's armed self-defense has evolved over the last decade: women who acquire guns for self-protection are misguided and/or incompetent; they are incapable of receiving or retaining the training that would allow them to use a gun in a safe, effective manner; they will shoot a spouse, family member, or innocent bystander "by mistake"; they will overreact and fire when unnecessary; they cannot be trusted to store a weapon in a safe manner. As gullible as children, women are unable to resist the lure of advertisements that offer the "false sense of security" of gun ownership. Even granting that women are appropriately afraid, they are deluded into trying to defend themselves when they should depend upon others to protect them. When danger threatens, help is only a 911 call away, after all.

The problem with all of this is its underlying subtext. These same demeaning assumptions about women should have feminists like Friedan howling with anger, and they do when the subject is just about anything other than firearms. Yet on this issue most feminists have perpetuated the same age-old gender stereotypes of female weakness and vulnerability that they quite rightly reject in other political and social contexts. The result is an odd sort of cognitive dissonance. Women who know perfectly well otherwise are willing to take as established fact that gun-armed women are naïve, childlike, and/or incompetent. It doesn't add up, somehow. But then, neither do many of the most frequently quoted statistics about guns and the people who own them.

The Numbers Game

What evidence is available for and against gun ownership in general, and women's gun ownership in particular? Many agencies collect data on aspects of the debate. Among them are such public sources as the Uniform Crime Reports data from the FBI, the Justice Research and Statistics Association (an organization supported by the U.S. Department of Justice), the Bureau of Justice Statistics, the U.S. Department of Justice Office of Justice Programs, the U.S. Census Bureau, and the ICPSR, which is affiliated with the Department of Justice. Private foundations also collect and distribute information, among them Handgun Control, Inc. (HCI), the National Council for a Responsible Firearms Policy, the Violence Policy Center, and the Coalition to Stop Gun Violence.

The political ideology of the private foundations is reflected in the figures they report. HCI's current chair is Sarah Brady, wife of James Brady, the presidential aide who was permanently disabled by a bullet intended for former president Ronald Reagan. While it occasionally issues statements regarding Americans' right to keep and bear arms for purposes like hunting, HCI's political agenda is and always has been clearly and explicitly anti-firearm, and especially anti-handgun. In an interview appearing in the July 26, 1976, issue of *New Yorker* magazine, Nelson Shields, then the HCI chair, described the organization's goal as making "the possession of all handguns . . . totally illegal,"[2] and that fundamental orientation has not changed. The Violence Policy Center and the Coalition to Stop Gun Violence share the basic goal of the abolition of handgun ownership. At the other end of the spectrum, of course, are the National Rifle Association (NRA) and Second Amendment Foundation, along with think-tanks like the Independence and Cato Institutes. Their agendas are just as clearly and explicitly pro-firearm. Each side of the debate has its own highly visible spokespersons, who marshal sets of facts and statistics to support their positions. Not surprisingly, the facts and figures they report are often widely divergent. Clearly, they can't all be true.

To demonstrate the conflict between data from politically differing organizations one need look no farther than the Internet. For example, the HCI website (www.handguncontrol.org/gunhome.htm) on Friday, November 12, 1999, listed the following as facts:

- In 1996, 13,788 people were killed using firearms and thousands more were seriously injured.
- Among young people, youths aged 10–19 committed suicide with a gun every six hours. That's over 1,300 young people in a single year.
- From 1984 to 1994 the firearm death rate for 15–19 year olds increased 222 percent.

Turning to other sources in the literature it takes relatively little effort to unearth statistics that appear directly to contradict, or at least create reasonable doubt about each of these assertions. For the first, regarding the number of murders in 1996, the Uniform Crime Reports published by the FBI says a total of 16,967 people of all ages were murdered in 1996, with 11,453 of the murders committed with firearms. HCI indirectly implies that its source is the Bureau of Justice Statistics, but in a close reading it actually cites no source for the 1996 figure. The question of how to account for the discrepancy in numbers is left to the reader—though most visitors to the web site, taking the figure at face value, would not be aware such a discrepancy even exists.

The second quote, on the gun-related suicide rate of 10–19-year-olds, is internally inconsistent. If one person is killed every six hours, then a total of four are killed per day. Multiply that by 365 and you obtain a figure of 1,460. (Ironically, this larger figure is actually more impressive, if one intends to emphasize the extent of the problem.) But how does HCI arrive at its figure? Again, no source is provided for the data. How many suicides are committed per year by youths in this age group? The Centers for Disease Control report a total of 2,105 suicides for youth between the ages of ten and nineteen for the year 1996.[3] However, it is difficult to determine how many of these deaths were gun related. Figures from the American Association of Suicidology divide age groups differently than the CDC, defining "youth" as ranging from fifteen to twenty-four years of age.[4] The inclusion of this older group (aged 20–24) inflates the figures, as this group alone had a total of 2,541 suicides in 1996, according to the CDC. The Association of Suicidology places the figure for firearms- and explosives-related suicides for youth at 62.6 percent. Taking the figure of 1,460 obtained from HCI's "every six hours" statement and comparing it to the total suicides reported by the CDC yields a figure of 69.4 percent, a figure even higher than the percentage derived from the larger sample. Something does not compute here.

The final figure cited by HCI regarding a 222 percent increase in the firearms-related death rate of teenagers over a ten-year period is, if accurate, certainly cause for concern. But rather than an increase in the rate of firearm deaths during the same period, attorney David Kopel of the Independence Institute (who clearly falls on the pro-gun side of the argument) cites a decrease in the incidence of firearms accidents from 1960 to the early 1990s.[5] In fact, Kopel's source for his figures—the National Safety Council—reports an absolutely level rate of gun deaths (.6 per 100,000) in the population in the years from 1986 through 1989. This figure dropped to a rate of .5 per 100,000 in the population in 1990, but only for the one year. The rate of accidental gun deaths returned in 1991 to the late 1980s rate of .6. This led the anti-gun faction to trumpet in 1991 that the firearms accident rate had increased an "alarming" 20 percent. What was not mentioned was that the base number of deaths was so small that a very small increase in that number presented in percentage form made the increase sound much greater than it actually was. It is all quite confusing, to say the least.

Then there is the statistic initially offered by Arthur Kellermann[6] that appears so ubiquitously in HCI's and other anti-firearms literature—that gun owners are forty-three times more likely to be shot or killed themselves, or have the same occur to a family member, than to be able to effectively use the firearm in defense of self and family. These numbers, if true, would indeed cast a serious doubt on the wisdom of arming oneself for self-defense. However, once again, figures in the pro-firearms literature either qualify or directly contradict Kellermann's findings.

Starting in 1986, Kellermann and a group of physicians affiliated with the Centers for Disease Control began to attack firearms from a public health perspective. Serving as the spokesperson for this group, Kellermann initially reported the risk figure of forty-three deaths, consisting of thirty-seven probable suicides, with the remainder being accidents and murders. In subsequent papers,[7] Kellermann repeatedly cited lower and lower estimates of the risk inherent in firearms ownership. He even admitted to an interviewer that if his own wife were in danger, he would want her to be armed with a thirty-eight special.[8] Nonetheless, despite several critics who have stepped forward to provide reasonable refutation of his findings,[9] Kellermann's "43-times-more-likely" factoid retains the aura, in press reports as well as in anti-gun fund-raising appeals, of gospel truth.

At the 1999 meeting of the American Society of Criminology, Gary Kleck presented a paper detailing his attempt to duplicate, and thus validate, Kellerman's estimates of the level of danger conferred on a home owner through the presence of a handgun in a household.[10] Giving every benefit of the doubt to Kellerman's assumptions regarding risk, Kleck combined figures from multiple sources to try to duplicate Kellerman's reported figures, but could not succeed. However Kleck manipulated the figures, he found no increased level of risk to the average home owner from his or her own weapons.

As Kleck and others have pointed out,[11] this is not surprising, since there is a clear and consistent pattern regarding firearms-related deaths: they occur overwhelmingly in households where violence is the norm. The "friends and relatives" who get caught in the crossfire are generally either partners in criminal activity or adversaries in drug deals gone sour. The typical murderer has a history of violent behavior, and a police record to go with it. The accidental killing of a child, or an adult for that matter, is the tragic exception rather than the rule. It only stands to reason, as James Wright has pointed out, that gun owners are by and large an extremely safe and safety-conscious group. Were they not, given the fact that approximately half of all U.S. households have one or more guns present, Americans would be up to their knees in corpses.[12]

It is possible to find, or massage, numbers that can support either a pro-gun or anti-gun stance, to pick and choose the figures that support the ideological position of your choice. Add to this the large number of studies conducted by academics on both sides of the gun issue and, to the uninitiated and the expert alike, there is a veritable buffet of facts from which to choose to support your position.

Quantifying Female Fear

How the numbers actually stack up depends on what information was collected, how it was interpreted, and toward what end. The array of data collection instruments employed to report the number of rapes and sexual victimizations provides a good example of the problems inherent in finding the "right" numbers to describe crime or other firearms-related phenomena. There are significant similarities and differences in the various surveys, and these have potentially important implications for the woman weighing her risks and contemplating different self-defense strategies.

Life in the United States can indeed be a dangerous affair. Violent crime rates have steadily declined over the last few decades; however, this decline offers cold comfort to the individuals who are victimized. Not all individuals are equally vulnerable. Males are more likely to be the victims as well as the perpetrators of violence. But while most violent crime is committed by men against men, other factors enter into the equation, creating some groups who are especially likely to fall into the victim category.

The only area in which women, as a group, are more vulnerable than men is that of rape and sexual assault.[13] A number of major surveys examine the phenomena of rape and sexual victimization—the National Crime Survey (NCS), the National Crime Victimization Survey (NCVS), the National Women's Survey (NWS), and the National

Violence Against Women Survey (NVAW). Three of these collect data from women eighteen years old and older; only the National Women's Survey includes girls from twelve to seventeen years of age. This is a not a trivial difference, since FBI figures indicate that a significant proportion of rapes are perpetrated against young women in just this age range. The National Violence Against Women Survey has also found that 54 percent of their participants were under the age of eighteen at the time of their first rape, 32 percent reporting rapes between the ages of twelve and seventeen, with the final 22 percent reporting rape before the age of twelve.

To further complicate matters, because of the unique characteristics of these crimes, it is extremely difficult to obtain accurate information. What constitutes sex as opposed to sexual assault is for many a highly personal matter. Plus, there is a social pattern of blaming the victim that makes many women hesitant to "cry rape." As numerous feminist critics have argued, it is extremely likely that crimes such as rape or sexual assault are seriously underreported. Estimates of the percentage of rapes reported to the authorities varies from a low of 8 to a high of 16 percent of the female population of the United States.[14] These differences in estimates may result from differences in design among the most commonly employed measures of sexual victimization.

The size of the samples employed in the four major survey instruments varies widely. The NCS and NCVS sample 50,000 households, interviewing two individuals, yielding a sample size of 110,000 for each. The NVAW interviewed 8,000 women and 8,000 men, for a sample size of 16,000. And, finally, the NWS interviewed 4,008 women. The accuracy of an estimate is only as good as the similarities between the sample and the population as a whole. As the size of a sample becomes smaller in proportion to the population being described, it is increasingly likely that the survey does not accurately mirror the population. Thus, the smaller the sample, the lower the level of confidence in the accuracy of its descriptions.

Method is as important a factor as sample size when it comes to collecting information. The NCS, the NCVS, and the NWS all depend at least in part on telephone interviews. They use random-digit dialing to reduce the problem of losing individuals with unlisted phone numbers from the sample. But the use of the telephone itself introduces a bias to estimates, by excluding those individuals without phones. Since individuals without telephones are more likely to reside at the lower income levels, and thereby fall into a group considered to be at higher levels of risk for sexual assault, this is not a random loss of subjects. To the extent that there is an association between socioeconomic class and the victimization of women, surveys which lose groups like poor inner-city or rural women risk underestimating the extent of the phenomenon.

Finally, there are different methods of reporting the occurrences of sexual victimization. Researchers calculate incidence rates by comparing the total number of rape events reported to the number of persons responding to the survey. If an individual reports multiple events (in this case rapes), she is counted multiple times and the incidence rate is inflated. Prevalence rates, on the other hand, are calculated differently. For prevalence rates, the number of persons reporting victimization is compared to the total number of individuals reporting. The number of rapes per victim is not considered, so a victim can only be counted once. For prevalence rates, then, victimization rates may be underestimated. When surveys do not indicate how they are reporting data and nonspecialists are unclear about the differences between incidence and prevalence, the potential for confusion obviously increases.

Not surprisingly, given all of these factors, there are large differences in these surveys' reported number of rapes. NCS reports the lowest annual rate, an estimated 130,000 rapes per year. The NVAW places the figure at 302,091 per year, the NCVS estimates 310,000 per year, and the NWS estimates 683,000 rapes per year. Which numbers are correct? There is, alas, no obviously correct answer.

Fear or Rational Concern?

Perhaps because women are especially vulnerable to sexual crimes, there is a significant literature that identifies them as being more fearful of falling victim to *all* crimes than are men.[15] According to some commentators, women as a result live in a state of "inordinate fear."[16] But from the vantage points of individual women, there is nothing "inordinate" about it.

The "female fear" is certainly not irrational. Awareness of the extent and frequency of rape and sexual victimization is relatively recent, and the implications are still not fully understood.[17] Even with their differences, and with the problem of underreporting, the surveys above report large numbers of women who are victims of sexually related crimes. These crimes can result in serious damage to these women: 31 percent of rape victims develop the psychological disorder known as Post-Traumatic Stress Disorder; and rape victims are 8.7 times more likely than their peers to attempt suicide.[18]

Further, the nature of victimization in rape is substantially different than other types of crimes. Rape is an act of power and control. The goal is domination, not sex. Forced sexual submission is used as a method of control and humiliation.[19] Fear of sexual assault restricts and controls the freedom of action of women and girls and socializes them to accept their subordination to men, and the ever-present possibility that they will fall victim to male violence. Women learn the safest clothing to wear, the safest places to occupy, and the safest times to move about. Their movements are limited and governed by their risk of victimization.[20]

Finally, the aftermath of a rape serves to revictimize women. Women who have been raped are stigmatized for having provoked the rape through inappropriate behavior or clothing, or for being sexually uncontrolled, or/and for not knowing "where to draw the line." This sets rape victims apart, since most crime victims do not need to convince others of the truth or validity of their victim status. In a study of convicted rapists, 84 percent continued to insist that their behavior definitely was not rape.[21] The police frequently doubt rape victims' honesty. The myth that nice women don't get raped is still alive and well.[22] A woman who manages to escape being badly bruised or otherwise injured during a rape is especially unlikely to be able to successfully press charges, since police officers are reluctant to believe a woman who has offered "less than extraordinary resistance."[23] While women of color are disproportionately likely to be the victims of rape and battery, they are less likely to be acknowledged as victims.[24]

Women's fear of crime in general derives directly from their fear of sexual victimization, because of the perceived likelihood of rape being associated with other crimes—as in the scenario in which a burglar happens upon a lone woman at home and proceeds to commit rape in addition to his intended original crime.[25] Crimes that might involve no sexual component when perpetrated against a man therefore present a greater level of danger to women. Women are, literally, more vulnerable because of their sex.

From a relatively early age, women recognize this increased vulnerability. Recent research has found that adolescent and adult women are equally afraid of crime. Interestingly, however, if fear of sexual victimization is factored out of the equation, the differential level between women's and men's fear of crime disappears.[26]

But why label this recognition "fear"? We generally employ the terms "caution" or "concern" when discussing precautions taken based on a perceived risk—no matter how probable the event. Parents take out life insurance based on concern for their children's well-being in the event of the parents' death. Individuals who are not expert swimmers are discouraged from swimming in deep water. Backpackers going on even a short hike are encouraged to leave their planned route and expected time of return with someone who can sound an alarm if necessary. We don't label these individuals "afraid." Instead, we see them as prudent or cautious. It is surely just as prudent for women to be concerned for their personal safety—and in some situations, more concerned than men would be. In fact, male and female gun owners are equally likely to report acquiring a handgun based on a concern about the danger they perceive in society.[27] Women's additional concern about the potential for sexual assault is in no way "inordinate."

Women and Children First

Arguably most Americans, and certainly most feminists, today grant that women have every reason to be concerned about their safety. They do not necessarily agree, however, that women should have to worry about taking responsibility for it. The phrase "women and children first," as applied to entitlement to seats in a lifeboat, identifies both groups as uniquely vulnerable and thus in need of protection. Conventionally, women and children are to be protected by male others: by fathers or husbands, or *in extremis*, by the society itself as represented by the police.

However, many women and children have no man available to provide protection. Women are generally marrying later than at any other time in American history, and many are choosing not to marry at all. Increasing numbers of women are divorcing and establishing single-parent households. A significant number of women neither have nor want a man in their lives, to whom they could turn for protection. And many who do have satisfying relationships with men do not include "knight in shining armor" in their mate's job description.

A growing number of women, across all the above categories, want to shoulder the responsibility for their own protection. They believe, along with shooting writer Susan Laws, "It is a sad fact that many women today, so quick to demand equal rights as citizens, refuse to take individual responsibility for their own safety and that of their family."[28] Or, to quote firearms instructor and cowboy action firearms competitor Heidi Smith, "It's pretty selfish to expect your spouse, a friend, or anyone else to take care of your personal protection."[29]

This is especially, and ironically, true in those cases in which the man in the house is a perpetrator of violence rather than a protector against it. Violence between intimate partners has only been the subject of study since approximately the late 1970s. That it took so long to examine this phenomenon may partly be due to the fact that in American culture men's violent or aggressive behavior, and women's tolerance of and submission to it, have been for most of our history viewed as "normal."[30]

In fact, one of the earliest studies published on domestic violence found that violence between family members is probably as common as love.[31] This finding was based on a sample of 2,000 families in which one-sixth of the married couples acknowledged that one partner or the other had engaged in at least one act of violence against their spouse. These numbers were in turn criticized as underestimates of the prevalence of familial violence, because divorced couples (among whom violence rates might be assumed to be higher or even possibly responsible for the divorce) were excluded, and because a certain number of people are unwilling to admit to such antisocial acts.[32]

The measuring instrument most commonly employed in this research was developed by sociologists Richard Gelles and Murray Straus, and is known as the Conflict Tactics Scale (CTS).[33] The scale consists of a list of increasingly violent acts; that is, acts carried out with the explicit intent of inflicting physical harm. They range from shoves or slaps all the way to acts resulting in severe injury or death. Rates of violence obtained using the CTS in 1985 appeared to fly in the face of the common beliefs about spousal abuse, which identified the wife as the primary victim.

Based on use of the CTS, in 1985, 12 percent of wives admitted to any of the violent acts (3 percent to the severe violent acts), and 11 percent of husbands admitted to any violence (with 4 percent admitting to severe violent acts). Multiplying these figures by census population figures yielded an estimated number of 6,250,000 assaulted wives and 6,800,000 assaulted husbands. This would appear to indicate that it is men, not women who should have a higher concern about spousal violence. Indeed, a number of newspapers and magazines leaped on this information; conservative publications like the *National Review* and *U.S. News and World Report* seemed especially eager to argue that men had more to fear from their wives than vice versa.

Proponents of what was for a time referred to as "battered husband syndrome" in the press failed, however, to take into account two pieces of information that author Gelles considered essential: that women are seriously injured at a rate *seven times* that of men, and that women are killed by their partners twice as often as men. True, Gelles and Straus concluded that "you are more likely to be physically assaulted, beaten, and killed in your own home at the hands of a loved one than any place else, or by anyone else in our society."[34]

However, the likelihood would still be considerably less if you are male and an adult.

The National Violence Against Women Survey (NVAW) also collects information on family violence. Data collected between November 1995 and May 1996 found 1.9 percent of women and 3.4 percent of men reporting a physical assault by an intimate during the previous year. Again we see the larger numbers for men. Because of methodological differences, the NVAW estimates of annual physical assaults are greater than the National Crime Victimization Survey (NCVS) estimates. The NCVS estimate for 1994 is 4.1 million aggravated and simple assaults of females age twelve and older, and 5.7 million aggravated and simple assaults of males age twelve and older.[35]

Figures like these have led some to ask, why be particularly concerned about women when the numbers indicate higher levels of overall violence for men? The answer is simple. Because of their average smaller stature and size, women generally inflict less damage with their attacks than men. Men, conversely, do far more serious damage to women. The U.S. Department of Justice reports approximately 130,000 aggravated assaults or assaults against women by their male partners that involve serious injury. One in twelve women who are treated in emergency rooms has been assaulted by her partner.[36] And 28 percent of female murder victims, according to the FBI, are killed by their spouses or boyfriends. More males may be slapped or shoved by women, but comparatively few are seriously injured or killed by their female partners.

Women in abusive relationships are often asked why they don't leave. The answer is complicated. Setting aside the obvious practical issues of where to go and how to support oneself and one's children, a primary reason for staying in the relationship is the fact that leaving increases the probability and severity of the violence. A 1980 report to the Wisconsin Council on Criminal Justice reported that leaving does not provide adequate protection for a woman. Thirty percent of the women in the report were separated at the time of attack. A study which compared a sample of women who had killed their husbands with a matched sample of women who had not killed (but had suffered equivalent abuse at the hands of their partners) found that 98 percent of the first group and 90 percent of the second group believed that their abuser could or would kill them if they left. By staying in the relationship, then, women are trying to protect themselves and their children.

Women who leave face the additional problem that their departure may be perceived as exacerbating the murderous behavior of their partners. In a case reported in the Denver *Rocky Mountain News* in June 1983, Pat Burns, an elementary school teacher, had tried to escape her husband of fifteen years. Finally, in August of 1982 she had managed to leave. Despite a documented history of abuse, and the fact that Ms. Burns had immediately sought legal assistance upon leaving, she was terrified of her husband's reaction. And rightly so. Her husband found her and shot her five times in the face at close range, killing her. At his trial, the judge stated that Ms. Burns had "provoked" the murder by leaving, and sentenced her husband to a total sentence of two years of work/release. In *Next Time She'll Be Dead*, Ann Jones catalogues dozens of cases with similar outcomes.

It is clear that for a substantial number of women, safety does not reside in the home. The men who could serve as protection from danger themselves represent the primary danger to which these women are exposed. If men won't protect women, what about the law? Can, or will, the police provide protection?

Call 911, an Ambulance, and Order a Pizza: See Which One Gets There First

Contrary to popular mythology, the police have no legal obligation to protect any single individual in this society. Indeed, there is a rich legal history denying the individual responsibility for legal protection by the police.[37] Attempts by victims to bring suits against the police for failing to provide protection are often summarily thrown out of court. This lack of police responsibility for the individual citizen's safety has been consistently affirmed by the courts, including the U.S. Supreme Court. In the *DeShaney* decision in 1989, the Court ruled that the due process clause of the Fourteenth Amendment exists to protect people from the state, not from each other. Police and other state authorities are, therefore, not required to intervene in domestic disputes—or, indeed, in any crimes-in-progress—their duty being, rather, to apprehend the offender after the crime has been committed. A frequently cited example of what this means in practice was the case of three Washington, D.C., women who were held hostage and repeatedly sexually assaulted in their own home for fourteen hours after the police had failed to respond to their call for help. In *Warren v. District of Columbia* (1981), the appellate court ruled that "the government and its agents are under no general duty to provide public services, such as police protection, to any individual citizen."

An even more chilling example of the victim's difficulty in holding the police accountable occurred in Massachusetts in 1986. When a woman went to the police for protection from the abuse and harassment of her husband, from whom she was separated, she was told that the police didn't "baby sit." The police suggested that she buy a gun. Over a fifteen-month period the harassment and stalking continued without the police ever arresting the husband even when he was caught in the act. When her husband threatened to kill her, she relayed the threat to the police, who responded by not responding. The husband broke down his wife's door and chased her out of the house and across the street through traffic. Though she sought help or protection from her neighbors, no one would give her shelter. The husband shot her three times in the face and neck, resulting in permanent paralysis, then turned the weapon on himself. The court ruled that the police had no duty to protect her and the case was dismissed.

A few years later, in a suburb of Buffalo, New York, a housewife called police to complain about threats from her estranged husband. The woman, a licensed gun owner, had fled to her mother's house. The police arrived there and confiscated her registered firearm "for her own protection." A few days later, her husband arrived on the scene. He murdered both the woman and her mother. These, unfortunately, are not isolated instances. But in order to successfully hold the police liable for injuries sustained when they have failed to provide aid or protection, it is first necessary to prove that the police had an obligation to provide this aid or protection. If the court determines lack of obligation, the case proceeds no further.

Some states have, however, created a "special relationship" between police and victims which establishes such obligation. "Special relationships" may include orders of protection; specific promises to take action; giving victims a false sense of security which caused the victims to fail to exercise vigilance or take action in their own defense; or an officer's failure to act when he can see that it places the victim at risk of imminent harm. Obtaining protective orders from the court often does not, however, create a sufficient duty for the police to protect a woman. Although these orders in theory require that offenders or stalkers maintain a safe distance from their intended victim, they are seldom effective or enforced. Texas has determined that for the police "'no duty' to protect means no duty to enforce a protective order against a violent criminal unless the police see the criminal actually violate that order."[38]

Five states (Alabama, Arizona, Montana, New Mexico, and Washington) allow suits to be brought against the police, with laws such that the victim might actually win. Others allow suits to be brought, but most are dismissed before reaching the trial stage. These include Idaho, Nebraska, New Hampshire, North Dakota, South Carolina, South Dakota, Vermont, West Virginia, and Wyoming. Four states (Alaska, Louisiana, New Jersey, and Oregon) operate under judicial decisions so inconsistent that it is difficult to predict in advance whether or not a suit would be successful. Thirty-three states and the District of Columbia provide for no tort duty to respond to individual citizens; in these states, a call to 911 in many instances can be ignored by the police with impunity.

What, then, is a woman, reasonably fearful for her own or her children's safety, to do? The former attorney general of Florida reported to Florida legislators that police responded to about 200,000 of 700,000 citizen calls for help—a frighteningly low 28.6 percent. When asked why so many Dade County citizens were arming themselves, he replied, "They damn well better, they've got to protect themselves." Former chief of police of Los Angeles, Ed Davis, is quoted as saying: "Crime is so far out of hand, we can't protect the average citizen. He [sic] must protect himself."[39] Not surprisingly, many women are seeing their options the same way.

Doing It for Themselves

Feminism is surely in some ways responsible for the fact that women are increasingly choosing to take the responsibility for their own safety, and learning self-defense despite the fact that society remains reluctant to accept the legitimacy of women's taking lethal-force power into their own hands. The large number of women who say they are taking steps to protect themselves are doing it out of a deep sense that their self-defense is worth fighting for. Rather than capitulating to the culture of male violence, these women are, as Naomi Wolf has suggested, fighting fire with fire.

As gun owner Leslita Williams, a middle-aged librarian, put it in an interview, "So much of nonviolent philosophy was dreamed up by men who didn't have to worry about the kinds of violence women face today. . . . Everyone has to decide for herself." Williams's own decision was based on the fact that in the mid-1980s a serial rapist was roaming her neighborhood in Athens, Georgia. She and seven of her friends, all of them "weaned on sixties-style nonviolence," enrolled in an armed self-defense course. They met together after each class, to talk over their feelings about the course and about guns. Ultimately, four of the women opted not to arm themselves, arguing that would amount to "stooping to the level of the enemy." Williams and three others decided that a pacifist approach was inadequate to the threat of a rapist-at-large; they bought handguns.[40] Two things stand out about Williams's experience. One is that it clearly exemplifies that the choice to arm oneself can certainly arise from a commitment to feminist politics and practice; that is, from the conviction that women's lives, safety, and peace of mind matter, and that it is up to women themselves to take responsibility for their own well-being. The other is that these women, in deciding for or against firearms ownership, had made an informed choice.

Many Second Wave feminists continue to regard the violence inherent in the concept of armed or lethal-force self-defense with a jaundiced eye. Like four of Williams's friends, they continue to take Audre Lorde's comment that the Master's tools cannot dismantle his house to mean that women must not embrace violence in any form. However, a new generation of feminists are beginning to think in different, almost revolutionary, terms about their relationship with violence.

One of them is Martha McCaughey. "I was once a frightened feminist," she remarks at the outset of her journey, both literal and theoretical, through the various options available to women for self-defense.[41] As McCaughey experienced self-defense courses ranging from padded-attacker, martial arts, and cardio-combat to firearms use, she discovered that while "enacting an aggressive posture felt empowering, it [also] felt taboo—in my case doubly taboo as a woman and a feminist." But she also discovered that an enhanced sense of her aggressive physical power felt good. "Getting mean," she remarks, "is fun."[42]

Research on the effects of women's self-protective skills on their self-image supports an idea of literal empowerment. After "Model Mugging" courses, women feel more capable of defending themselves physically in the event of being attacked, which leads to a reduction in the number of limitations women place on their everyday activities. They now take risks with their behavior that would have been unthinkable before the training. McCaughey suggests: "If contemporary feminism has enabled the transformation of women's consciousness, and has spawned a critique of the way the female body has been treated, represented, and thought of, self-defense training reveals how the traditional sexist ideas find their way into the functioning of the body itself. . . . Feminists have long considered the ways in which gender seems like biology but really isn't; self-defense illuminates the ways that gender is an ideology inseparable from, and alterable through, the lived body."[43] Women who learn self-defense techniques not only see themselves and experience their bodies differently; they carry themselves differently, with more self-consciousness and self-confidence. Interestingly, believing you are safer can actually make you safer; rapists and muggers know how to read body language when selecting potential victims.

Yet because aggression is perceived as a male prerogative, women who become aggressive—even in the service of their own self-protection—risk being accused of "trying to be like men" and copping to patriarchal notions about power. McCaughey argues that "much feminist discourse has maintained a central assumption of bourgeois liberal individualism, namely that the body is an appendage of the self subjected to property rights. . . . This assumption turns the body into an object rather than an agent, thus rendering women's self-defense training irrelevant, inconsequential, or even antithetical to feminist politics."[44] But accepting aggressive power as something of which women are and should be capable, far from being antithetical to feminism, creates a new "physical feminism." Women begin eagerly to accept their power to protect themselves from assailants, and will disrupt the societal "scripts" that define women as vulnerable victims and men as powerful and entitled.

McCaughey is not the only feminist to discover the liberating power of self-defense. Ellen Snortland encourages women to find the "warrior within" through physical self-defense training. Her book, *Beauty Bites Beast: Awakening the Warrior within Women and Girls*, avoids discussion of firearms, save for a brief mention in a question and answer appendix. When asked how one should respond to an attacker armed with a gun or a knife, she responds, puzzlingly: "One of the most potent aspects of learning full-force, full-contact self-defense is the ability the trained person has to talk to a potential assailant."[45] Snortland does not explain the connection between a full contact self-defense course and the ability to converse, or how such a course would increase that ability. When asked about the wisdom of obtaining a gun instead of learning self-defense, as if the two were mutually exclusive, Snortland admits her anti-handgun bias. She suggests instead learning how to make weapons out of available household objects. But it is difficult to understand why this sound advice rules out using the most effective weapon available, a handgun, to break off an attack.

Certainly physical training for self-defense is a good idea. It not only provides women with an opportunity for exercise and developing physical fitness, it also helps them develop a stronger sense of their own strength and agility. But basic size and strength differences between men and women cannot be denied. Many if not most women would not or could not train themselves to a level of proficiency that would make them truly equal to a man in hand-to-hand combat. And it is difficult to imagine any, except the most highly trained and physically fit among women, successfully fighting a man armed with a knife, bludgeon, or gun. Research has shown that a woman who forcefully resists stands a better chance of fending of an attacker than one who tries to talk her way out of the situation. However, the level of forceful resistance must be equivalent to the ferocity of the attack.[46] And a handgun, as Arthur Kellermann himself acknowledged, is by far the most reliable self-defense against a potentially lethal attack.

Additionally, not all women are able to undertake physical self-defense training. For older women and those with disabilities, a firearm may represent their only choice for active self-protection. In each issue of its membership magazines *American Guardian* and *American Rifleman*, the NRA's "Armed Citizen" page features clippings from newspapers around the country, focusing on ordinary citizens' uses of firearms to thwart crime. Over the years an increasing number of these stories have been about women. The two following anecdotes are similar. These, however, were taken from a website on the Internet on "Women and Self-protection."

*Geneva Littlefield, 61, and her 95-year-old mother are quiet women who keep to themselves in their East Hall, Georgia, home. Geneva keeps a .38 cal. revolver in case others don't do the same. After cutting the phone lines of the elderly women's home, a man broke in early one morning. Geneva heard him coming and was waiting for him. He began to choke her mother, so she shot him in the groin. Unable to call police and unwilling to leave her mother alone with the wounded burglar, she held him at gunpoint until she could alert passing neighbors. (*The Times, *Gainesville, GA, 10/18/97)*

*The burglar ransacked 81-year-old Alberta Nicles' Muskegon, Michigan, home before waking her up and ordering her around the house to search for money. Ending up back in her bedroom, the intruder—a suspected crack addict with a long history of criminal activity—removed the widow's pajama bottoms and was preparing to rape her when she informed him that she knew where there was some money. Her assailant let her up and followed her to a closet where the woman instead retrieved her late husband's .38. She turned and shot her tormenter to death. Nicles then went to a neighbor's home to call police because her own lines had been severed by the intruder prior to his breaking in. "This was not just a random breaking and entering. He was planning on taking advantage of the vulnerability of an elderly person. She was clearly acting in self-defense," Muskegon County Prosecutor Tony Tague said. (*The Chronicle, *Muskegon, Michigan, January 2, 1997)*

In neither of these two cases would these women have been able to physically deter their attackers or protect themselves in any other way. One not uncommonly hears anti-gun feminists say they would rather die than own a gun. As these anecdotes demonstrate, that could represent a very real possibility.

Elderly and disabled women are not the only ones at a disadvantage when it comes to being able to actively defend themselves. As we have already had occasion to remark, the generally anti-gun tenor of mainstream feminism reflects, and is to a large degree insulated by, a comfortably middle-class, white perspective. It is surely easier to forswear violent resistance if one belongs to a group that is statistically less likely to fall prey to violent attack. According to Bureau of Justice Statistics, although women are one-third less likely to be victims of robbery or assault (excluding sexual assault) than men, certain women are far more vulnerable than others. These include women in the following risk categories: women aged 20–24 years; African-American women; divorced, separated, or single women; urban dwellers; women who never graduated from high school; and women who earn less than $10,000 a year. Women of color and poor women, many of whom share several of these risk factors, seldom have the luxury of debating about whether or not the Master's house can be dismantled using the Master's tools.

White liberals like to pontificate about the need to get "Saturday Night Specials" off the streets and out of the hands of criminals. The problem is, these relatively inexpensive handguns are generally not the ones involved in the commission of crimes; felons tend to steal, or to illegally buy on the black market, far more expensive sidearms. As law professor Robert Cottrol remarks: "Bans on firearms ownership in public housing, the constant effort to ban pistols poor people can afford—scornfully labeled 'Saturday night specials' and 'junk guns'—are denying the means of self-defense to entire communities in a failed attempt to disarm criminal predators. In many under-protected minority communities, citizens have been disarmed and left to the mercy of well-armed criminals."[47] And in these communities, a disproportionate number of households are headed by single women. If police will not protect them, they should at least have access to the tools with which they might protect themselves and their families.

The Right Tool for the Job

A gun is simply a tool. Although anti-gun literature frequently treats firearms as if they were talismans, with magical powers of their own, the fact of the matter is that firearms in the home are dangerous only if used or stored irresponsibly. Guns can save lives as well as take them. Bear in mind, in this connection, that the defensive use of a firearm frequently does not require that it be discharged. Merely the threat or the sight of a firearm can terminate an attack. People, quite appropriately, fear handguns. Any felon will be the first to tell you this.

Research shows that the fact that potential victims might be armed represents a risk for assailants that often affects if, when, and where a crime is committed. In one survey of over 1,500 incarcerated felons, over 80 percent agreed that smart criminals attempt to ascertain whether the intended victim is armed.[48] More than half of the inmates reported they would change their target if they discovered, or even suspected, their original target was armed. Burglars reported that if they determined that a home was occupied they would avoid trying to break into the home because of the specific fear of being shot. And perhaps most interesting of all, more than half of the criminals reported being more concerned about running into an armed victim than into a police officer.

So a firearm can be a deterrent to crime by its mere presence. How many times a year are crimes thwarted or not committed for fear of an armed victim? As with the other statistics we have discussed in this chapter, this question is difficult to answer conclusively. As of 1995 at least fifteen surveys had attempted to measure the number of defensive gun uses each year.[49] While it is relatively easy to obtain reliable statistics on actual crimes, it is extremely difficult to find solid data on crimes that weren't committed. The smallest estimate for the number

87

of these defensive gun uses is 700,000 per year,[50] but some others range far higher.

The largest academic interview study of its kind, undertaken by criminologist Gary Kleck, found 2.5 million incidents of defensive handgun uses in the United States between 1988 and 1993.[51] Fifty-four percent of these uses were reported by women, which when multiplied by the population yields 1,180,586 defensive gun uses.[52] This number may seem amazingly large, even to those who favor armed self-defense, given the fact that there are no figures that would indicate that women own anywhere close to half of the firearms in our society. However, there is no mistake. Unlike other surveys that asked about gun use by any household member, this study specifically asked if the woman herself had used the gun. It's important to remember that in addition to the between eleven and seventeen million women who own firearms themselves, far more have access to and experience with guns owned by other members of their households. It is equally important to remember that, as in cases of sexual assault, surveys about gun use tend to be subject to a certain amount of underreporting. Kleck's work indicates that the civilian experience with defensive use of handguns appears to be approximately three times as common as the experience of victimization.[53] The defensive value of the gun's mere presence is demonstrated by the study's finding that in only 8 percent of the 2.5 million defensive uses of guns, the firearm was actually fired.

If women are, in fact, responsible for over a million defensive uses of guns over a six-year period, who are these women? According to most studies, gun owners tend to be male, middle aged, and relatively affluent. The women in one 1999 sample of firearms owners[54] ranged in age ranged in age from 23 to 71. The median age was 48, which makes this sample comparable to previously reported samples of male gun owners. Household incomes ranged from $10,000 to

$180,000, with a median of $55,000 for the combined household income. Only seven women reported incomes below $30,000, while eleven reported incomes over $100,000 per year. These relatively high incomes are likely related to the fact that half of the sample (sixty-one women) reported having completed college or an advanced degree. Not surprisingly, since the sample was composed of readers of firearms magazines, almost all (97 percent) own handguns. Over two-thirds of the sample bought their own handgun; 17 percent received their weapons as gifts.

The women were almost equally split between owning revolvers and semi-automatic pistols. Revolvers are the familiar "cowboy"-type of handgun where cartridges are loaded into a cylinder which advances each time the trigger is pulled. Semi-automatic handguns hold the cartridges in a magazine that is inserted into the grip of the gun; the firing of each round loads the next round into the chamber. For both types, only one bullet is fired by each pull of the trigger. The primary difference is that a larger number of bullets can be contained in a semi-automatic handgun. Gun women preferred a .38 caliber handgun, while men often prefer the heavier .45 caliber weapon.[55] Four out of five had undergone formal handgun training and described their skills as either intermediate or expert.

Over half of the women also own at least one rifle and at least one shotgun. However, for a variety of reasons, long guns are less effective as self-defense weapons than are handguns,[56] so it is reasonable to assume they owned these guns for other purposes, like hunting and target shooting. When asked why they obtained a handgun, 60 percent of the women cited self-defense over competition, recreation, and hunting as their primary reason for handgun acquisition. This closely matches the reasons given by men in a number of studies.[57] These gun women generally were not responding to an incident or attack they had personally experienced, although 22 percent reported having been victims of a serious crime. Most cited a general concern for their personal safety. Of those women who reported using their handgun for self-defense (eighteen women representing 13 percent of the sample), only four had fired the weapon. As discussed earlier in regard to the deterrent value of firearms, most either displayed the weapon or informed the attacker that they were armed.

Most of the sample (111 or 82 percent) reported carrying the handgun. Of this group, 40 percent (forty-four women) reported carrying the gun at all times; an additional 43 percent (forty-eight women) reported carrying their gun when they expected to be in an unsafe environment. In other words, for most of these women, the handgun is an integral part of their daily routine. Unlike men who often carry their handguns in holsters, women reported various methods for carrying their guns, including regular purses or briefcases, purses or briefcases specially equipped with an internal holster, fanny packs, even diaper bags.

In terms of citizenship, this sample of gun women reported an unusually high level of civic involvement. Ninety-three percent were registered voters. Forty-six percent had written to a lawmaker in the past eight months, and an additional 13 percent had written both to a lawmaker and a letter to the editor. Thus, almost 60 percent were vocal in expressing their views and actively involving themselves in the democratic process.

Three out of four said they did not approve of gun control. Yet a small minority reported favoring waiting periods, mandatory firearms training for gun owners, banning certain types of weapons, and keeping guns out of the hands of children (no more than twenty favored any one type of control). It bears noting, regarding these responses, that there is a considerable disparity of opinion, among gun owners, regarding the phrase "gun control." Some interpret it to

SISTERS ARE DOING IT FOR THEMSELVES

mean reasonable regulation, while others see it as inordinate government intrusion into individuals' Second Amendment rights.

Both sides have a point. There is obviously a need for the lawful regulation of instruments as powerful as firearms, which helps to account for the fact that there are nationally over twenty thousand gun laws on the books. Indeed, some of the controls favored by some of the women are already federally mandated, including instant background checks (which in 1999 superseded the Brady Law's waiting period), the prohibition of the sale of handguns to minors (as well as to convicted felons and persons deemed mentally incompetent), and the banning of certain models of guns that fall legislatively under the category of "assault weapons." Other controls vary by, and sometimes within, states. The most common argument cited by those who oppose gun control in any form is that the states and federal government should focus on strictly enforcing existing statutes and punishing those who commit gun-related crimes to the full extent of the law, rather than further restricting the rights of the majority of gun owners who procured their guns legally and who abide by the law. Citing the cautionary adage, "When all arms are outlawed, only outlaws will be armed," some opponents of gun control further argue that the more deeply the state intrudes into individuals' decisions to keep or bear arms, the more likely individuals are to become de facto lawbreakers, by opting for legitimate firearms use even in the face of the law.

Whatever the validity of this latter argument, its force came through loud and clear in the survey. Asked "If it were illegal for you to carry a handgun for personal protection, and you felt threatened, would you carry anyway?" *86 percent* (116 women) replied they would. It is, of course, a different matter to actually break a law than to report that you would hypothetically do so. A follow-up question therefore asked whether these women had actually broken the law by carrying illegally. Two-thirds reported that they had indeed carried illegally for the purpose of self-defense.

This sample presents an image very much in contrast to the stereotypes of gun owners. These women are well educated, relatively affluent, politically active, and responsible. Most carry handguns, apparently often illegally, for their own self-defense. They are assuming the responsibility for their own personal safety, even if it means taking their chances with the law. As several of the women stated, citing another cautionary adage: "It is far better to be judged by twelve, than to be carried by six."

Weighing the Risks

Advocates of restrictive gun control most commonly cite three reasons for limiting the availability of firearms: the potential for accidents; the use of the firearms in suicides; and the contention that the more guns there are in society, the higher the likelihood is that crime will occur. We have explored the potential positive effects of firearm ownership for women. Do these positive effects outweigh these three negatives? What do the statistics tell us about these problems?

The argument regarding accidents usually revolves around the question of children finding a gun and injuring themselves or someone else with it. Most reports of such gun-related accidents suggest that the firearm involved was stored in an irresponsible manner—that is, it was both accessible and loaded or with ammunition easily available—leaving open the question of whether these accidents occurred in the homes of responsible firearms owners.

The NRA's Eddie Eagle program, nationally the most widely distributed gun safety program for children, emphasizes to children that if they happen upon a firearm unexpectedly they should stop, not touch the firearm, leave the room (or wherever the gun was found), and immediately tell an adult. The police department of Lakewood, Colorado, in 1998 ran an experiment to determine whether children who have received the NRA's, or similar, firearm safety training would actually behave differently than children who had never been exposed to educational information about firearms. In a simulation involving a real though thoroughly disabled gun, the children who had received training generally remembered and followed their training, leaving the room to report the presence of the firearm to an adult. Children who had not received safety training—who had been told, for example, only that "guns are bad"— were consistently more likely to approach and handle the firearm, even going so far as to aim it at themselves or another child.[58] It would appear that failing to educate children on firearms safety in a society where approximately half the households contain firearms, rather than keeping these households safe, is more likely to render them scenes of accidents waiting to happen.

How often do accidents with firearms actually kill children? Anti-gun public health physicians who have framed gun ownership itself as a national "epidemic" contend that almost a thousand children die each year from gun accidents.[59] However, the only way to attain this figure is to expand the category "children" to include youths between the ages of eighteen and twenty-four. These young adults can hardly be considered children; they represent not only a risk for firearms accidents, but also, particularly if they are male, an increased risk for almost every other form of accident.

Using a more reasonable cut-off point of fourteen years old to describe children, the National Safety Council (figures for the year 1993, released in 1996) reports firearm-related accidents as a distant sixth cause of death, taking the lives of 205 children. The leading causes of accidental deaths in children include car accidents (3,044 deaths); drownings (1,023 deaths); fires and burns (1,015 deaths); mechanical suffocation (449 deaths); and ingestion of food or an object (223 deaths). The NSC figures suggest that a public health epidemiological approach would more appropriately be aimed at automobile and swimming pool safety than at firearms, since the combined deaths by auto and pool (4,067) represent almost twenty times the risk that firearms present to children. And approximately five million American homes have swimming pools,[60] whereas an estimated 43 million households contain firearms.[61] This is not to say that any child's accidental death by firearm is anything less than tragic. But it does put these tragedies, which almost invariably could have been prevented by the combination of gun safety education and a routine of responsible gun storage, into perspective. It also suggests that in the vast majority of households where there are both guns and children, gun owners are doing their part to keep firearms out of little hands.

What about suicide? Recall that of those forty-three deaths Kellermann attributed to the presence of a gun in the home, thirty-seven were suicides. Indeed, firearms are used more frequently for suicides than for homicides. In 1993, gun deaths accounted for 48 percent of all suicides. Guns clearly represent a "serious" method of suicide highly likely to result in death, as compared to often "nonserious" methods such as ingestion of sleeping pills. However, increases in the numbers of firearms available in American society do not relate in any systematic way to the number of suicides. Between 1972 and 1993 the number of guns per capita increased 54 percent.[62] During this same time period the suicide rate was virtually flat—moving from 11.8 to 13 per 100,000.

The big question, of course, is if firearms were unavailable, could suicides be prevented? Perhaps. Another possibility is that the individual would simply choose another method. One of the research studies often cited by anti-gun physicians compares the cities of Seattle, Washington, and Vancouver, British Columbia, in terms of their accident and death rates.[63] Although there are reasons of culture as well as laws controlling firearm availability (Canada has extremely restrictive firearm laws), the suicide rates for the two cities are virtually identical. The difference is in the method of suicide. As might be expected, very few of the suicides in Vancouver result from firearms. So although some in the psychiatric community argue that the suicidal are deterred if a firearm is unavailable (and it is the method of choice),[64] at least in these two cities approximately equal numbers commit suicide; they simply do it differently.

Of course, cultural comparisons are always to some extent problematic. But the ready association between the presence of firearms and an increased likelihood of suicide is clearly refuted by the fact that in Japan, for example, where guns are a rarity, the suicide rate is considerably higher than in the United States. In Israel, on the other hand, where virtually every household has one or more firearms, the rate is considerably lower. Switzerland, another heavily armed country, has a rate comparable to that of the U.S. Guns may facilitate suicide, but they do not cause it.

One factoid that made the rounds in the anti-gun press toward the end of the 1990s was that persons who purchase handguns are, within a few days of the purchase, at considerably higher risk of suicide than the general public. This ostensibly made waiting (or "cooling off") periods sound like a reasonable idea. But, as suicide researchers have long affirmed, the fact is that people do not spontaneously decide to end their lives. Rather, the decision in favor of self-annihilation is arrived at over a period of time, and often in the context of clinical depression. The man or woman who purchases a handgun on Monday, and uses it to end his or her life on Tuesday, had already made that decision before walking up to the gun counter. The gun is the means, not the cause, and logically can hardly be considered a "risk factor."

Granted, on some level it is difficult to reduce the social and emotional cost of suicide to anything comprehensible by the term "logic." But the difficult fact remains that restricting access to handguns will not deter persons who are determined to end their lives. Some of these persons will be women. That, as appears to be the case, more women may be using guns to kill themselves than formerly is perhaps a bitter "down side" of changes occurring in American society. These changes, however, have to do with far more than women's increased gun ownership. In any event, the argument that putting a gun in a woman's hands will turn her into a potential suicide is demeaning, trivializing, and insulting.

Do the number of guns available increase the likelihood of crime? This question needs to be asked, if one is to decide whether guns are a public menace or a desirable option that some might reasonably choose for self-protection. The question became somewhat less murky in the late 1990s with the publication of research conducted by John Lott and David Mustard, first in a relatively inaccessible form (heavy on the statistics in an academic journal),[65] then in far more approachable style in Lott's book, *More Guns, Less Crime*.[66]

Lott and Mustard analyzed data from the more than 3,000 counties in the United States for over twenty crime variables, over a period of fifteen years. These were further broken down on a number of demographic variables that included population, racial distribution, economic factors, crime rates, and, most importantly whether the state allowed concealed carry (for example, in a covered holster or in a purse) of firearms. The results of the study confirmed the intuitions of firearms owners and experts. Crime rates fell for violent crimes almost immediately after the passage of the concealed-carry laws and continued to drop over time. Presumably, this occurred in part because more citizens took advantage of their right to bear arms, in part because more criminals assumed they had. The average decreases were 7.7 percent for murder, 7.01 percent for aggravated assault, and 5.3 percent for rape.

The gains from these laws were not evenly distributed across all of the groups in the society. Lott observes some irony in this: "Women and blacks tend to be the strongest supporters of gun control, yet both obtain the largest benefits from nondiscretionary concealed-handgun laws in terms of reduced rates of murder and other crimes."[67] Concealed carry changes the rules of the game of criminal victimization. As we have seen, when criminals know that their potential victim may be armed, that victim becomes a greater risk and far less appealing.

Perhaps the strongest example of the increases in safety that can be obtained from firearm ownership and responsible use can be illustrated by a program that was run by the Orlando police department in 1966.[68] The police trained 2,500 women in the defensive use of handguns. The program received a great deal of media attention, so potential criminals in the city were aware of the fact that any woman they chose to target for victimization might be a trained gun woman. The rate of rapes dropped by 88 percent in 1967 as compared to 1966, while the rate of rape in the rest of Florida remained at 1966 levels. Follow-up studies conducted five years later found the rate of rapes still 13 percent below the preprogram rate in Orlando. In the surrounding areas, however, the rate had increased 300 percent in the intervening five years.[69]

The evidence is clear that in the hands of untrained or irresponsible people, firearms can represent a hazard to life and limb. For those individuals who train themselves and follow safety rules, however, firearms can offer not merely a sense of increased safety, but an actual avenue to increased safety. And this may be especially true for women. Feminism at its best represents the opportunities for individuals to make choices: about their careers, about their life-styles, and about reproductive rights. Not everyone will make the same choices. But for those willing to play by the rules, a woman's choice to protect herself with a firearm should be equally respected. And for today's gun women, whether they call themselves feminist or not, armed self-protection is a responsibility they are willing to assume.

Snapshot

Vivian B. Lord, *Becoming a Police Officer—1975*

I was born into a family of musicians, scientists, and teachers. I had hoped to become a veterinarian, but flunked out of veterinary school at the young age of nineteen. The university I was attending offered "Catch-Up," a program funded through the now defunct Law Enforcement Education Program (LEEP). The program paid females and minorities in college a small stipend to complete basic law enforcement training. Upon completion of basic training and a bachelor degree from the university, participants in Catch-Up could be hired as sworn officers by police departments within the state of Georgia.

My family was not particularly happy with my new nontraditional profession, and it was my police boyfriend, not my parents,

Vivian B. Lord, Ph.D., is Professor of Criminology at the University of North Carolina—Charlotte.

who attended the Catch-Up graduation. When my boyfriend presented me with a .38 Smith and Wesson Revolver on my twenty-first
birthday, my entire family was appalled. My brother would not speak
to me for a year, but by then I was a police officer.

Needless to say, guns were not part of my family's traditions. I
had heard a story in my younger years that my brother had been in-
vited to go hunting when he was in his teens. He evidently killed a
rabbit, which traumatized him for quite a while (of course, if the
reader has ever heard a rabbit scream as it is dying, he or she will probably understand my innocent brother's crisis). So it was up to my
boyfriend and the instructors of the basic law enforcement training
(BLET) unit to teach me about weapons.

Before beginning my basic training, my boyfriend introduced
me to both his service weapon, which was a .357 Smith and Wesson
revolver, as well as a 20-gauge shotgun. I found his revolver to be
rather cumbersome, but discovered this awkwardness could be attributed to its grips. I am a small woman with small hands. In 1975
it was difficult to buy grips to fit women. Needless to say, my aim
remained average until I was able to practice with my own .38 that
had small grips.

Another discovery I made was the fact that I saw two targets
when I shot. The Weaver stance was not commonly used three
decades ago, so both my boyfriend and my BLET instructors taught
me the isosceles stance. I would look at the target first to decide where
it actually was, then look down the barrel, and point the weapon at
the "real" target. Many years later, I was taught the Weaver stance
when the firearms instructor heard me joke about finding the "real"
target. It turns out that individuals, male and females, whose strong
eye is the same side as their strong hand, have difficulties sighting
down a barrel without seeing a double target. The Weaver stance
places the shooter perpendicular to the target, instead of pointing

straight at it. It changes the way a shooter will view the target and thereby narrows the target to one, real target.

Holding and shooting a shotgun was an intimidating experience for me, at least until my boyfriend taught me to shoot from the hip, *Rifleman* fashion. Unfortunately, shooting from the hip was not allowed for qualifications. Cradling the shotgun in my shoulder and placing it near my face was pretty scary. He began my instruction with bird shot, which was not too bad. I shot at a number of targets, becoming pretty comfortable with the weapon's slight recoil. Suddenly, after I fired, I was lying on my back with a large swelling beginning to protrude on my shoulder. My boyfriend had decided it was best to introduce me to buck shot without giving me any warning. The problem with this plan was that I had become too relaxed with the slight recoil of bird shot and had not kept the shotgun snug on my shoulder. It took quite some time after that for me to feel comfortable with a shotgun, and I can't say that I have ever liked qualifying with one.

I had received my new .38 Smith and Wesson revolver in time to allow me to train and qualify with it during BLET. With my use of the smaller grips and my numerous practice sessions with firearms, I was probably the most experienced student in the class. Because Catch-Up was only for African American males, and for females in general, none of the students had had much early experience hunting with male relatives. The firearms instructor let us walk through the firearm qualification series without being timed. The instruction only occurred during the day. My scores never fell below the mid-to-high 90s.

When I was hired by a police department in North Carolina in 1976, the firearms instructor took me out to qualify. The qualification was timed on both a day and a night course. My scores fell apart. Timing the course made it more difficult for me to find the real target quickly, and my night vision has always been poor. I was working for a small university town police department that was accepting of female officers. The firearms instructor continued to work with me, and after some time my qualification scores improved. The instructor's remediation helped me to the point that when I was promoted to investigator and had to qualify with a two-inch snub-nose revolver, I still qualified with scores in the high 80s. Shooting a revolver with a two-inch barrel accurately at 25 yards is not easy.

I have not been a police officer for over twenty years. I continued to qualify when I was training officers myself, but I have not shot a weapon in about six years. The experiences of a new female officer are probably very different from mine.

Snapshot

Jennifer Gwyn, *Becoming a Police Officer—1999*

Nobody in my family is in the law enforcement profession, nor do any of my family members use firearms for recreational purposes. Before entering basic law enforcement training (BLET), my only experience with firearms was one practice session with a 12-gauge shotgun in the backyard with my sister's boyfriend.

In my BLET class, three out of the four female recruits needed remedial work with firearms; none of us had had any previous experience. I was particularly uncomfortable with the 12-gauge shotgun. In addition to the remedial training given to me by the firearms instructor, I was also able to work out a trade with another student. He had military experience and was very proficient with firearms, but he was struggling academically. He worked with me on the firing range during lunch and breaks, and in return, I helped him study.

Jennifer Gwyn is an officer with the Charlotte-Mecklenburg Police Department.

Slugs in the shotgun were particularly painful, and I was not sure if I would ever make the qualifying score. When we were preparing to qualify, the instructor announced, "If you qualify today with slugs, you will never have to shoot with slugs again unless you want to be on the SWAT team." What a motivation! Both times I scored 50 out of 55, which placed me well within the qualifying score.

As of January 2000 I have been working with my field training officer (FTO) for about eight weeks. I have only had to take my service weapon out of its holster once. We had been hearing some discharging of firearms that appeared to be used to welcome in the New Year, but after answering a domestic call around 0100 hours on January 1, we heard more shots. My FTO and I ran to where we had heard the shots and saw a man with a shotgun. We announced our presence and yelled, "Drop your weapon." He ran toward his house, but then turned to face us. Another officer came up behind him, tackled him, and took his weapon from him.

Could I use deadly force? I am fully confident that I could and would fire my weapon if a citizen's life, another officer's life, or my own life were in danger.

3   In the Line of Fire

Women in Law Enforcement and the Military

From the *New York Times*, Sunday, February 27, 1994:

On Valentine's Day, Arlene Beckles and Steve Imparato gave new meaning to the term "shotgun wedding." The couple, who met in 1988 while working as New York City Housing Authority Police officers, had been engaged for about three years but were in no rush to marry until she almost died in a gunfight.

Detective Beckles is the petite, soft-spoken 30-year-old cop who was sitting under a hair dryer at Salon La Mode Beauty Parlor in downtown Brooklyn on February 5 when three armed robbers walked in. She pulled out her off-duty revolver and shot at the intruders with such accuracy that she earned a new nickname, Dirty Harriet. One of the robbers wrestled her to the floor and held a pistol to her face. He pulled the trigger, but the pistol misfired. He pulled again—it jammed.

Nine days later, Mr. Imparato and Detective Beckles were at the altar. "It made me realize we should get married right away," the bridegroom said. "Some people don't realize how short life is. This made me realize it."

. . .

Mayor Rudolph Giuliani officiated at the wedding in a City Hall meeting room decorated with oil portraits, American flags and crystal chandeliers. The benches were filled with about 150 people, including reporters: hard-bitten detectives in tan raincoats, chewing gum; friends of the couple; and rows and rows of police officers in blue dress uniforms.

"Weddings are almost as traumatizing as what she went through," said Officer Angel Silva, an instructor at the Police Academy. . . .

Detective Beckles walked down the aisle gingerly, almost like a Victorian lady making her mannered way across a dance floor. Her long nails were painted with white-on-white stripes. Drop pearls hung from her headband and dress like icicles. She seemed to be flaunting the fact that she is a very feminine sharpshooter.

"Arlene is the best thing that ever happened to female police officers," said Officer Patricia Keating of the New York Police Department. "It shows everyone that women don't run away. They face danger just like the guys do."

The ceremony also broke stereotypes. The Mayor praised the bride for her grit and heroism while he commended Mr. Imparato, a bearish man who cries easily when talking about Detective Beckles's ordeal, for showing his emotions, even in front of television cameras. . . .

"Being a police officer at all is incredible," said Denise Lopez, a singer who performed at the reception. "But for her to act alone, sitting under a dryer, taking care of her female business, it reminds me of that song 'Woman': 'I can bring home the bacon, fry it up in a pan and stop the perpetrators and come home and look good for my man.' That sums it up."[1]

Fairy-tale happy endings don't come much better than this one. Nor do illustrations of the gender uncertainty surrounding the participation of women in previously male-identified professional fields like police work. Note that unlike the gum-chewing, presumably male detectives at her wedding, Detective Beckles is petite and soft spoken. She is a woman who takes care of her "female business," and as a bride "flaunts" her femininity. Thwarting a robbery-in-progress she may have swung into action like a commando, but in her wedding dress she looks like a character out of Dickens. Except that there is something aggressive about the way she goes about being feminine: those long nails, the abundance of icicle-like pearls . . . that off-duty revolver she was packing in the beauty salon, and for all we know had strapped to her thigh under her voluminous skirt, or tucked discreetly into her bouquet. No wonder Rudy Giuliani was impressed.

While American society is generally disinclined to put guns into women's hands, historically this has been even more the case regarding arming women to do traditionally male work like law enforcement or military service in combat roles. The wedding singer was right to observe that for a woman, "being a police officer at all is incredible." Up until quite recently in American history, it would have been impossible. In large part, Detective Beckles and her female colleagues across the country have feminism to thank for giving them the opportunity to become "Dirty Harriets."

One of the pivotal issues of the Second Wave of feminism beginning in the 1960s was the right for women to choose whether to opt for a career outside the home, and what career paths they would take.[2] Women had traditionally been either relegated to the role of housewife or forced to take one of the jobs that was considered appropriate for females. These "pink collar" jobs often mirrored the sex-role stereotypic traits, like nurturing or serving others, that were attributed to all women. They included the sorts of work one would find in the then-familiar "Help Wanted: Female" classifieds: nurse, social worker, secretary, teacher, child care worker.[3] These jobs had in common lower levels of social status and lower pay than such stereotypically male jobs as physician, attorney, corporate executive, or engineer.

As women began to make inroads into jobs conventionally held by men, they encountered resistance from society in general and from their male colleagues in particular.[4] Law enforcement and the military turned out to be two professions women had a particularly difficult time entering. Not only had these occupations traditionally been dominated by males, but both were perceived as essentially masculine because of the aggressive behaviors they involved, perhaps primary among them the use of firearms. Any women choosing to enter these professions were simultaneously choosing to adopt behaviors generally perceived not only as the antithesis of femininity, but also as threats to their male colleagues' masculinity.

Social scientists have extensively documented the reactions to women entering nontraditional occupations. When there are only a few persons in a profession, their rarity casts them in the role of "token." Female tokens tend to be highly visible, and experience performance pressures, exclusion, and stereotypic treatment from which their male colleagues are exempt. They are often penalized for their failure to comply with sex-role stereotypes by being portrayed in reductive roles like "mother," "pet," "seductress," or "bitch."[5] All of these reactions can be identified in both law enforcement and the military, although the two professions emphasize different stereotypes.

To Protect and to Serve

Alice Stebbins Wells, who was hired by the Los Angeles Police Department in 1910, is generally regarded as the first woman to be a sworn police officer rather than serving in a support role such as secretary.[6] However, in reality her hiring was the culmination of a period begun in the 1820s, when Quaker women in the United States followed the example of their English counterparts and entered into prisons to provide education and religious training for female inmates.[7] By the 1880s these women had succeeded in creating another new profession for women: police matron. In the decade following Wells's 1910 hiring, approximately 125 policewomen served in thirty American cities. These policewomen were assigned to controlling behaviors that had not previously been seen as falling within the purview of the police, including "prostitution, sexual morality, dance halls, penny arcades, curfews for minors, and temperance."[8] As women, they were seen as occupying a kind of moral high ground, and as being naturally inclined to help the less fortunate. That is, their official duties fell squarely within the stereotypically appropriate behavior expected of women.

Moral reform under the guise of police work continued to be women's lot until the period following World War II. In 1956, the International Association of Women Police (IAWP) began to move away from the social work role of earlier policewomen and toward the roles played by male officers. Policewomen realized that men in traditional uniform patrol had a greater range of career options, as well as enhanced opportunities for promotion. In a pivotal case in 1961, two female police officers were barred from taking the test for promotion to sergeant. They sued the New York City Police Department, and after a two-year litigation, they won. Both subsequently gained promotion to sergeant, and in 1967 both were promoted again, becoming the department's first female lieutenants.[9]

Several pieces of legislation were passed in the 1960s that prohibited discrimination against women in selection, assignment, and other conditions of employment. The 1963 Equal Pay Act required equal pay for equal work; the 1964 Omnibus Civil Rights Law's Title VII prohibited discrimination in the private sector based on sex, race, color, religion, or nationality; and Executive Order 11478, signed by President Richard Nixon, extended that protection to federal employees. All these laws helped pave the way for women to move into traditionally male roles in police and federal law enforcement agencies. In 1968, in Indianapolis, Betty Blankenship and Elizabeth Coffal were "the first policewomen to wear uniforms, strap gun belts to their waists, drive a marked patrol car, and answer general-purpose police calls for service on an equal basis with policemen."[10] In theory, then, women had moved into a position of parity with male police officers. The reality proved to be quite a different matter. Women in police work continued to encounter discriminatory treatment in their training and service as officers.

Learning to Walk the Walk

Entry into work in law enforcement involves passage through a training academy. The requirements vary across federal, state, and local agencies, but at a minimum include arrest tactics and firearms training. Prior experience with firearms is not a prerequisite for entry into police training. While the physical fitness or strength requirements may be modified for female trainees, the firearms requirements for graduation are identical for males and females.

Typically, trainees must gain proficiency with both a handgun and a shotgun. Training begins with the use of standing targets, and it may advance to use of tactical shooting exercises like the Firearms Training Simulator (FATS) and "Hogan's Alley." FATS training involves a large-screen interactive video simulator that can project situations that police officers might encounter on patrol, allowing trainees to practice reacting to targets and identifying whether the targets represent a dangerous or a benign situation. Hogan's Alley is a real-life training simulation with instructors playing the roles of ei-

→❋ ANNIE OAKLEY. ❋←
(LITTLE SURE SHOT.)
J. WOOD, Photo.,   208 Bowery, N. Y.

1. Annie Oakley, America's first high-profile gun woman, circa 1885, the year she joined Buffalo Bill Cody's Wild West exhibition. In 1914, Oakley wrote in *Sports Afield* magazine: "I can truthfully say I know of no other recreation that will do so much toward keeping a woman in good health and perfect figure than a few hours spent occasionally at trap shooting." "Annie Oakley, Little Sure Shot," by J. Wood, reproduced with permission of the Buffalo Bill Historical Center, Cody, WY.

2 *(left)*. Women frequently were featured in early 20th century advertising for firearms and ammunition, as in this 1909 poster for Winchester's .22 caliber autoloading rifle. Gift of Olin Corporation, Winchester Arms Collection, reproduced with permission of the Buffalo Bill Historical Center, Cody, WY; 3 *(right)*. This cowgirl, circa 1914, promoted Winchester arms and ammunition in Spanish-speaking countries. Reproduced with permission of the Buffalo Bill Historical Center, Cody, WY.

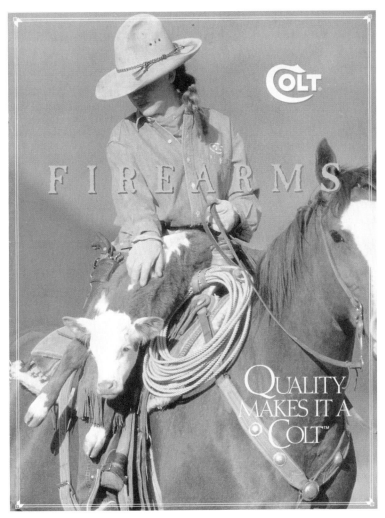

4. By the close of the 20th century, cowgirls were back in firearms advertising–here, on the cover of Colt's 1996 catalogue. Copyright © by Colt's Manufacturing Company, Inc. Used with permission. All rights reserved.

5 (left). "Osa Brings Home the Dinner," from Osa Johnson's 1941 safari memoir, *Four Years in Paradise*. Hardly the image of the unwilling or unhappy hunter some feminist critics have made her out to be. Reprinted with permission of Martin and Osa Johnson Safari Museum; 6 (right). Mary Zeiss Stange with her .270 Sako and the pronghorn buck she shot with it in October 1988. Like the majority of current American women hunters, Stange began hunting as an adult. Reprinted with permission of Doug Stange.

7. College student Carrie Krull was a member of her high school rife team, and now shoots recreationally. She is one of a growing number of young women who use firearms—in this case, a Mossberg Model 590 Shotgun—both for pleasure and for self-protection. Reprinted with permission of John Krull.

8. Eleven-year-old Vanessa Noble with 9mm Ruger P89 before her first Practical Shooting competition, On Target Shooting Range, Laguna Niguel, CA, 1996. Interview: "My next IPSC match, which will be my second one, I'm going to shoot the .45. It's weird because now it's so easy to shoot the .45 but it was so hard to shoot the .22 when I first started. IPSC gives me something to do against other people who are a lot older than me and have more experience. Shooting is so fun because people are proud of me and they say that I'm a good shooter. I think it's a good sport because you have to learn a lot. I like moving and shooting. It's kind of weird being the only girl against all these men who have been shooting for a long time. It's kind of harder shooting with men because women are easier to be around and most of the men are a lot older and they're interesting and stuff, but it's, I don't know, for some reason it's easier to be around women.

"Lindsay's six and she's shooting the .22. It will probably be a couple of years before she shoots IPSC because she's still not mature enough. She's learning a lot though, which is good. Last week she got to shoot the .38 Diamondback, the revolver, and she said she was so excited because, you know, it's pretty neat." Copyright © 1996, Nancy Floyd.

9. Gail with .45 cal. Colt Gold Cup National Match, 1994. "I am personally in a help-less position. I can't run away from anybody. This makes me feel just a tad more un-easy, for instance, driving in my van. Since I do display the handicap placard very prominently, and I do park in all the handicap places, someone might think that I'm a much easier mark and that I could not defend myself.

"It's a shame that one has to break the law in order to protect oneself, but I'm willing to take that chance. If trouble comes to me, I don't intend to just sit there or lay there screaming, 'Help me!' I'm going to grab, as fast as I can, for my loaded weapon. And, believe me, I have made up my mind that, in order to protect my life, I will shoot to kill." Copyright © 1994, Nancy Floyd.

10. Officer Audrey Jenkins with 9 mm Smith & Wesson, Atlanta, GA 1997. "The first thing that most people do is they size you up. They look at you to see how you are built, what kind of physique you have. In their mind, they're saying 'I wonder if I can take this person?' That's kind of scary, especially if you're walking up to a guy who's six five and 300 pounds. You're looking at him like, man, if he grabs me, he's going to break me in half. Just by nature I'm a serious person, so when a person sees me, I think they say, 'Oh, she's a no-nonsense kind of person.' It's pretty much my normal everyday look. I'm not a smiley-type person. And I think that helps me a lot. People don't try to take advantage of me because they wonder, 'What is this person really made of?' I think my look kind of intimidates them.

"Male police officers are pretty fair. I think most just want you to do your job. They want everybody to do their job and be proficient and just be able to handle any situation. If they get into anything, just be there to back them up. That's the main thing that everybody wants, is that back up, you know. Be there." Copyright © 1997, Nancy Floyd.

11. Single-Action Shooting Society member Jubilee Montana with Model 1894 Winchester Rifle and Montana Territorial Centennial, Diamond Jubilee Edition Colt .45 at the 1994 End of Trail. "First and foremost, I like the people involved in SASS. I grew up with cowboy action shooting, so I feel very close to everyone in the club, and I feel close to the sport. I mean, there is such a strong feeling of camaraderie and people are so supportive of each other. There's a nice balance of people out there, of people who are into it strictly for the competition and those who are there just to have fun.

"SASS is a very controlled sport. It's very precise and what I like about it is that it requires a lot of fine tuning, both with the firearms you use and with yourself. It's more mental than a lot of people think because you have to be very focused while you're shooting. There's a lot of things to remember, from your stance to your sight picture, to how you're holding your gun, to ways to improve your speed. So I guess what I really like about it is the challenge. I've certainly never won a match, but it's a good feeling when you clean a stage, meaning you hit everything that you were aiming at, and you do it in pretty good time." Copyright © 1994, Nancy Floyd.

ther "bad guys" or innocent victims, and trainees armed with paint pellets. Trainees must show appropriate judgment in the simulations. They must also achieve an acceptable level of accuracy with their firearms in order to graduate from training.

As sworn officers, they must continue to qualify on a regular basis by demonstrating firearms proficiency. Some agencies require annual qualification, while other agencies, including the Federal Bureau of Investigation (FBI), require that agents qualify four times a year (reduced from six times a year in 1999). Trainees at the FBI Training Academy at Quantico, Virginia, train with a semi-automatic .22 caliber pistol manufactured by Glock, and an MP5 12-gauge shotgun. Qualification requires 80 percent accuracy with both, firing from various positions and distances.

Trainee classes at Quantico begin with forty students. Usually, women make up 15 to 20 percent of a class. Currently 16 percent of FBI field agents are women. While most of the men are married with children, of the six women in a typical class, two are married (usually without children), two are in long-term committed relationships, and two are not in relationships.

In the fall of 1999, one of the authors had an opportunity to interview a number of women trainees at various stages of their Academy training. Several of the women chose to remain anonymous, but two of the women agreed to be interviewed for attribution. The trainees were informed that the focus of the interview would be on their firearms experiences; however, a number of the interviews evolved into long conversations about the Academy experience of the women and their perceptions of the different experiences of their male counterparts.[11] The women ranged in age from twenty-seven to thirty-one years old and all had earned advanced college degrees. This makes them better educated and older than the trainees for most law enforcement agencies. But then, the

FBI is perceived by many—and certainly by the trainees—as "the Cadillac" of law enforcement agencies.

Colleen Fina Calves had never handled a firearm before entering the Academy. Although her grandfather hunted and took along some of his grandchildren, he only included the boys. Colleen completed both bachelor's and master's degrees in International Affairs before entering the Academy. She chose the FBI not because she was particularly interested in what she referred to as "traditional police work," but rather because she was interested in the problem-solving and investigative aspects of the agent's role. When she entered the Academy she had eagerly anticipated learning to handle firearms, but was finding the actual experience difficult. It brought home to her in a way she had not anticipated a feeling of added responsibility, based on the fact that introducing a firearm into a confrontational situation "immediately ups the ante."

Colleen's family was supportive, but couldn't understand her choice of an FBI career. They had what she termed "old-fashioned" expectations for her, including school, marriage, and staying at home with children. Colleen had satisfied the familial expectation that she marry, and her husband was very supportive of her career choice. She reported that her mother-in-law was nervous about the whole idea of her handling and carrying a firearm. Other married women reported supportive husbands who were willing to follow where the FBI might send them, and to forgo the possibility of having children. Several commented that it felt unfair that they might be forced to choose between the FBI and motherhood while the male trainees faced no similar choice.

Samantha ("Sam") Koval was a special education teacher with a master's degree specializing in gifted children's education when she entered the Academy. Sam's father was a "cop" and Sam had always wanted to follow in his footsteps, but not at the local level, which she saw as "too militaristic." She had shot a .22 occasionally with her father, but felt that her lack of experience was her "biggest asset." She reported that some of her male classmates who had extensive experience with guns from law enforcement or the military had to "unlearn" bad habits with the firearms. This fits very closely with the experiences reported by numerous firearms instructors—that women are easier to teach to shoot because they don't assume that they know more than the instructor.

Sam's family was supportive of her choice to enter the Academy, but like several of the other women interviewed, this choice cost her a relationship. She had been involved in a serious long-term relationship with a man who wanted a traditional wife, not an FBI agent. He continued to be a source of support for Sam during a difficult period early in her training, when she injured her knee severely and had to be "recycled" (left back to a later class). But it was clear that the relationship had shifted to a friendship. During the time she was recovering, instructors from the Academy kept in touch with Sam and assigned her to a local FBI office. The experience of seeing what life would be like after training strengthened Sam's determination to return to the Academy.

What did the women trainees report about their experiences with the firearms training? Several stated that it was very important to them that there were female firearms instructors to serve as role models. They reported that the women trainees spent more time practicing shooting on their own time than did the men. Those women who had firearms experience helped those without. They also reported, after some deliberation, that they were treated differently on the firing line than the male students. However, they did not believe the instructors were conscious of this differential treatment. One recalled an incident when she and a male trainee were having what seemed to be identical difficulties with their shotguns. Neither was shooting accurately. She was small and slight while he was large and muscular. He was told by the instructor he was "muscling" the weapon. She was told she was not being sufficiently aggressive. It was hard to determine to what extent the fault lay in the trainees' shooting, to what extent in the instructor's perception of the trainees themselves.

Interviewees also cited differences in the behavior of male and female trainees on the FATS and Hogan's Alley courses. Some of the women felt that here, too, the instructors displayed stereotypic expectations. They expected the women to be timid and unwilling to employ deadly force. As the students completed the course, they were allowed to remain and watch subsequent students' performance. The women reported that female students were as willing or more willing than the men to use appropriate force on the FATS training. The male students shot slightly faster, but were more likely to shoot an innocent victim. Descriptions of their initial team experiences on the Hogan's Alley brought wry smiles to their faces as the women described how they had continued to work together as teams, while some of the male students had become so immersed in the exercise that they abandoned the team concept entirely, and struck out on their own into the woods chasing the instructors portraying "bad guys."

Several women reported being amused at the reactions they evoked from the male students. The men had harbored their own stereotypic expectations about their female colleagues, expecting them to be masculine or "super jocks." The men were surprised when they saw the women in feminine civilian clothes, and they treated the women "like ladies." Several of the single men were adamant that they wouldn't allow *their* girlfriends to become FBI agents, and the women reported encountering a few of the men who felt women didn't belong in the Bureau. A few of the women reported mixed reactions on the part of the male students' wives to the presence of female classmates.

Sam was not the only woman who reported feeling a strong sense of responsibility to future women who might choose the FBI as a career. When the women were discouraged, or needed a shoulder to lean on, or wanted advice, they reported seeking out women in senior classes. They did not share their problems with less senior women because they reported they did not want to discourage those women who followed. As Sam stated, "Each class makes it a bit easier for the next females."

Assuming the Position

Women entering into law enforcement in the 1970s faced a very macho environment. Policing was perceived, both by practitioners and the public, as a masculine activity that went against the very nature of women.[12] If women could equal men in the performance of police work, then what did that mean about the work itself? As one criminologist phrased it, "if women can do it, the value of the practice as a means for exhibiting masculinity is cast into question."[13]

Critics commonly employed a metaphor that symbolized the perception that women could not possibly be successful as police officers: the image of the "250 pound man in an alley."[14] In interviews with female officers in numerous agencies, communications expert Connie Fletcher found this image ubiquitous. The assumption, of course, is that a physical confrontation is inevitable, and that the woman will just as inevitably be overpowered by her larger assailant. This assumption, of course, discounts both the presence of the officer's firearm and the possibility that the situation can be resolved without resorting to physical aggression.

Women officers reported that in fact they felt better equipped than their male counterparts or partners to deal with the alley scenario. One of Fletcher's respondents put it this way: "Policing is like a chess game. The whole goal is to outsmart people. . . . It's a game of finesse, of skill, or luck. It's not a game of brute force." Another observed: "It doesn't mean we can't also be physical. But our first choice is verbal. Second choice is hold the gun in your hand. . . . Third choice is knock 'em cold."[15]

In other words, women think first and attempt nonconfrontational means of solving problems before they engage either in fisticuffs or gunplay. This is the same deliberation before shooting mentioned by the FBI trainees in the FATS and Hogan's Alley training. This tendency to think first and shoot second was described by Marlene Dreifke, who served with the Madison, Wisconsin, police department from 1979 through 1995. A detective when she left the force, Dreifke stated that her experience led her to believe that this propensity on the part of female officers, to exhaust all other reasonable alternatives before employing the use of the gun, led to far less self-doubt and questioning in cases where a gun was used.

In one circumstance, however, men tend to be more hesitant to shoot than women. This is when the call involves a female perpetrator. Interestingly, women do not seem to make tactical shooting decisions based upon the sex of the offender, as men do. Robert Dreifke, who served with the Dane County, Wisconsin, police from 1974 to 1995 as a firearms instructor and supervising lieutenant, and John Roberts, currently a training officer with the Macon, Georgia, police, both commented that they had to remind male recruits that female offenders can be as dangerous as men, and that the same criteria should be applied to the use of firearms against both.

Black women police officers have been described as suffering from the "additive" effects of the combination of the two stigmatizing characteristics of race and gender. Recent feminist critics, however, believe the effects are less additive than "interactive."[16] That is, the differences in the relationships between white men, and white and black women, create variations in the women's experiences of discrimination. White women share the power and status of race with their white male colleagues, and hence have greater potential to rise in a masculine organization like the police. Similarly, black men share their white male colleagues' masculinity. Black women lose on both accounts, and their relationships with colleagues of both races and genders are often more problematic.[17] In addition, the stereotypic image of the black woman lacks the elements of gentility and helplessness associated with white women (recall the petite "Victorian" detective-bride). Significantly, Fletcher found that the problem of the 250-pound man in the alley was raised with regard to white female officers, but not to women of color.

In 1980, Susan Martin examined the ways that police women in the 1970s had adapted to the hostile environment they encountered in police work.[18] She reported they reacted to the stress by becoming either *police*women or police*women;* that is, they chose which stereotypes to conform to. *Police*women emulated the role of male officers by becoming tough and masculine. Police*women* emphasized their femininity by avoiding masculine behaviors or taking any risks. Black women officers might be more attracted to the first role, while white women might fall into the trap of the second. As one black woman officer commented to Fletcher: "The Joe Public—when they think of danger on this job, they may be thinking of a Caucasian female; they think that she's not gonna handle it. They're not gonna think that way about a black female police officer unless somebody has inside knowledge. . . . They figure a black woman can handle herself."[19] Another group that tended to adopt the more macho role (at least in one Midwestern city) was the openly lesbian officers.[20]

However, there may be inherent problems ahead for women who choose to emphasize the "police" (masculine) aspect of their role. Susan Miller quotes one officer:

In my experience, the women that try to do the job as men do are not successful. Obviously, they're not successful as men, and they're not really successful as women, either, because they're not approaching things the way that a woman would and in the way that they probably would if they just let themselves be themselves.

But sometimes I think they feel the pressure that—"I have to prove myself to the men on the job, and I have to prove myself to the other women on the job, I have to prove myself to the public"—and they might see some men that have been there before them and so they try to emulate them instead of really relying on their own strengths. So they fail on both counts.[21]

Another officer told Miller:

In my own personal experience—and not to divide the sexes—but there were a lot of times when I felt more comfortable on the street with a female than with a male. And the reason for this is that some males are not challenged— their fear level is not challenged as much as a female's fear level. And when that fear kicks in—it takes a whole hell of a lot of thinking to get control of yourself. And if you can't get control of yourself, you're gonna lose the battle. Bottom line.[22]

This last statement identifies an advantage ironically conferred upon police women by the "female fear" we addressed earlier. Because women are more experienced in the emotion and experience of fear, it apparently does not take female police officers by surprise. The implication is that because male officers are not so accustomed to the experience of fear, they are potentially more likely to lose control of themselves, and of the situation, in fear-provoking contexts. To shoot first, in other words, and ask questions later.

New Directions in Policing—Community Policing

During the 1980s a new, far less masculine approach to the role of police officers emerged. The traditional model "celebrated as masculine crimefighters who were brave, suspicious, aloof, objective, cynical, physically intimidating, and willing to use force and even brutality."[23] Traditional law enforcement rejected stereotypically feminine characteristics such as gentleness and a focus on establishing connections. The new approach, known as community policing, shifted the values away from the traditionally masculine and toward the traditionally feminine. The goal was to create closer ties between the community and the police through increased contact. One of the more popular forms of the approach involved reintroducing police on foot patrol in communities. In establishing increased familiarity with the police and a higher police profile in the community, it was hoped that community members would come to experience higher levels of trust in the police. This, in turn, should lead to greater satisfaction with the police, reduced levels of fear within the community, more willingness on the part of community members to provide information about crimes committed, and more community members willing to serve as informants and witnesses.

A detailed study of one of the earliest implementations of community policing was conducted by Susan Miller in a midsized Midwestern city she referred to with the pseudonym "Jackson City." As might be expected, given that the style of policing could be construed as more feminine than the usual police role, the first officers to volunteer for the program were all female or minority group members. The majority of the police force did not welcome the program, which they perceived as an idea being forced upon them by a new chief. They resisted the break from traditional police roles. However, when the program was expanded with two subsequent waves of additions to the original corps of community policing officers, more white male officers applied for inclusion. It wasn't hard to figure out why: the community policing program had become a fast track to promotion.

The adoption of community policing by more cities may increase the number of women and minorities entering and advancing in police departments. In part, this is because of the style of the work itself. Also, since one of the principles of community policing is to match the officers to the community in which they serve, those cities with large minority neighborhoods will bring in more minority officers. The city of Madison, Wisconsin, instituted a community policing program in 1986 and directed hiring efforts explicitly at women and minority group members. By 1993, 25 percent of Madison's police force was female.

For other cities, such as Boston and Washington, D.C., legal decisions that require the redressing of past discrimination against minorities have resulted in increases in the number of minority women in police departments. In Boston, the consent decree demanding that more minority (not explicitly female) officers be hired resulted in more than half of the females on that city's police force being either black or Hispanic. In the District of Columbia, the majority of the department's officers, and over 80 percent of the women, were black.[24]

Departments with a significant number of women continue, however, to be in the minority. According to James Stinchcomb, the numbers of women as sworn officers in American police forces remained relatively static at approximately 10 percent for the two decades from 1973 to 1993. In addition to the cities mentioned above, however, several urban departments such as Detroit (with 19 percent females) and Los Angeles (with 14 percent) had hired proportionately more female officers. Suburban, generally county, departments averaged 12 percent females, and rural departments 7 percent.[25]

Are women finding a more hospitable environment in police work? Not necessarily. Robert Dreifke, retired firearms instructor with the Dane County, Wisconsin, Police Department, reported that he had seen a definite change in the attitudes of male trainees toward women on the force. When he began as a trainer in 1974, he reported a high level of open resentment toward women recruits. During the late 1970s and the 1980s, the level of discrimination steadily declined. By the time he left the force in 1995, however, he reported there had been a dramatic resurgence in negativity toward women recruits. He attributed the change to the fact that in the 1970s men didn't believe that women could be good cops. As more women entered the profession, they proved their abilities. Almost too well, it appears. Dreifke associated the recent high levels of resentment with the fact that the male recruits had come to believe that women were not only able to function capably as officers, they had become credible threats to the men's own opportunities for advancement in police careers.

How far women have come, and how far they may go, in law enforcement is still an open question. Clearly, the way to success in police work will continue, for the foreseeable future, to be strewn with stereotypic expectations. And women's traditionally problematic relationship with firearms will no doubt continue to function as a symbol of the risks taken by any woman who ventures into the masculine domain of policing. Another more recent profile of a police woman, also from the *New York Times*, helps illustrate this point. But it also helps show the distinctly different angle of vision a female officer brings to her work out on the street. The story was headlined "Tough Truant Officer Is Also True Romantic":

Though you have to pass a metal detector to reach her grim cinder block headquarters, a former darkroom at the High School of Graphic Communication

Arts on West 49th Street, Lt. Helen Rossi, the hard-talking matriarch of New York City's truancy task force, is a romantic at heart.

The lipstick, eyeliner, and hennaed hair (after she's happily liberated it from her no-nonsense police cap) hint at it. So do the diamond rings that decorate four of her fingers.

"Anybody tries to steal my rings, I'll shoot 'em," she snarls. But she doesn't mean it. Lieutenant Rossi, a 28-year member of the New York Police Department and an icon in her specialty, truant adolescents, has never once fired her weapon in the line of duty. "Not ever," she emphasizes, knocking on the pocked wood of the anonymous school desk that doubles as her desk. "I don't even use handcuffs unless I have to. I'm not about harassing kids. I'm about getting them off the streets before they become crime victims themselves or get involved in one."

. . .

Lieutenant Rossi, a petite 53-year-old mother of two daughters, 15 and 11 and ensconced in Catholic school, lives in Astoria, Queens, with her husband, Anthony, a bartender. She has never taken her gun home from work. "No guns in my house," says Lieutenant Rossi, who finds them offensive to the romantic within and also does not want them around her children.

. . .

When, after dating an officer who died in 1969, she joined the N.Y.P.D. in 1973, the first year the academy permitted women to graduate as actual patrol officers rather than matrons, her role model was Angie Dickinson from television's "Policewoman" series. The job didn't turn out to be as romantic, or dramatic, as Ms. Dickinson's scripts suggested, but Lieutenant Rossi isn't complaining.[26]

Women Warriors

Law enforcement and the military have two things in common that have conventionally helped to define them as men's work. One is that both fields involve aggression and the use of firearms, as well as other weaponry. The other is that both exist, at least in theory, to protect the more vulnerable members of society. As political scientist Judith Hicks Stiehm has pointed out, this latter role gives both professions a lot of power: "Those who exercise society's force are given great discretion and formidable instruments. They are often given honor and high position as well. They describe themselves as protectors—police are said to protect citizens from robbery, murder, rape and riot; the military protect against invasion, rebellion, perceived threats to international order, and occasionally natural disasters."[27] The exclusion of women from both fields has been attributed to the natural order of things, in which men are the protectors, women the "protectees." So long as this model was by and large accepted, gender stereotypes shaped public policy. With the advent of Second Wave feminism, however, questions regarding women's "natural" subordination came to the fore, in ways that distinctly challenged the status quo. At about the same time women were making significant inroads in the field of law enforcement, the debate over women's military involvement came to a head.

The issue was President Carter's reintroduction of draft registration, in 1979. Feminists had spent the previous decade asserting the equality of women to men in all fields of endeavor. Equal opportunity, of course, went hand-in-hand with equal responsibility. Having applauded the elimination of women-only branches of the armed services in 1973, the National Organization for Women (NOW) in 1979 came out in support not only of registering draft-age women along with men, but also of assigning them to combat duty.[28] The prospect of one's daughter carrying a draft card in her wallet was an unsettling down side to the vision of her making the same salary as a comparably skilled male. Columnist Ellen Goodman confronted the issue head-on in a 1980 editorial on "Drafting Daughters":

I don't want anyone registered, anyone drafted, unless it is a genuine crisis. But if there is a draft, this time it can't just touch our sons, like some civilized plague that leaves daughters alone to produce another generation of warriors. . . . So, if we must have draft registration, I would include young women as well as young men. I would include them because they can do the job. I would include them because all women must gain the status to stop as well as to start wars. I would include them because it has been too easy to send men alone.

I would include them because I simply cannot believe that I would feel differently if my daughter were my son.[29]

The key issue at work in the question of the drafting of women was, as NOW had recognized and Goodman eloquently expressed, the prospect of women in combat. But there was a deeper concern as well. The surface debate was over policy issues: Should women be drafted? Should they serve in combat? But as Stiehm points out, a more basic question was: "Should men monopolize legitimate violence?"[30]

Many feminists, then as now, were of course happy to let them do just that. As we have already observed, there is something very attractive about assuming a position of moral superiority that relegates violence and aggression to the male half of the species. The problem is, some violence is legitimate in some contexts, and females are arguably as capable of engaging in it as are males. Only the most stringent—or the most naive—pacifist would argue otherwise. And when it comes to feminist arguments for exempting women from combat, feminist pacifism has too frequently amounted to what Stiehm astutely dubs "pseudopacifism":

A truly pacifist position commands respect. It does not flinch from reality; it challenges and risks; it accepts suffering too. In contrast, pseudopacifists choose safety; they refuse to hurt others but they permit others to hurt for

them. Women accept, even expect, the police and military to provide protec-
tion. They only superficially accept Camus' charge to be neither victims nor
executioners; they do not accept the responsibility he assigns the moral
human being. Pacifism is not the issue for women, as most are satisfied to
be protectees.[31]

But not all women have been satisfied to sit along the sidelines in times of war. Today's young American women entering into the service academies, and serving on the front lines, can look back on generations of foremothers.

Amazons in Real Life

While the entrance of women into police work in roles equivalent to male officers has been a relatively recent phenomenon, there are numerous historical references to women who entered into military action in various capacities. Women have been drawn into warfare by the need to protect themselves, their families, or their communities. Because of the relatively chaotic environment of war, these women have often been able to function as warriors with their identity as women going unnoticed. As historian David Jones notes, "The primal power of the warrior ideal is fueled by tradition and myth. History . . . demonstrates that the warrior's mantle is a woman's birthright as surely as it is a man's and that the hand that rocks the cradle can also wield the sword."[32]

The Revolutionary War produced a number of women warriors, although they often are excluded from mainstream histories of the period. While Paul Revere's ride to warn the colonists of the invasion of the Tories is the subject of song and story, Sybil Ludington, Lydia Barrington Darragh, and Emily Geiger also rode through the countryside carrying warnings of invading armies to troops in, respectively, Connecticut, Pennsylvania, and South Carolina.³³ Yet these women remain relatively unknown.³⁴

Immediately after the beginning of the war, in 1775 Prudence Wright organized a corps of women in Lexington, Massachusetts. She and her troops dressed in men's clothes and defended the town of Pepperell with pitchforks and muskets, in the course of which they captured a British spy. Other Revolutionary-era warriors included Margaret Cochran Corbin and Mary Ludwig Hays, both of whom fought beside their husbands and took over the fight when the men were wounded. Both women were awarded postwar military pensions. Mary Hays is believed to have been the inspiration for "Molly Pitcher," the plucky woman who changed her role from bringing pitchers of water to the soldiers (thus the name) to cannoneer when her husband fell. Legend has it she remained poised and controlled when a cannonball ripped through her skirts between her knees as she fired at the British.

Women of the Revolutionary era were not above utilizing their womanly wiles in order to serve their cause. Nancy Morgan Hart was surprised by five or six Tory soldiers in her Georgia home in 1779. The soldiers insisted that she cook them a meal, which she did. After sneaking her daughter out of the cabin to alert neighbors, Hart plied the soldiers with her homemade whiskey. Intoxicated, the soldiers let down their guard, and Hart took up a musket, killing one who attacked her, fatally wounding another, and guarding the rest until help arrived.

During the Civil War, women served as nurses and laundresses; but they also served in the military ranks incognito. Among the women who fought disguised as men were Loreta Velazquez (as Lieutenant Harry T. Buford), Mary Scaberry (as Charles Freeman), Sarah Roseta Wakeman (as Lyons Wakeman), and Jennie Hodgers (as Albert D. J. Cashier). Hodgers managed to sustain the masquerade until she was identified as a woman when she moved into an old-soldiers' home.

Other women played the important and dangerous role of spies. Rose O'Neal Greenhow hid plans for the Battle of Bull Run in her hairdo, in an attempt to tip off the Confederate army. Placed under house arrest, she continued to manage a spy ring and flew a Confederate flag from the window of her Washington, D.C., home. Actress Pauline Cushman gathered intelligence for the Union forces as she traveled to several Confederate camps in Tennessee, ostensibly searching for her brother. And the well-known African American Harriet Tubman played three important roles in the war: as nurse, spy, and guide for a troop of several hundred black soldiers commanded by Colonel James Montgomery on a raid in South Carolina to free eight hundred slaves.

World War I marked an important change in the role of women warriors. With the more highly organized military forces, women were not as able as formerly to sneak into the warrior ranks. However, the U.S. government began to set up separate female military units. These women did not see combat, but rather assumed duties such as nursing and clerical work. Some were camouflage designers. The Navy called the women in its program "yoemanettes." The Marine Corps swore in their first "marinette," Opha Mac Johnson, in 1918. Approximately 12,500 yoemanettes and 300 marinettes served before the end of the war. The Army, which had no similar program largely because its enlistment-authorizing legislation specified "male persons,"[35] would not enlist women until World War II.

The Women's Army Auxiliary Corps (WAAC) was established in 1942 based on a bill introduced by Representative Edith Nourse Rogers. It was initially intended as an auxiliary with no military status and no benefits. However, in 1943 the name was changed to the Women's Army Corps (WACs) and the group was given full military status. The corps was racially segregated and served no combat role. The Navy created the WAVES (Women Accepted for Volunteer Emergency Service—or, as they also liked to be known: Women Are Very Essential Sometimes) in 1942. The WAVES reached a numerical strength of 86,000 at their peak. Like the WACs, they saw no combat action.

Two civilian women's pilot groups joined forces to create the Women's Air Service Pilots (WASPs) to aid in the war effort by flying planes from factories to air bases, training male pilots, and towing targets for gunnery practice. Approximately 2,000 women served as WASPs during World War II, but they were denied military status and benefits until 1977. All told, approximately 350,000 women served with the military during the war without status or benefits. In the postwar years, women's service roles shrank considerably, with most serving in secretarial positions. By 1948, only 14,000 women remained in the armed services.[36]

In a little-known action during World War II, U.S. Army General George Marshall had experimented with the use of women for anti-aircraft artillery duties. The experiment was kept secret partly because classified equipment was used, but also because of the fear of negative publicity generated by the use of women in combat roles. According to David Jones, "The results of this experiment showed the superiority of women in all functions involving delicacy of manual dexterity, such as operation of the director, height finder, radar, and searchlight control systems. They performed routine repetitive tasks in a manner superior to that of men. Morale was also generally higher among the women."[37] Despite these overwhelmingly positive results, the information was buried and women continued to be denied combat-related duties.

This experiment was not the only evidence in favor of women's expanded service in the military. Women in the military auxiliaries lost less time from work than men, their rate of sexually transmitted diseases was practically zero while the disease rates were high for male soldiers, and women's rates of alcoholism and desertion were far below the rates for men.[38] The Germans were not ignorant of the excellent performance of American military women. Albert Speer, Hitler's weapons production chief, was quoted as saying: "How wise you were to bring your women into your military and into your labor force. Had we done that initially, as you did, it could well have affected the whole course of the war. We would have found out, as you did, that women are equally effective, and for some skills, superior to males."[39]

To fast-forward through decades that included the Korean War and the Vietnam War, 1973—toward the close of the latter conflict—was when the women's branches of the armed services merged with the men's. About 10,000 women had served in Vietnam as nurses, Red Cross workers, journalists, and social workers. During this same year the first six Navy women earned their pilot's wings. They were limited in their assignments, however, and could not be assigned to combat ships, even to deliver the mail.

Legislation passed in 1975 required all the service academies to admit women, and the following year marked the entry of the first women into the U.S. Naval Academy, West Point, and the Air Force Academy. The first classes containing women thus graduated in 1980. In 1984, Kristine Holdereid was the first woman to graduate at the top of her class from a military academy, the Naval Academy. She was followed in 1986, by Terrie A. McLaughlin as the first female outstanding cadet at the Air Force Academy; Kristin Baker as the first woman named captain of the West Point cadet corps in 1989; and Lieutenant Rebecca Marier as the first female at the top of her class at West Point in 1995. These positions were not won easily. We will discuss below the barriers these women overcame in their rise to excellence in extremely hostile environments, and the changing roles women played in the military in the decade of the 1990s.

Military Culture—The Ultimate Men's Club

Opponents of admitting women into the military ranks on an equal basis with men have generally argued the existence of, and need to maintain, a strong male "military culture." Each branch of the armed services, they explain, has a culture that is "manifest in the rituals we observe, the jokes we tell, the clothes we wear, the food we eat, the work we do, and the ways we interact with others who share our workplace."[40] Some aspects of organizational culture are by-the-book aspects of etiquette, like the rules for greeting based on rank, whom you should salute, and, equally important, whom you shouldn't. But there is also an informal, shadow culture:

For example, at the end of Airborne training a soldier receives his wings from a military mentor or relative whom he has chosen to fasten onto his uniform the small metal pin that from then on will attest to his accomplishment. Back in the barracks another ceremony follows the official one. Here fellow soldiers award the same wings a second time: one by one the soldier's buddies step up and punch the wings, their tacks exposed, directly into the proud pincushion's flesh. Only then, when pricked by his peers, has the soldier earned his "blood wings."[41]

Many of the rituals of the shadow culture, like the ceremony described above, emphasize brutality. Proponents justify such behavior by appealing to the need for cohesion within the military unit, and they argue for excluding women from military service because their presence would disrupt this necessary cohesion. The same argument was made in the past regarding African Americans, and more recently regarding homosexuals.

American military culture has always prized stereotypically masculine characteristics like aggressiveness, independence, risk taking, and sexual bravado. Students of military culture point out that "the stereotype of masculinity has acquired additional power because it fits nicely with another central value of modern militaries, the love of uniformity."[42] Women in the ranks obviously break the uniformity of the male unit.

However, a close examination of the literature on the dynamics of group cohesion casts serious doubt on the accuracy of this assumption. Among the several functions served by military culture, two especially support discrimination against women; these have to do with creating commitment and reinforcing boundaries. High levels of commitment relate to the desirability of membership in a group, the exclusivity of the group, and the hurdles that must be overcome or costs paid to enter the group. In the ceremony above, for example, members of the Airborne are ostensibly bonded together less by the formal ritual, than through having endured the informal "pinning" ceremony. The important question is whether these informal mechanisms actually create the commitment, or whether an already high level of commitment to an organization is what spurs the individual to submit to such ordeals.

Two important types of cohesion characterize groups like military units: social cohesion and task cohesion. The first refers to whether the group members like each other and have a feeling of closeness. Task cohesion, meanwhile, relates to the feeling of a shared goal and a joint commitment to achieving the goal. Social science research conducted on different types of military units, such as ROTC cadet squadrons and rifle teams, has shown that while the presence of task cohesion is indeed associated with group success on a task, social cohesion is irrelevant to success.[43] In fact, if anything, social cohesion is more likely to "undermine a group's effectiveness."[44] Rituals whose goal is to increase the social cohesion of men in the military and thus exclude women do not deserve protection, and should be eliminated. Unfortunately, thus far the military has not recognized this reality, partly because of another function of military culture: reinforcing boundaries.

It is clear that the presence of an outside threat will cause a group to become more cohesive. The threat may be real, as when Islamic fundamentalists captured the American embassy in Iran. Or it may be illusory, as when Jim Jones was able to persuade over nine hundred members of the People's Temple to commit voluntary suicide because of the supposed presence in the surrounding jungle of CIA sharpshooters who, Jones claimed, were planning to execute Temple members.[45] The point is that there is an outsider who is perceived as both different from the group and dangerous to it.

In the past, the emphasis on masculinity and macho attitudes and behaviors served to identify anyone not white and not male as not belonging to the military group. Their proposed inclusion in the group constituted a threat. But blacks, women, and gays are now members of the military. It is neither functional nor productive to identify a group member as a threat. By discriminating against some of its group members, the military therefore risks a negative effect on the cohesion of the entire group. The informal or shadow culture emphasizes the link between attitudes about women and women in combat.[46] Excluding women from combat excludes them, as well, from the informal aspects of the military culture and encourages discrimination.

Major Rhonda Cornum was the only American woman soldier to be taken as a prisoner of war during the Gulf War. She recounts a story that illustrates the importance of group task cohesiveness. Cornum's battalion had been housed together in a parking garage. She was approached by a woman officer from another unit who suggested that all of the women should be moved to live together in a separate place, perhaps the basement of the structure. She asked Cornum as the ranking officer to make the request to the executive officer of the 101st Airborne Division. Instead, Cornum demonstrated a recognition of the importance of keeping the functional groups together: "When I met with the executive officer, Lt. Col. Richard Gill, I argued that putting the women in a separate area was a terrible idea. The commanders wanted to enhance unit integrity and cohesiveness, so segregating people according to sex was obviously not the way to do it."[47]

Another method of enforcing boundaries that has been endemic in the military is the use of sexual harassment to emphasize the masculinity and prowess of the men, and to minimize the value and power of women. Sue Guenter-Schlesinger differentiates two "generations" of sexual harassment in the military.[48] The first generation spanned the late 1970s and 1980s and included overt physical, verbal, and nonphysical harassment. The women's supervisors and peers were equally liable to be sources of this harassment:

Many were frightened for their physical safety, fearing the harassment would elevate to assault or rape. On one army base in Germany, women soldiers could not walk from their barracks to the education center to take university evening courses because of their male counterparts hanging half-nude out of barracks' windows, yelling profanity and verbally intimidating them.[49]

This is the type of harassment that resulted in the 1991 Tailhook scandal and the problems identified at the Aberdeen Proving Ground. While this type of behavior may increase the bonding of the male personnel, victimizing and marginalizing group members reduces the task effectiveness of the group.

The second generation of harassment identified by Guenter-Schlesinger is less overtly sexual in nature, but continues to marginalize women through their hostile and prejudicial treatment.

Instead of direct attacks, this form of harassment is based on isolating women from mainstream military life. It especially targets those women who have demonstrated ability and might threaten the military establishment through promotion based on performance. According to a retired Defense Equal Opportunity Management Institute commandant:

Senior leaders may be less prepared today than ever to have women as close associates. I fear they may think they run the risk of being accused of sexual harassment. In light of recent allegations against the Sergeant Major of the Army and the drill sergeants at Aberdeen Proving Ground, I am concerned that this type of "backlash" may occur even more. As a result, women will have even less opportunity to work at the level and in the positions to which they normally should be assigned.[50]

The Price of Admission: Jodie Calls and Cat Calls

Entry into the military proceeds through either boot camp or the military academy. In these contexts, two other aspects of military culture enter in, having to do with cognitive and control functions, or "creating automaticity and predictability within [the] organization."[51] The entry points into the organization serve to inculcate these aspects of the culture. Boot camp is an example of what sociologist Erving Goffman referred to as "total institutions."[52] During boot camp, fledgling soldiers are taught military skills such as shooting and fighting, but they are also taught how to do everything in a military manner: "how to walk, eat, dress, speak . . . make their bed, shine their shoes, and fold their clothing."[53] The goal is to create uniformity under conditions of extreme stress. "Drill instructors, the engineers of their transformation, control every minute of the recruits' days: they deprive them of sleep, tax them physically, infantilize them, and, if these recruits are male, feminize them through a ritual humiliation designed to impress on them that to be degraded is to be a woman ('Come on, ladies')."[54]

The message is clear. To be a woman is to be inferior. And to be a female in the military is to be inferior. The message is reiterated everywhere. The marching chants, known as jodie calls in the Marine Corps, are often misogynistic, along the lines of "Three-zero-five-six/We don't need no stinkin' chicks!"[55] Traditionally, both boot camp and academy have faced the task of turning boys into men, which appears to entail turning them into misogynists as well:

From the familiar "This is my rifle, this is my gun; one is for killing, one is for fun," to "The Marines need a few good men," pride of manhood is a part of recruitment and training. When an institution tries to organize and control large numbers of unruly young men, when it tries to teach self-regard to young men who have little, it is helpful to be able to tell them that they are, by nature, better than half the population.[56]

To the extent that it requires such misogyny to forge the warrior spirit, accepting women or gays into the ranks obviously disrupts the process.

A related governing theme of both boot camp and the service academy is that warriors are forged in these institutions through the application of stress. Military analyst Paul Roush explains the logic:

[I]f one learns to deal with one kind of stress, one is assured of being able to deal with all other kinds of stress. . . . The argument goes something like this: Being abused physically by those in power is stressful. Combat is also stressful. Learning to respond to physical abuse without being debilitated by the resulting stress will therefore allow one to face the stress of combat without being debilitated by it.[57]

Roush was here refuting premise of a 1979 article by James Webb in *The Washingtonian*, defending physical abuses practiced at the Naval

Academy and entitled "Women Can't Fight." Not only is this line of reasoning ludicrous, it is also dangerous for the unity of an integrated military force. This premise encourages the brutality of training and of the rituals that mark passage into the services. Other than tradition, there is no support for this concept, which finds its logical conclusion in debacles such as the Tailhook convention. The psychological literature is clear that exposure to brutality and abuse serves to condition the individual to mete out brutality and abuse in their turn. "To the extent that the military brass have permitted training to operate as a male rite of passage, they have furthered a culture hostile to women."[58]

Keeping Women in Their Place

Military culture employs various other strategies to disadvantage women or to tokenize them. Uniforms are a good example. The function of uniforms is to "separate soldier from civilian, private from general, pilot from submariner, and man from boy as well as from woman."[59] And the potent symbol of the military uniform provides an equally potent example of the ambivalence toward women in the military. When women began to enter the service academies, one of the first questions that arose was how they ought to dress. The problem pivoted on the issue of the desired uniformity (literally) of what had become a nonuniform group. One option was to dress the women in the same uniforms as the men, but that was immediately rejected, apparently because the idea of women looking like men was sufficient to raise concern about the sexuality, or sexual orientation, of the female cadets. Among the service academies, West Point was the only one that allowed women to wear trousers. But that changed with the 1976 "Plebe Hop," the traditional dance for first-year cadets. There, men and women, both with short hair and both wearing trousers, were dancing with each other. Subsequently, according to the amended rule book, female cadets might attend dances in trousers only if they did not intend to dance with men; if they did, they had to wear uniform skirts.[60]

Skirts provided a very effective way to mark women military personnel as different. At Annapolis and at the Air Force Academy in Colorado Springs, women were required to wear skirts in marching formation. Of course, skirts required appropriate footwear. Marching places a strain on the feet, a strain that could have been minimized by requiring female recruits to wear flat-heeled shoes. All of the service academies, however, required the women to wear high-heeled shoes. The Navy did take the step of commissioning a podiatrist to examine the most appropriate footwear for female midshipmen. The memo returned on the topic read: "This shoe, with our altered heel, produces a shoe that does not trap correctly. This incorrect trap causes the individual woman to feel off-balance when standing at attention."[61] This is perhaps an appropriate metaphor for the entire uniform problem. The point was to keep women off balance.

The 1990s: A Turning Point

High heels notwithstanding, women kicked open the doors to parity in the military through their accomplishments during several military actions during the last decade of the twentieth century.

Desert Storm witnessed the greatest deployment of women warriors in modern times. The thirty-five thousand American women in the Gulf War did everything that men did, including taking part in combat. In addition to their service in communications, nursing, and various logistical operations, they piloted helicopters, tankers, and other types of aircraft over the machine guns; repaired M1 tanks and Bradley fighting vehicles; loaded laser-guided bombs on F-117s; guarded bases from terrorist attacks; commanded prisoner of war facilities; operated heavy equipment; and led platoons, brigades, companies, and battalions.[62]

In short, women did everything that the military brass had long claimed they were incapable of doing. They shattered the myth that women cannot be effective warriors. Their demonstrated competence was "instrumental in the legislative action and subsequent military directives that eliminated the restrictions on women serving as combat pilots and on surface warfare ships."[63] During Desert Storm and Operation Just Cause (the phrase used to justify the American incursion into Panama), many individual women committed acts of noteworthy bravery.

Among these brave women are Captain Linda L. Bray, Lieutenant Paula Coughlin, and Major Rhonda L. Cornum. Captain Bray served with the Army in Panama during the 1989 military action in that country. Bray was assigned to lead thirty military police to take control of a kennel for attack dogs that was incorrectly believed to be only lightly guarded. The battalion captured the kennel after a three-hour firefight. Bray resigned from the Army after receiving negative reactions from other army officers.[64]

Lieutenant Coughlin was the officer who brought the Tailhook scandal to public attention in 1992, after the Navy failed to respond to reports of the sexual assaults committed at the 1991 convention. The publicity and subsequent investigations resulted in the resignation of the Secretary of the Navy and reprimands for a number of officers. The top admiral who was present retired with a full pension. In 1994, Coughlin won $6.7 million from the Hilton Hotels in damages for inadequate provision of security. She found it impossible to remain in the Navy and resigned.[65]

Major Cornum, a flight surgeon stationed in Saudi Arabia during the Gulf War in 1991, was taken as a prisoner of war when the eight-passenger helicopter on which she and her crew were flying to rescue a downed American pilot was shot down behind enemy lines. Despite two broken arms and other major injuries, Major Cornum provided support and comfort to fellow prisoners during her eight-day captivity.[66]

What is striking about these three stories is the fact that two of these three heroic women were forced to leave the careers they loved because of the backlash they experienced to their behavior.

Other women have been forced to resign from their military careers despite outstanding records because of their sexual orientation. Colonel Margarethe Cammermeyer was the chief nurse of the Washington National Guard. A Bronze Star Vietnam veteran, she was dismissed when she disclosed her lesbian sexual orientation. A federal court ordered reinstatement in 1994. Colonel Cammermeyer was a victim of President Clinton's ill-advised "Don't Ask, Don't Tell, Don't Pursue" policy, which has actually resulted in an increase in the number of courts martial of gay and lesbian military members.[67]

As of 1997, women represented 13.6 percent of all military officers and 13.7 percent of enlisted personnel. African Americans represented 8 percent of all officers and 22.1 percent of enlisted personnel, and were most heavily represented in the Army, with 11.6 percent of all officers and 29.7 percent of the enlisted personnel. Almost half of all army women were African American. In 1997, 60 percent of women officers served in traditionally female areas of medicine and administration; the number was less than 50 percent for enlisted women.[68] An assessment of the interaction of women and men in the military concluded that while the wrinkles have not been worked out of the system, the presence of women in the military has had a net positive effect on the "readiness, cohesion, and morale" in the units studied.[69]

Women have proven their value to the military, as in police departments, by surmounting hurdles thrown in their way purely on the basis of their sex. But even when women win, they sometimes eventually lose. Honest, courageous, honorable behavior is as often punished as celebrated. However, as the military and police agencies continue to become more diverse simply based upon the population from which they are drawn, the luxury of discrimination based on gender, sexual orientation, or race will eventually become impossible. Demographics may effect what decades of accomplishment have been unable to achieve.

Ellen Goodman argued a generation ago that the presence of women in the military might at least have a mitigating effect on the military's propensity for war. Whether or not the presence of more women will make for a less aggressive military remains to be seen. But, like neighborhood police units, it can only be a good thing for armed services to more genuinely reflect the constituencies they claim to protect. Even if that means, as it did in the Gulf War, women fighting and dying alongside men. Regarding this "de-gendering of war," Barbara Ehrenreich has observed:

The de-gendering of war does not mean that "masculinity" will cease to be a desirable attribute; only that it will be an attribute that women as well as men can possess. . . . The division of humanity into "masculine" and "feminine" may persist, but these categories may have less and less to do with the biological sexes. This is not an entirely negative development, from a woman's perspective: With the admission of women to warrior status, we may be ready for the long overdue recognition that it was not only human males who made the transition from prey to predator, but the entire human race.[70]

Women as predators? Now, there's an interesting thought.

Snapshot

Susan Ewing, *A Woman's Place*

I lashed the buck's front hooves behind his head and wrapped my wooden-handled pull rope around the base of his antlers. His blood was pressed into the swirls of my fingerprints.

I wasn't strong enough simply to drag him along behind through the snow, so I walked backwards, pausing after each two steps to pull him toward me; backwards along the trail through bare rose bushes and cottonwoods and red-osier dogwoods, two steps at a time.

Nose running, sweat soaking the waistband of my long johns, I moved through the frozen morning in a state of feminine grace. When I hunt I still feel like a splinter member of the female tribe, but the path along which I pulled the deer is crowded with the tracks of a history of women. Most traditionally, women have been linked with the processing tasks of the hunt—butchering and preserving meat,

Susan Ewing is a writer. She lives in Bozeman, Montana.

rendering oil, tanning hides, preparing food. The chores, rather than the traveling as a hunter, fit more realistically into a mother's life. But I'm a restless sort, and not a mother. In a sense, hunting has given me a tiny shred of the connection I've missed by not having children, causing me to consider my life in the most basic of biological terms and human behaviors. Hunting has given me a stake in the cycle of blood, life, death, and nourishment; it is a devotion—an act of responsibility and courage. But these sorts of words are more easily twisted than understood, so I have to look to my own heart for the truth and just hold on. Hold on and pull, two steps at a time.

This particular weekend happened to be the beginning of a very popular cow elk season, and the snow-swept roads crawled with trucks full of orange-hatted men. It was rolling, open, Montana cattle country—mostly large ranches with irrigated hay fields, and some national forest in the background. The Musselshell River gave the local landscape a center, as rivers do.

One of the biggest ranches was running guided hunts, and another large landowner was letting on fifty elk hunters a day, first come first served. Hunters piled out of trucks and busied ranch offices like orange-crested magpies. While the elk hunters waited their turns for access to the higher country on private land, many of them cruised the county roads for deer. The situation was closer to a competitive shoot than a hunt.

A certain section of river bottom was open to shotguns and archery only, so I had somewhat skeptically brought slugs for my single-barrel 20-gauge, even though I had only used the shotgun for birds—mostly missing them. All my hunting experience has been Out West, where long shots and brawny calibers are, ironically enough, equated with hunting skill. It was hard to imagine making a true shot on a deer without looking through a scope. Besides, I had just gotten a new Remington .243 and was eager to hunt with it. But before I left home I fired some practice slugs, which merely proved it was possible to punch holes in cardboard from atlatl range.

After passing yet another truckload of hunters stopped by the side of the road to glass, I stopped at the ranch office to ask about hunting the river bottom, just in case. The woman handling check-in made a little dot on a photocopied map. I could park next to the sheep barn but not by the little house, so as not to disturb the Peruvian family living there. No, she said, no one else had requested permission to hunt the bottom.

Pat and I met up at the old roadhouse where we were staying. He was chasing upland birds on a nearby Hutterite colony while I looked for deer. The warm café was crowded with red-faced, boisterous hunters. Bringing the shotgun and slugs had been Pat's idea; I've never liked him telling me now to hunt. When we crawled into the old iron bed after dinner I was still wavering. Well before dawn I creaked out of bed and headed toward the river.

A light was on in the Peruvians' tidy, blue-sided trailer house, and I tried to look like a woman going to work. I wondered what life was like for the woman in the house. Did she feed and water the animals and chase away coyotes? Did she shear, sort, and carry wool? Butcher sheep? Pull difficult lambs from struggling ewes?

No one appeared at the window as I walked by in the frigid dark and turned down an alley between drifted-in breeding pens. The dry snow was deep but easy to walk through, and a string of deer tracks led me to a narrow path through cattails taller than me. Like Alice going down the rabbit hole, I made myself small, turning my shoulders into the passageway. The cattails gave way to willow whips, then the path turned out into a small clearing.

A doe flushed as I moved too quickly into the open space. She seemed surprised to see anyone in there, and not too alarmed. I slowed down and began meandering the river bottom, ducking on and off deer trails, over and under fallen cottonwoods. At a giant cottonwood snag, I bent around onto another trail burrowed through the shrubbery and eased along. Fifteen feet ahead, the tunnel-like trail opened onto a frozen beaver pond, and through the tangled jumble of winter-bare tree and shrub I saw a buck standing out on the ice. The trail had already forced me into a crouch, so I hunkered more solidly, brought up my shotgun and pushed off the safety. If he stepped up to the trail, he would walk right into my shot. Through the dense sticks I watched slivers of him move closer. I both desire and dread this moment of hunting. I will get to shoot. I will have to shoot.

He stepped up to the entrance of the trail and peered in at me— a huge-bodied whitetail with wide, symmetrical antlers. The bead was lined up right behind his shoulder.

I squeezed the trigger. The deer blinked. I squeezed the trigger. The deer sniffed. I squeezed harder. The gun may as well have been cast in a single piece of bronze. I fingered the safety. Off. For sure. I squeezed the trigger again. Nothing. Holding my breath I clicked the safety on, back off, and squeezed the ossified trigger. The deer swiveled his ears and bobbed his heavy head.

In blind-minded panic, I pulled back the action with a loud, metallic *schlllk*. The startled buck reared backwards and galloped, whistling in alarm, across the pond, disappearing into dense cover on the other side.

I wanted to scream. I wanted to cry. I wanted to slam the goddamned gun against a tree and break it into freeze-dried bits. Instead, with great effort, I got up and skated across the pond after the deer. If the ice had held him, it would hold me. His trail led through the brushy edge into the woods, past a tree where a single hawk feather hung solemnly from a bare branch. The sight was somehow soothing, and I ghosted through the brush for several more hours in the close company of does and a small buck or two, listening to occasional rifle shots far off in the distance.

The Peruvians' lights were on as I walked past their house and into the cattails the next morning. Feeling part of the habitat by now, I was halfway through a small clearing when I noticed some deer in a willow clump forty yards away. Breaking away from the group, a doe angled in my direction, passing on the other side of some trees. A small, two-point buck followed a minute behind. As soon as the other deer put their heads back down to eat, I crossed the rest of the clearing and ducked next to a bush with a view of where the two had passed. Five minutes later a doe walked by, seventeen yards away, followed by a fawn. The young one paused on the trail and jumped when it saw me, but just trotted up to the ambling doe and the two walked on. I could still hear does talking in the willows, and maybe the grunt of another buck. Deer bodies flashed brown in the vertical slices of sight afforded through the trees. Stripes of soft gray-brown and then a hard gleam; tines, then snatches of a head. *That* deer. His dark eye caught the light. A red-tailed hawk landed on a tall snag opposite my hiding place and seemed to wait with me as the buck fiddled around at the edge of view. Finally, I caught a white wag of tail as he turned around and trotted away, deeper into the woods.

When my breath came back I realized how truly, deeply happy I was to be there, nestled in the snow like a cottontail—warm and dry in my army surplus pants with that elusive, sagacious buck, and the hawk, and the rose hips.

A few more deer lingered in the bushes and I continued to wait, having decided to accept any antlered opportunity, should one arise. Antlers are beautiful mementos but I'm not a trophy hunter. A doe walked past and before she had quite disappeared a buck nosed into my two-second chance. I pulled the trigger and he crumpled to the ground. The hawk flew.

Lowering the gun I wondered at what I had done. There are so many proud, sorrowful ways to answer the questions around this ancient transaction—this most precious exchange.

I went to the buck and after sitting awhile, rifled through my pack and found everything I needed: sharp knife, saw, rope. As I rolled up my sleeves I found everything I needed inside, too—a sense of my own feminine self, solid, complete, and grounded. Dressing him out was a peaceful communion and in forty-five minutes I was ready to go, two steps at a time, down the whispering path.

4 Babies and Bullets in the Same Conversation

American Women and Hunting

It used to be so easy to talk about gender roles. The formula was simple: men hunt, and women gather. Men, that is, being innately audacious, like to venture forth into the wide, wild, dangerous world, to explore and stalk and kill. Women, meanwhile, being by nature less adventurous, prefer to stick closer to home and hearth, tending their children and puttering around with plants and flowers. Men like to quest, while women would rather nest.

This has been the pattern since the origin of the human species, or so the story—the so-called hunting hypothesis of human origins[1]—went. The idea at the heart of it was that our species could never have originated at all had it not been for the sexual division of labor. As anthropologist Desmond Morris remarked, it was essential hundreds of thousands of years ago that proto-human females "stay put and mind the babies," if their male mates were going to be able to get on with the serious business of evolution: inventing, through their hunting activity, such uniquely human behaviors as upright posture, tool use, language, cooperation, and so on.[2] Male hunting at the dawn of the human species made us what we are today, in terms of qualities like courage, and our ability to employ technology to conquer nonhuman nature as well as the occasional human enemy. Females contributed the softer side to this story of human evolution, being simultaneously more nurturing and less aggressive than men and thereby more in need of male protection.

It was a neat picture, and quite satisfying to the post–World War II Western mentality that developed it. Rosie the Riveter might have helped us win the war, but with the men returned from the front, and seeking to regain their jobs in business and industry, women were expected to return home. And since those same men carried memories of unspeakable atrocities, they may have had an emotional as well as economic stake in asserting the essential tenderheartedness, and vulnerability, of their wives and daughters. It had to be reassuring for them to know that during the last Ice Age, forty thousand years ago, male hunting bands naturally ventured forth to bring chunks of mammoth meat back to the camp, where their eagerly waiting women would prepare it and complement it with the fruits of their foraging. According to the hunting hypothesis, it was just as natural for modern men to venture forth into the asphalt jungle to bring home the bacon, which their housewives would lovingly fry up, maybe with a side of hash browns harvested from the backyard garden.

The problem with this picture was that our ancestors were far more complicated than the Flintstones, and so, of course, are we. The idealized image of swarthy Man the Hunter and his dainty helpmate Woman the Gatherer accorded with neither the Paleolithic then, nor the modern now, of human social reality. In her book *Primate Visions*, science historian Donna Haraway brilliantly exposes the political and social agenda that had driven this line of thinking: With the advent of the Cold War, "Third World" countries were up for grabs and were choosing sides between "Free" and "Communist" allegiances in an incredibly high-stakes geopolitical game. It was certainly comforting for Westerners to know that in the long run, evolution was on the side not only of capitalism, but of Euro-American culture. The anthropological research that resulted in the hunting hypothesis was funded largely by the United Nations. In the wake of the Holocaust, fascism, the atom bomb, and Stalinism, the U.N. sought scholarly input on what it means to be human. If one could find the common denominators, perhaps we could all learn to get along. Man the Hunter, the essential human being (Haraway calls him "UNESCO-Man") was the result. As his image developed in the anthropological literature of the midcentury, he just happened to look an awful lot like your typical middle-class capitalist nuclear family man. And, as a number of feminist anthropologists were quick to point out, his little woman looked suspiciously like the lesser half of a classic patriarchal marriage.[3]

Not that these feminist critics were anxious to claim hunting, or other such male-identified activities as warfare, as anything women—modern women anyway—would want to be caught dead doing. They championed Woman the Gatherer as the standard of true humanity, and located the "essentially" human precisely in women's apparent disinclination to engage in violent or aggressive behavior.[4] They were willing to acknowledge that it was likely that some women must have hunted in Paleolithic times, just as women in some present-day hunter-forager societies (the Mbuti Pygmies, Philippine Agta, Tiwi Aborigines, some Native American tribes) engage in hunting. Historically, for a lot of practical reasons, pregnancy and child rearing no doubt among them, many women may have opted out of hunting, long before they were assumed to be incapable of it. Yet at the same time, throughout history in Europe and America, some women have always hunted. Female hunters have, for at least as long as history has been recorded, been in the minority. But they have always been there. Hunting, perhaps especially in American cultural history, has never been an exclusively male prerogative.

One can only wonder, then, why feminist critics of the tired old story of Man the Hunter failed to see, let alone to celebrate, the existence of women who so radically challenged the acceptable canons of femininity. Here, as elsewhere in the story of women's relationship with guns, the reason seems to lie less in perception than in gender politics. By the late 1970s, no one in the field of anthropology was taking the hunting hypothesis seriously. Too much evidence was coming to light in ethnographic and animal behavioral studies, and in the emerging field of sociobiology, that challenged the simple equation: aggressive man hunts, passive woman gathers. Yet even as scientists were abandoning the Man the Hunter idea, some feminists as late as the 1990s were eagerly embracing it.

Why? One obvious reason for ignoring the existence of female hunters is that it makes it easier to identify hunting with "male violence." Numerous feminist writers,[5] especially those espousing one form or another of the philosophy that has come to be called ecofeminism, have equated hunting with rape—and not only the rape of women, but by extension the "rape" of nature and man's domination of the nonhuman environment. It's a seductive line of thinking, to the extent that it tends to exempt women from any real responsibility for the negative environmental impacts of their own existence, and places them on a moral high ground of sorts. Women, in this view, are incapable of the sort of domination that characterizes men's interactions with the natural world—interactions epitomized by hunting.

It is no accident, of course, that most of the proponents of the hunting-as-rape idea are also animal rights advocates. The "vegetarian feminism" for which they argue arises from a vision of the way human beings relate to nonhuman animals that relies upon the same erroneous assumptions about gender differences as did the hunting hypothesis. One of the most influential vegetarian feminists was the late Andree Collard. Writing that "no woman will be free until all animals are free and nature is released from man's ruthless exploitation," Collard affirmed her allegiance with the nonhuman:

I am first of all always on the side of nature. Her innocence (in the etymological sense of "not noxious") may derive from the fact that she acts not from choice but from inherent need. Whatever nature does that seems cruel and evil to anthropomorphising eyes is done without intent to harm. . . . Where the human hand has not greedily tinkered, nature is spontaneous, awesome, refreshingly unselfconscious, magnificently diverse. For thousands of years, nature has been the measure of our humanity, providing much of our self-identity.[6]

In this worldview, the human hand that "greedily tinkers" cannot be the same one that rocks the cradle. And the hand that rocks the cradle would never, unless driven by extreme circumstances or seduced by fantasies of male power, take up a gun and venture into field or forest with the intent of killing. The death and violence that happen in nonhuman nature are acceptable, because nature is unconscious of "herself." Women at their best share in nature's "refreshing unselfconsciousness"—an unsettling idea, to be sure, for those of us who thought feminism was about advancing women's equality with men.

But there's the rub. If women really are like men, when it comes to their desire for hands-on engagement with the natural world about them, then that would seem to imply that women are as capable as men of exerting harm to that world. And viewed from the outside— that is, from the perspective of the non-hunter (let alone the anti-hunter)—using a firearm to kill a "defenseless" animal certainly looks like harm. Better, then, that women's capacity for harm remains un-selfconscious: it is, after all, easy enough not to think about the environmental consequences of one's eating habits, whether they have to do with the number of wild animals killed or displaced to create the soybean field in which one's tofu originated, or the prehistory in factory farm, feedlot or slaughterhouse of the meat one buys shrink-wrapped in the market.

Indeed, from this vantage point, a feminist need not be a vegetarian or subscribe to the philosophy of animal liberation to see hunting as the province of men only. It is hardly news that ours is a consumerist, death-denying society, in which the majority of Americans are living at ever greater remove from the sources of their day-to-day sustenance. This distance is as mental as it is physical. Most people are either unaware of, or would rather not look too closely at, the amount of killing it takes to keep them alive. To the extent that killing can be identified as something that men do and women don't, it is tempting for feminists to lapse into the same gender categories that they might criticize in other spheres—equal employment, say, or child care.

Add to this the fact that hunting generally entails the use of some form of weapon. A review of existing hunter-forager cultures reveals a consistent pattern: the tools that men make for their own use are also tools that can be used as weapons, whereas women's tools cannot.[7] Weapons use is generally recognized as an advance in the direction of technological sophistication and development, so we may read an economic message here: women's more primitive tools, coupled with their lack of access to and training in advanced technologies, mean they have to work longer and harder, and for less compensation, than men. This is as true in advanced societies like our own as in tribal cultures. Only the tools differ. Instead of being hampered, as tribal women are, by digging sticks and infants in carrying slings, women in industrialized societies occupy the majority of low-skilled, low-paying jobs, after which they come home to the "second shift" of housework and child care. Women's subordination to men arguably begins and ends in the denial of their access to and training in advanced technologies.

But more than that: another clear implication of this comparison between tribal and advanced cultures, and one more to the point of this chapter, has to do with the tools, or the weapons, available to women. Here, once again, we bump into the problematic image of the woman armed and dangerous. However, hunting adds the dimension that the woman who knows how to kill is able not only to defend herself against attack, but to fend for herself when it comes to putting food on the table. She doesn't need Man the Hunter around to protect her *or* to provide for her. It is easy enough to see why patriarchy needs to suppress this kind of woman. The question is, why would feminism shy away from her?

A-Hunting She Will Go

It just may be that women hunters present more of a challenge to conventional conceptions of appropriate female behavior than do either women who arm themselves in self-defense on the one hand, or who work in gun-related occupations on the other. After all, women who have made the decision to own or carry firearms for protection are reacting to actual or potential external threats to their safety; women in the military or law enforcement have opted for traditionally male-identified careers in which guns happen to come with the territory. Firearms proficiency in either of these cases can be viewed as a gun owner's duty and responsibility. But in both cases, though a woman may derive satisfaction from practicing shooting at inanimate targets in order to gain that proficiency, she will generally affirm that she would much rather not have to use her gun in a real-life situation. She can imagine shooting to kill an assailant or an enemy, but at the same time she hopes she'll never need to. As one woman who keeps a handgun for self-protection observes: "My pistol is fun to shoot at targets; however, since I keep it for personal protection, it's not got a fun job description. In other words, I would rather not have to use it for its intended purpose."[8]

Hunting is altogether different. In this case, while target practice or shooting clay "birds" may indeed be enjoyable activities in their own right, the woman's ultimate purpose is to use her gun against another living being. Her goal is to shoot to kill. She is not doing this out of need, since she could always buy her meat in a store. She is doing it out of desire, because she has chosen to hunt, and because she takes pleasure in hunting.

Now, it was a truism of the hunting hypothesis that "men enjoy hunting and killing, and these activities are continued as sports even when they are no longer economically necessary."[9] That idea fit the conventional wisdom, and it has not been an aspect of that wisdom that feminism has particularly sought to change. But to say that *women* enjoy hunting and killing, and will opt to hunt for sport when there is no economic reason to, is to challenge contemporary gender norms in a way that makes a lot of people—among them, many self-identified feminists—decidedly uncomfortable. It suggests a cultural can of worms they would rather not open up.

Women hunters have not always been so invisible. From the late 1800s up until roughly the outbreak of the Second World War, if you were to open up the average issue of a hunting magazine like *Outdoor Life* or *Field & Stream*, you would likely find articles or hunting stories by women, pictures of women engaged in various "blood sports" or posing with their trophies, or advertisements for companies like Winchester and Remington, selling guns and ammunition, and featuring women shooters. You might even find a woman on the cover. Women may have been a minority in the hunting community, but they were obviously a very real and openly welcomed part of it. Given the pioneer heritage of the United States, and its predominantly rural population base up until the mid-twentieth century, it only stands to reason that a fair number of women joined men afield, or even hunted on their own. Annie Oakley was exceptional not because she was female, but because she was such an extraordinarily good sharpshooter.[10] Oakley, of course, honed her shooting skills by hunting to support her family when she was growing up in Ohio farm country. In her later life, she made it her mission to teach as many women as she could to shoot, and to develop the skills that make an outdoorswoman self-sufficient.

Oakley's enthusiasm was shared in print by a number of prominent women outdoor writers. Grace Gallatin Seton-Thompson's *A Female Tenderfoot* (1900) gave practical guidance for the outdoorswoman who wished to be both functionally and stylishly turned out in hunting camp and on the trail, along with advice about the best caliber rifle to take on a large-game hunt. Elinore Pruitt Stewart followed up her immensely popular Wyoming memoir, *Letters of a Woman Homesteader* (1914), in 1915 with *Letters on an Elk Hunt.* In her autobiography *Cross Creek* (1942), Marjorie Kinnan Rawlings, author of the Pulitzer Prize-winning novel *The Yearling*, recounted with evident relish her hunting adventures in the Florida backwaters she had decided to call home. In *Trails of Enchantment* (1930), widely regarded as one of the finest deer-hunting narratives ever written, Paula Brandreth chronicled years of hunting whitetails in New York's Adirondack Mountains. Meanwhile, writers like Delia Akeley (*Jungle Portraits*, 1930), Mary Jobe Akeley *(Carl Akeley's Africa*, 1929, and many others) and Osa Johnson (*I Married Adventure*, 1940, and *Four Years in Paradise*, 1941) published popular accounts of their experiences on safari in Africa.

Around the close of World War II, things changed. Female images and voices disappeared abruptly from the outdoor press, and the assumption took hold in the public imagination that hunting was a males-only thing. During the fifties and sixties, girls and women were for the most part actively discouraged from such pursuits. Fathers took their sons out, as part of a male rite of initiation, and the men-only hunting camp was depicted as a safe haven, a refuge from the wife and kids back home. Hunting came to be so identified with manliness that in1968, *Outdoor Life* editor William Rae, reviewing issues of the magazine from the turn of the century and noting the presence of a perplexing number of women, wrote, with tongue not entirely in cheek: "One wonders whether men really were men in those days, as we have been led to believe."[11]

Of course, Rae wasn't the only man who was feeling uneasy, circa the late sixties, about women's invasion of male territory. The women's liberation movement was by then challenging conventional gender roles and expectations on several cultural fronts. Some male hunters probably saw themselves as the last bastion of American malehood. Even for those who didn't, hunting culture had become so identified with conventional masculinity that it would have been surprising had the women's movement *not* been perceived as somehow threatening to the "hunting fraternity."

The feminist threat took two forms. The first, of course, was anti-hunting activism. Spokesmen for the hunting fraternity were prepared for this. After all, women who were opposed to hunting were acting and thinking in female-appropriate ways. Outdoor writer John Mitchell, in an influential series of essays that originally appeared in *Audubon* magazine in the late seventies and subsequently were published under the title *The Hunt*, explained that, with some reluctance, he had to give up hunting because he found himself living with "female children who would acquire their mother's loathing of guns and would stare at their father with ill-concealed contempt as he ineptly explained how he had once enjoyed walking in the woods with a rifle in the crook of his arm." Throughout *The Hunt*, Mitchell blithely assumes that to be female is to be averse to guns and to hunting.[12] It seemed at the time an altogether reasonable assumption. So it would surely have come as no surprise to Mitchell, or to his fellow sportsmen, if feminists were to argue against hunting.

In some ways, a greater threat to the hunting fraternity's self-image was the prospect of feminists in favor of hunting, and more specifically women's hunting. Not that many were. In the 1960s and '70s, Second Wave feminism was more concerned with issues like affirmative action, reproductive rights, and passage of the Equal Rights Amendment. But feminist "consciousness raising" was in the air, and even the outdoor press was not immune. In a striking departure from convention, in January 1973 *Field & Stream* initiated a new department, "Especially for Women." Its editor, Margaret G. Nichols (a trailblazer in her own right, who had begun her career with the magazine in the 1963 as the gender-neutral M. G. Nichols), wrote in the inaugural column that it was "designed to present ideas and information of particular interest to women, and to encourage them to stretch out, forgetting any 'men-only' ideas that may be keeping them from the fullest enjoyment of the outdoors."[13] The column, an anomaly in the outdoor press, ran monthly through the spring of 1976.

Not until the 1990s would women again begin to acquire some room of their own in major outdoor publications. *Bugle*, the magazine of the Rocky Mountain Elk Foundation, commenced a "Women in the Outdoors" feature in 1995. *Outdoor Life*, the outdoor monthly with the largest circulation, launched a bimonthly "Women Afield" department in 1998. In 1999, Petersen's Publishing Company (now EMAP), which produces such magazines as *Hunting* and *Guns & Ammo*, in conjunction with the Women's Shooting Sports Foundation began quarterly publication of *Outdoors for Women*. And throughout the nineties, feature articles by and about women hunters appeared with regularity in virtually every national and regional outdoor publication.

What accounted for this change in outdoor publishing? First and foremost, shifting demographics. Owing at least in part to the legacy of the women's liberation movement, female hunters were once again visible as a distinctive minority within the hunting community. They were unembarrassed about engaging in hitherto male-identified activities, and as a group these women had more mobility, more leisure time, and more disposable income than ever before. More women were single heads of households, and they were looking for outdoor activities to share with their children, including hunting, fishing, and camping. Though there appeared to be a slow decline in the number of male hunters nationally, the number of women hunters was growing dramatically. And these outdoorswomen were looking for information about hunting, and for the kinds of goods and services traditionally available for men. It made obvious economic sense for publishers and advertisers to pay attention to this market.

It also made good political sense. For the most part, outdoor editors and their colleagues in the hunting industry were, like American men in general, becoming somewhat less jealous about guarding their masculine turf. And they were now uncomfortable with the ready equation between masculinity and boorish behavior that, for perhaps too long, they had tolerated with a wink and a chuckle. Surveys had begun to show that while the nonhunting public in general approved of the idea of *hunting*, especially when the hunting yielded food for the hunter and his or her family, growing numbers of people were inclined to say they disapproved of *hunters*.[14] The problem was the image of the "slob hunter"—the macho guy who mixes guns and alcohol, shoots up road signs, trespasses on posted property, disobeys game regulations, and makes a general nuisance of himself. One could argue that these types have always been in the minority, but no one could deny they were out there. Throughout the 1990s, in sporting trade publications and in venues like the annual Governor's Hunting Heritage Symposia, outdoor writers, fish and game officials, and hunting industry representatives argued that hunters needed to "clean up their act." One of the best strategies for doing this, as far as public perceptions of hunting went, was to emphasize the presence, and enthusiastic participation, of women in the hunting community.

This was not the first time women hunters had been called into service to help justify hunting in the mind of the public. During the late nineteenth and early twentieth centuries, the idea of sport hunting was being consciously developed by hunter-conservationists to counter widespread public disapproval of the excesses of market hunting—excesses that led to the extinction of species like the passenger pigeon and near-extinction of the American bison.[15] One way to demonstrate that sport hunting was a healthy and morally defensible activity was to highlight the number of women who took pleasure in it. A similar strategy had been evident in British hunting publications of roughly the same period; there, the issue was fox hunting.[16] In both these earlier cases, familiar gender stereotypes of feminine gentility and moral rectitude were intentionally, if somewhat ironically, called into play to serve the interests of the predominantly male hunting community.

The situation in the nineties was similar, to the extent that the general consensus was that "women are the future of hunting." That is, if hunting was going to survive in an increasingly urban-centered society in which women were wielding more economic and political clout all the time, then women had best be a prominent part of the hunting community, both in fact and in popular perception. The increase in numbers of female hunters represented, in this sense, a trend to be celebrated and encouraged. And evidence suggested that the presence of women in the field did indeed seem to correlate with better hunter behavior overall.

Additionally, by the 1990s, anti-hunter sentiment had been growing nationally, largely as a result of the animal rights movement. Although many of that movement's more prominent leaders were men, at the grassroots level women comprised approximately 80 percent of animal rights activists.[17] Organizations like People for the Ethical Treatment of Animals (PETA) and the Fund for Animals targeted hunting as not only an animal rights, but also a women's rights, issue. They could be successful in doing this, however, only to the extent that they were able to define hunting as a males-only, or at least a male-dominated, activity. Women hunters in growing numbers were, therefore, a public relations asset to the hunting community. They were, simultaneously, a theoretical thorn in the side of ecofeminists and animal rights advocates. And therein hangs a tale.

Outdoorswomen, or Babes in the Woods?

In 1990, Christine Thomas, then an associate professor at the University of Wisconsin–Stevens Point College of Natural Resources, organized a day-long conference on the subject of "Breaking Down the Barriers to Participation of Women in Angling and Hunting." Thomas had several colleagues on the project, among them Tammy Peterson of the Wisconsin Department of Natural Resources; psychologist Robert Jackson of the University of Wisconsin–La Crosse, who had conducted a series of studies of Wisconsin women deer hunters; and Frances Hammerstrom, who as a student of the originator of modern wildlife management, Aldo Leopold, was one of the first American women to pursue a career in wildlife ecology. Following Thomas's lead, they were working from the assumption that women's traditional nonparticipation in hunting and fishing had less to do with lack of interest than with negative external pressures and lack of opportunity. Their assumption proved correct, based upon brainstorming in focus groups made up of wildlife managers, hunting professionals, and interested members of the public who had been drawn to the conference by its title. Wisconsin is historically a big hunting state, and so, not surprisingly, the conference attracted the press and generated considerable public interest.

The following year, Thomas and Peterson offered a three-day women's outdoor-skills training workshop, at Treehaven Field Station in Tomahawk, Wisconsin. They called it "Becoming an Outdoors-Woman," or BOW (as in bow and arrow) for short. The idea was to create a female-friendly atmosphere in which women could get hands-on experience and training in a variety of hunting-related skills, from shotgunning, riflery, and archery, to non-"blood-sport" activities like compass-reading, backpacking, and outdoor photography. The September 1991 workshop, attended by just over a hundred women, became the model for what rapidly evolved into a national Becoming an Outdoors-Woman program. Working under the aegis of state fish and game agencies, BOW organizers draw on the expertise of hunting and fishing professionals, as many as possible of them women, who volunteer their time to keep participant costs low. For women who cannot afford the fees (generally between $150 and $300), scholarships are available, funded by organizations like the Rocky Mountain Elk Foundation. Course offerings vary somewhat from state to state and region to region, but in all BOW workshops hunting and recreational shooting figure prominently. Today, one or more BOW workshops are offered annually in forty-four states and nine Canadian provinces, as well as a growing number of "Beyond-BOW" programs for women with more advanced skills. Diane Lueck, who for the last several years has been the BOW national coordinator, estimates that by the close of 1999, fifty thousand women had participated in the BOW program.[18] BOW has in turn inspired other women's outdoor skills training programs, some of them sponsored by hunting organizations like the National Wild Turkey Federation and Safari Clubs International, others by local rod and gun clubs, still others by merchandisers like Orvis, which runs somewhat more costly shooting and fly-fishing clinics for women.

All of this has been a source of consternation for those critics of hunting who feel a woman's proper place is on the animal-rights picket line. So it is hardly surprising that the most vociferous critics of the BOW program have been animal liberationists, chief among them Heidi Prescott, national director of the Fund for Animals, the anti-hunting animal-rights organization founded by the late Cleveland Amory. In 1995, Prescott sent letters to the directors of the wildlife agencies of all fifty states, demanding that they cease financial support of the BOW program. Reasoning that the workshops were designed "to entice women to hunt—whether the enticement is blatant or subtle," Prescott objected that "although these programs are spin-doctored as an opportunity to 'get-acquainted-with-nature,' the obvious intention is to recruit women hunters or, at the very least, to increase women's acceptance of hunting." She further accused these agencies of trying to play the role of "social engineer."[19]

Prescott could point to the statements of wildlife professionals and hunting industry spokesmen to buttress her claim. Every year since 1992, the annual Governor's Hunting Heritage Symposia, sponsored by state governments and held at various locations around the country, have featured presentations on one variation or another of the general theme of "recruiting and retaining" new hunters. (Prescott herself had addressed the fourth symposium in 1995.)[20] Whereas for hunters, introducing women and youth to hunting is a way of preserving a cultural tradition that is inherently important and worth sharing, for the Fund for Animals it represents a thinly veiled exploitation of women and children to further the financial interests of the state (through license sales) and the hunting industry (through tapping new markets for guns and hunting gear).

As we saw in chapter 1, one of the most familiar anti-gun arguments has been that in its advertising the firearms industry plays on the legitimate concerns women have for their own and their children's safety. Women, according to this argument, are deceived into buying a false sense of security with a gun, and the deception supposedly works because women are fundamentally naive about the facts of firearms use and ownership. The idea of women's essential innocence with regard to guns and women's aversion to gun-related activities persists among advocates of strict gun regulation or abolition, as a sort of necessary fiction. Prescott and the Fund for Animals have called into play the same sort of fiction, in reaction to the growing number of women participating in such traditionally male-identified "blood sports" as hunting, fishing, and trapping.

On Mother's Day 1999, the Fund issued a report, "Money, Motherhood and the Nineteenth Amendment: The Hunting Industry's Open Season on Women,"[21] pitched as an exposé of the way women are being duped into taking up hunting by an industry that wants their money (women, according to the report, spend $1.8 billion a year on hunting-related activities), their children (whom they, in turn, will "entice" into hunting), and their vote for anti-gun control legislation. This report was a sequel to the Fund's 1997 report, "Killing Their Childhood: How Public Schools and Government Agencies Are Promoting Sport Hunting to America's Children," which argued, among other things, that the promotion of hunting to children is important because, unless people are "desensitized" to killing at an early age, they are unlikely to take up hunting later on.

"Money, Motherhood and the Nineteenth Amendment" claims hunting, "the quintessentially masculine pursuit—throughout recorded history," is a rite of manhood that is "being seriously challenged for the first time in history. Today in the United States we are witnessing the world's first large scale campaign to turn women into hunters." The report goes on to explain that, given decreases in the overall number of male hunters and changes in public perceptions of hunting, "leaders of the hunting industry are willing to swallow their male pride and open their ranks to women. If they can't hang on to Nimrod, they are going to need Diana." Thereafter, the report focuses most of its attention on the BOW program, in which "the hunting industry in the role of Henry Higgins [is] trying desperately to remake American women as Eliza Doolittle cum Diana: the huntress created in their own image. Is the female hunter campaign really a form of empowerment for women," the report asks, "or is it just a self-serving effort by male hunters and the leaders of the hunting industry to manipulate women for their own benefit?"

What is surprising, in a document that claims to be pro-women, is the way the report arrives at its foregone conclusion. Picking up where the Fund's 1997 "exposé" of hunter education programs for children had left off, the 1999 report focuses on the recruitment of young people into the ranks of hunters. It is a "very peculiar characteristic of hunting" that "people who do not hunt when they are children are unlikely ever to become hunters," because the idea of "killing animals for recreation [is] so repugnant that if they are not desensitized to it at an early age by an older family member in whom they vest moral authority, they will never become reconciled to it." The trusted older family member is now the mother; hence programs like BOW, which are patently designed "to turn them into supporters of hunting who will encourage—or at least not discourage—their children in taking up the sport. In most families, mom now has a veto, and the hunting industry wants to make sure she doesn't exercise it."

This seems a plausible line of argument, until one asks what it implies about the women themselves, who are being duped by the dastardly hunting industry, only in turn to lead their children down the bloody path. If the normal adult finds hunting "repugnant," and if only children can successfully be "desensitized" in this regard, then the women who become hunters through BOW or some other venue are either morally depraved with regard to killing, or stunted in their moral development. Either would be a disturbing conclusion to have to draw, given the fact that the majority of the two million or so women who currently hunt began to hunt as adults.

This, of course, is why the Fund for Animals finds the success of the BOW program so vexing. The report goes on to make it clear that, like the women supposedly manipulated by handgun advertisers, female hunters are putty in the hands of their deceivers: "Just as the fashion industry has convinced millions of women that their personal worth is dependent on the latest styles and most expensive make-up, the hunting industry is trying to convince women that their independence and self confidence depend on killing defenseless animals." And the mastermind behind all this (although according to the report she, too, was merely the pawn of manipulative males) turns out to be none other than Christine Thomas, who at one point in her memoir *Becoming an Outdoors-Woman* remarks that "I cry every time my hunt results in a kill. I can't explain this."

Taking Thomas's comment out of its context (an elaborate narrative of her first experience of hunting elk), the report proceeds to "explain" it for her: she cannot recognize that her tears arise from guilt feelings to which she has blinded herself, because that guilt is "buried so deep beneath the lies and myths of the hunting culture that only death is powerful enough to bring it to the light of day."

The Fund for Animals is here using the same tactic to which op-ponents of women's armed self-defense resort: they demonize the manufacturers of guns, and in this case the entire hunting commu-nity, in order to portray women as either willing collaborators with their oppressors, or hapless victims of male oppression. The problem is, female hunters are neither hapless nor helpless. They can defend and fend for themselves. These women have blood on their hands and on their consciences. And, while—like Thomas—they acknowl-edge that the killing that hunting entails can generate some complex emotions, these women are happy about what they do. And they are having fun doing it. It's enough to drive an animal-rights activist off the deep end.

Changing the Conversation

Picture the hunter, fresh from the field in dusty camouflage. She props her now-unloaded rifle in the gun rack, kicks off her muddy boots, and tiptoes into the nursery to look in on her baby. The hand now tenderly stroking her daughter's cheek has traces of blood under its nails; an hour before, it was wielding a finely honed hunting knife, deftly eviscerating a whitetail doe. That deer may or may not have had a fawn tucked away somewhere; just because you don't see a youngster with a doe doesn't mean she doesn't have one. Still, she wasn't lactating, so if there was a young one, it should be able to make it on its own. A saddening thought, but a fact of life. It was a good day, and the hunter smiles wearily as she adjusts the blanket covering her infant daughter.

It's an image as intricate as life itself. And it is so challenging to conventional ideas, or ideals, of femaleness that one needn't be an animal rights activist to find it unsettling. And yet, women who hunt will tell you it makes perfect sense to them. Disconcerting as the picture might look today, embedded in it is a primal intuition about human participation in the cycle of life and death. The ancient Greeks recognized Artemis, and the Sumerians Ninhursaga, as goddesses of both hunting and childbirth. The Nordic "Snow Queen" Skadi, often depicted with children, was first of all goddess of the hunt. Historically speaking, the idea that a woman must be as soft and as pink as her baby's nursery is a relatively recent invention.

Among the participants at the first BOW workshop held in Texas (in 1993) were a middle-aged mother and her adult daughter from Houston. The mother's name was Rosemary; she had come at the urging of her daughter, a reporter who was covering the workshop for one of the Houston daily papers. Rosemary had been hunting for several years by that time, always with her husband and his male friends. Used to being the only woman in deer camp, she was skeptical that she would derive much benefit from spending three days "with all these women." She had never felt discriminated against, was by no means a feminist, and didn't believe women would know any good hunting stories. But by Sunday afternoon, as she and her bunkmates were packing up to head home, Rosemary's perspective had changed. "With men," she said, relishing the insight, "you have to be one-dimensional. Here, you can be multifaceted. You can decompartmentalize your life. You can talk about babies and bullets in the same conversation!"[22]

Patriarchy has wanted to keep the gender conversation far more simple in this regard, of course, and, too often, so has feminism. Few feminist scholars take note of the existence of female hunters, and those who do generally do so in such a way as to make excuses for them. Donna Haraway, for example, in *Primate Visions* portrays avid hunters Mary Jobe Akeley and Osa Johnson as somewhat unfortunate collaborators in "Teddy Bear Patriarchy," forging their respective identities as the wives of hunter-naturalist Carl Akeley and of his nature-photographer protégé Martin Johnson. According to Haraway, these women hunted to some extent despite themselves; but their hunting served the higher purpose of science. In Akeley's case, she was collecting specimens for the Africa exhibits in the American Museum of Natural History in New York. Johnson took up a gun to feed the camp, thus freeing her husband's hands and eye for the camera. Haraway implies that, given the choice, these women would have preferred not to hunt. Delia Akeley, Carl's first wife, presents a more problematic picture because, as Haraway acknowledges, she was "a joyous and unrepentant hunter" who mounted African expeditions of her own after her divorce from Carl.[23]

Along comparable lines, historian Vera Norwood argues in her study of American women naturalists that for Akeley and Johnson, as well as for many female hunters, "the hunt posed a major problem. . . . Their narratives reveal a continuing struggle to match gender codes with the bloody results of the chase."[24] Norwood's personal bias appears to be against hunting. She notes that novelist Mary Hastings Bradley "carefully distanced herself from any bloodthirsty imagery" in her hunting narratives—yet perhaps for Bradley there was nothing "bloodthirsty" about hunting. Norwood similarly remarks that women like Bradley, Delia Akeley, and nineteenth-century Colorado naturalist Martha Maxwell (who said she never hunted for such a base purpose as "carnivorousness," but in order to "immortalize" through the art of taxidermy the animals she killed) present a particular problem for the historian, because "each took up a gun and hunted, not as frontierswomen might for meat, but for intellectual pursuits with unsettling links to sporthunting." These links appear more "unsettling" to Norwood, however, than to the women about whom she writes.

Take, for example, her discussion of Osa Johnson. Norwood quotes Johnson's self-effacing story in *I Married Adventure* about how, since the real purpose of their photo safari was Martin's camera work, she would "really . . . have to learn to shoot," and her subsequent discovery that she happened to be a superb gun woman. Although Johnson's two books about her experiences in Africa are filled with hunting narratives, and with pictures of Osa with the results of numerous hunting forays, Norwood chooses to quote one passage in which Johnson reflects—as hunting writers male and female not infrequently do—on the ambivalent feelings generated by the killing that hunting necessarily involves. Osa has just procured her and Martin's Christmas dinner:

There lay the giant bustard. Thirty-five pounds of delicious African turkey. I held him up. He was a beauty. The feathers of his tail were spotted, his handsome chest a pearl grey. His long beak and proud little white pompom crest on his head were splotched with red where the bullet had entered. As I looked at him, I realized as never before that there was more joy in shooting with a camera than with a gun."[25]

Of course, Osa and Martin subsequently savored the bird. And Osa continued, unabashedly, to hunt. But Norwood focuses on how this passage implicates Osa in "the violence attached to the trophy hunt," on how "even bringing home Christmas dinner was a hollow victory." Oddly, and perhaps unintentionally revealing her own bias, on the page facing this discussion in Norwood's book is a picture of a beaming Osa Johnson with shotgun and not one but two dead birds, which Johnson herself titled "Osa Brings Home the Dinner" when it appeared in her 1941 book, *Four Years in Paradise*, the same volume in which the bustard story appears. There is nothing of "hollow victory" about the woman in this photograph; she is strong, vibrant, capable, and appears, if anything, quite delighted with herself, her gun, her kill. (See illustration no. 5.)

Norwood and Haraway are both right that women like Delia

Akeley and Osa Johnson were aware of transgressing rigidly defined gender boundaries—the same ones as had professional sharpshooter Annie Oakley. Oakley was always at pains to project a feminine image, what she called her "ladyhood," in order to "woo . . . to her side" a public that did not generally believe women belonged in the rodeo arena. Oakley's biographer Glenda Riley depicts a woman in many ways years ahead of her time, who, although she would not refer to herself as a feminist or a suffragist, argued for women's right to arm themselves both for protection and in order to pursue sports like hunting and trapshooting.[26] Up until her death in 1926, Oakley—who as a seven-year-old child had hunted to feed her widowed mother and five siblings—wrote about hunting and shooting as activities for women for outdoor publications like *Sports Afield* and *Outdoor Life*.

Yet in her recent book about women's role in American environmental history, Riley downplays Oakley's and other women's hunting. Riley gives the impression that for the nineteenth and early-twentieth-century female adventurers about whom she writes, hunting was at best a side-effect of camping and hiking, something they only undertook because of the men in their lives. Left to their own devices, one gets the feeling they would just as soon have taken a vigorous hike, *sans* gun. But—as was the case with Delia Akeley and Osa Johnson—the women themselves tell a different story. Grace Gallatin Seton-Thompson, for example, was an enthusiastic big-game hunter, something she wrote about at length in *A Woman Tenderfoot*. Riley neglects to mention this when she describes the book as, basically, a travelogue. Riley's outdoorswomen shoot, but they don't hunt. This seems, in large part, to be because Riley believes a hunter cannot simultaneously be an environmentalist, or nurture the sort of intimate kinship with nonhuman animals that for her characterizes women's relationship with nature.

This leads Riley to either misread or misrepresent her history. "Like English women," she writes, "American women gradually championed animal rights and rejected trophy killing as a desirable goal. By the 1900s, even Annie Oakley, who once took pride in shooting energetic, English blue-rock pigeons, switched from live birds to clay pigeons." An attentive reader here will note that Riley is talking about live target shooting, not about hunting. Yet the very next example she gives is of Fannie Sperry Steele, a turn-of-the-century hunter and outfitter in Montana's Blackfoot Valley, who "had gained sympathy for such animals as elk, as well as enormous enmity toward people who misused the environment, especially trophy hunters who simply wanted animal heads for their walls. 'I will prosecute them every chance I get,' Steele proclaimed at age seventy-four."[27] It is clear here that Steele regarded trophy hunting as a problem; it is not at all clear that she renounced hunting in general. Riley seems to feel that hunting itself is a "misuse" of the environment, and implicitly to approve of the animal-rights position against it. This leads her to distort or simply erase the pro-hunting views of many of the women she writes about. And that is too bad, because these women and their sister-outdoorswomen have much to say for themselves and their sport, much that would enliven and enrich our current, some would say "postfeminist," debate about gender roles and realities in American society.

Why do otherwise astute feminist critics such as Haraway, Norwood, and Riley have a blind spot regarding women and hunting? Apparently, it's a hangover from feminism's flirtation with the hunting hypothesis. The belief that hunting must necessarily be a male-defined activity leads them not to take women's statements about their hunting at face value.

But what happens to our views of women hunters if we do take their statements about hunting seriously and assume that they are neither deluded nor naïve, nor suffering from false consciousness, regarding what they are doing and why they are doing it? What, in short, happens if we put babies and bullets into the same conversation? As big game hunter Mary Coleman, mother of three, remarks: "Not every woman can nurse a baby, bake a cake, and then go out and kill. But some can."[28] What do we know, then, about the ones who can, and do?

Women Afield

Somewhere between one and three million American women hunt. It would be nice to be able to be more specific when it comes to numbers, but as we saw in chapter 2, the answer to the question "How many?" is frequently "It depends on whom you ask." State fish and game agencies, the most logical places to look for raw numbers, do not employ a uniform system of record keeping about hunters. In fact, fifteen states don't even specify sex on hunting license applications, and many of those states that do, fail to do anything with that information.

Every five years, the U.S. Fish and Wildlife Service (USF&WS) compiles the *National Survey of Fishing, Hunting and Wildlife-Associated Recreation*, recording trends in hunting and other wildlife-related outdoor activities. According to the most recent survey, between 1991 and 1996 the overall number of hunters in the U.S. remained constant at around fourteen million. By way of comparison, the number of anglers held steady at thirty-five million. "Nonconsumptive" wildlife watchers decreased 18 percent over the same period, to a total of about 63 million. This figure includes activities as various as nature photography, wilderness hiking, and keeping a backyard bird feeder. The 1996 survey estimated that women comprised 9 percent of the total hunting population, or roughly 1.2 million. This figure diverges from another USF&WS report, *Participation and Expenditure Patterns of*

Black, Hispanic, and Women Hunters and Anglers, which in 1995 placed the number of women hunters at 1,069,000.

Meanwhile, a 1995 survey sponsored by the National Shooting Sports Foundation (NSSF—the firearms industry's major marketing group) estimated that 2.5 million women hunted with firearms.[29] Another report, issued by the National Sporting Goods Association, reckoned that between 1989 and 1997 the number of female firearms hunters increased 15 percent, from 1,752,000 to just over 2 million (in that report, female bow hunters numbered 391,000), or 11 percent of the hunting population. In a widely cited 1992 *Fortune* magazine article on the hunting industry, provocatively titled "A Bang That's Worth Ten Billion Bucks," Alan Farnham, citing "marketing experts," put the figure at "11% and growing."[30] Although compared to government figures numbers like these appear to be inflated, market analysts with an eye to the bottom line may have a better handle on actual numbers than do state or federal bean counters. The reality probably lies between the extremes.

This much is clear, at any rate: women account for approximately 10 percent of the hunting population, as all sides of the debate over hunting seem to agree. As the number of male hunters appears to be gradually declining, the number of female hunters appears to be increasing. Most of these women hunt with firearms—primarily long guns, that is, rifles and shotguns, though a small but enthusiastic number of female (and male) hunters use large-caliber revolvers or semi-automatic pistols for hunting. Some women hunt with bows rather than guns, or bows in addition to guns. And most female hunters learned to hunt from men in their lives: perhaps as children from their fathers, but more typically as adults, from male friends or partners.

Outdoor writer and editor Diana Rupp cherishes the memory from her Pennsylvania girlhood of the deer season when her father set aside his own quest for a buck to devote all his energy to helping her bag her first deer, a doe, at the age of thirteen. Sue King, the founding director of the Women's Shooting Sports Foundation, has a photograph of herself at age five or so with her first gun: a Winchester Model 67A .22 caliber rifle her father had given her and taught her to shoot; more than fifty years later, the gun still hangs on her wall. Growing up in Colorado, freelance writer Marilyn Stone was taught to shoot by her brother:

When I was in the second grade, I asked for and received a B.B. gun of my own for my birthday. I told everyone in Show and Tell and couldn't figure out for the life of me why no one else was particularly impressed. I was one of the few country kids there and had a decidedly different perspective on "fun."

Just how different the female perspective is from the male one, on the "fun" of guns and hunting, is a complex question. The late psychologist Robert Jackson, who for years surveyed the attitudes of Wisconsin deer hunters, found that while women and men tended to cite the same primary reasons for hunting—getting out in nature, putting food on the table, participating in the life cycle—men tended to place greater emphasis than women on "the 'macho' factors: men found greater satisfactions in getting shooting, marksmanship . . . , killing a deer, telling hunting stories, displaying a trophy, and in doing better than friends."[31]

These "macho factors" may well account for why, in years past, it didn't even occur to many men to introduce their daughters to hunting, along with their sons. BOW coordinator Diane Lueck remembers, for example, that although her father took his three daughters fishing and camping, she didn't learn to hunt until she met the man she would eventually marry. "Squirrel hunting," she says, "was part of our courtship." Recently, her father and brother-in-law came for a visit and brought along some shotguns and clay targets. "I had never done any shooting with my dad," Lueck reflected afterward. "We all had a wonderful time, and he told Gary [her husband] he had no idea I could shoot so well. I have a great relationship with my father, but wonder what it could have been like if we had hunted together when I was young."

The times, of course, are changing. It's more common, for example, to see articles in outdoor magazines about introducing children of both sexes to hunting. Despite what the Fund for Animals imagines, this is less a reflection of firearms-industry manipulation than of the social realities of these magazines' readerships. And those realities are complex. Katherine O'Riley, a Midwestern thirteen-year-old, began learning to shoot at the age of ten from her dad: "It gave me a sound mind/body/spirit, and made me aware of my surroundings," she says. "Considering that before shooting, I had none of the above, I am thankful for being taught to shoot." Her mother was learning to shoot and hunt at the same time and recalls: "I was 48 on my first hunt. . . . When I took a deer within the first few hours of my first hunt, I felt incredibly competent—I'm not well coordinated or involved in any other sports." She and her husband have since divorced, but mother and daughter continue to shoot, and now hunt, together. They took the state's required hunter education class together in 1999, and they are self-consciously creating a family tradition with hunting at its center, sharing their "girl-gun" (a Winchester .243 rifle) for deer hunting. Their names, along with the dates they have taken deer with it, are engraved on the gun's stock.

Businesswoman Brenda Potterfield, who had hunted small game for twenty years, took up big game hunting ten years ago, when she realized her husband, son, and daughter "had a special bond due to their hunting. I also realized the great possibilities for family time as we traveled to hunts and sat around the campfire at night sharing the hunt." Brenda finds hunting has strengthened her marriage: "I see couples married for twenty-five or thirty years separate because once the children are gone, they no longer have anything in common. Larry and I will always have a common love for the hunt." Their twenty-something daughter Sara began shooting at the age of four and hunting at nine. She is also a world-class competitive shooter.

How do women like these feel about the guns they own and use? Sara Potterfield talks about her favorite hunting firearm:

My double rifle. It is a Charles Boswell 450/400 double rifle. [This is a heavy, large-caliber long gun.] My parents purchased it for me when I was nineteen, for elephant and buffalo hunting in Africa. . . . This gun is fantastic. Dad says it was made between the wars, so it is an old gun with good history, and probably several owners before me. I have carried this gun for up to eight hours a day while in Africa, balanced on my shoulder where I can pull it into shooting position quickly if I need to. When you are on a twenty-one day safari, carrying your gun every day, you certainly develop a fondness for it.

Marilyn Stone's favorite hunting gun is a 12-gauge Savage shotgun she nicknamed Sara. "It's not pretty or fancy," she says, "but I'm more interested in utility. I have taken geese, ducks, doves, turkey, huns [Hungarian partridges], pheasants, squirrels, and rabbits with that gun. . . . I learned to hunt with this gun. It carries the memories of my first hunts, my first accomplishments and the first 'partnership' I felt with a gun." Montana outdoor writer Susan Ewing, who began hunting in her thirties, strikes a kindred note when she remembers her first hunting rifle:

I loved my first hunting rifle—a youth model 7mm Remington. Though it did make me wonder if I was supposed to pretend to be a boy, rather than a grown woman. I shot my first deer with it and it's also the rifle with which I first hunted alone. That rifle felt somehow animate to me, more akin to a companion than a tool. I never thought of it as a weapon. Especially since I had just started hunting, that rifle was evocative to me in the way of—at risk of sounding high-flown—a religious icon: a seemingly inanimate object imbued with some essential force of its own.

Not all women experience their guns so intimately. Maggie Hachmeister, a South Dakota wildlife educator and director of that state's BOW program, says, "I look on my guns as tools, which need to be cared for correctly and enjoyed correctly. Beyond that, I have not found myself having any strong feelings towards them." Minnesota deer hunter Annette Pullen is similarly dispassionate regarding her Winchester Model 1400 semi-automatic rifle, remarking simply, "I use it for deer hunting and then it goes back into its case 'til next year." Texan Sue King takes a hard-headed approach to both guns and hunting:

It is my impression that the human species tends to mystify and romanticize all sorts of activities, as well as hunting and guns, unnecessarily. . . . I can tell you what kind of relationship I do not have with my guns. They do not empower me as a woman. Sex has nothing to do with the finger on the trigger. They are not a phallic symbol. They do not define my character, my essential self, any more than does the fact that I am appalled by those who permit hollandaise sauce to be slathered over their Oysters Rockefeller.

Asked why she hunts, and what satisfaction she derives from it, King cites both the personal pleasure of doing it skillfully, and the role hunting plays in wildlife conservation. "Besides," she quips, "it beats the hell out of housework."

Gearing Up

Among Robert Jackson's findings about Wisconsin women deer hunters in the 1980s, two things stand out that appear to apply to the female hunting population in general. One is that women are more likely than men to rank "appreciation of wildlife and nature" as a primary reason for their hunting. The other is that these women hunt with passion and are willing to overcome considerable obstacles in order to do it. "Seventy percent stated they would miss hunting more than most or all other recreational activities. It should be noted that most of them reported their most obvious role model, their mother, didn't even have recreational interests. Their development as hunters is almost revolutionary."[32] Add to this the fact that this "revolution" has occurred, for the most part, in the face of genuine barriers: not only social disapproval of women's hunting, but also the scarcity of guns and gear tailored to fit women.

Firearms makers and outdoor clothing merchandisers have, in the last decade or so, begun to respond to the women's market. It is possible now to find good-quality, affordable hunting clothes, boots, and accessories for women, although it takes some looking and the variety is still far from what is available for men. And guns can still be a problem. Just as handguns are generally designed to fit the "average man's" hand, long guns are designed for men's generally larger torsos and longer arms. Some manufacturers refer to smaller-scaled guns as "youth's and ladies' models," and these guns do work for some women.

However, for many women the choice of the right gun for hunting is a blend of fit, utility, and taste. A woman may be looking for a particular caliber or gauge not available in a "ladies'" gun. Issues like weight (composite stock or wood?) and recoil (semi-automatic or bolt-action?) may or may not figure in her choice of a gun. Issues of quality and taste may be important. She may be looking for an aesthetically pleasing firearm, with beautiful hand-finished wood and fine engraving on case-hardened metal. She may desire excellence of craftsmanship, an innovatively designed action, perfect wood-to-metal fit. In other words, she may want and expect, in a hunting gun, the same sorts of things and in various combinations, as a man.

If she is not built like the "average man" (many men are not, either), she will have to either put up with a gun that does not quite fit her and learn to adjust her shooting to this fact; or she will opt (as some men do, too) to have a gun custom fit to her. This generally entails cutting down and/or repositioning the stock, modifying the sights, perhaps shortening the barrel. The results, in terms of hunting success and hunter satisfaction, can be dramatic.

Jodi Bishop, who works for the Rocky Mountain Elk Foundation in Montana, lucked into the right gun when her husband introduced her to hunting fourteen years ago: "My favorite gun is my .308 rifle. It was my husband's first gun. He got it when he was twelve and they cut the stock and barrel down for him so it fits me perfectly." Arizona attorney Sandra Froman, five foot two with small hands and short arms, found that even youth rifles had stocks too long for her. This didn't prevent her from becoming a firearms collector; in addition to an array of pistols, rifles and shotguns, she owns and shoots machine guns. But she didn't find the right gun for hunting until she had a .260 Remington caliber rifle built especially for her by Dakota Arms, "downsizing it to fit me perfectly. The first time I ever raised the gun to my shoulder, I was astonished at how much a part of my eyes and arms it felt. I realized that this was the feeling that most men experience when they shoulder a long gun that fits them—but I had never felt that before, so it was a real thrill." Diane Lueck tells a similar story. She started hunting with her husband's gun, and had a terrible time with it. When it came time to choose her own deer rifle, she picked out a .44 Ruger; the overall size and caliber of the gun were right for the Wisconsin swamp conditions in which she stalks her deer, but the stock was too long for her. She had it shortened, and "I was ecstatic to have a firearm that fit. The following year I put a low-power scope on it, and now wouldn't rifle hunt without it. Yes," she says, "it's temperamental as to what bullets it likes. Yes, it has a bullet drop of about two feet at a hundred yards. But it fits me, fits my style of hunting, and I love it."

Some women find the technical side of firearms appealing. Judy Clayton Cornell, a Montana outdoor writer, admits to a fascination with ballistics—bullet weight, velocity, "knock-down power," and so on. Susan Ewing loves to clean her rifle:

I used to clean it all the time. I love the mechanics of things, so I really enjoyed getting out all the cleaning tools and screwing the cleaning rod together and taking out the rifle bolt. I loved the smell of the cleaning fluid and oil. It was a meditative exercise. But then I learned you weren't supposed to clean your gun after you sight it in because it can throw off the first shot afterward. So now I just clean my guns after the season.

Whether they see their guns as mere tools or as trusted companions in the field, women hunters realize, as a group, that the instruments in their hands involve them intimately, and urgently, in the primal business of life and death. It is, therefore, crucial that the guns are in good operating condition, and that the women know how to use them. What they use them for, ultimately, is to kill, efficiently and cleanly. But, to evoke Spanish philosopher Jose Ortega y Gasset's oft-cited observation in his *Meditations on Hunting*, like their male counterparts these women do not hunt in order to kill, they kill in order to have hunted.[33]

Women hunters generally cite two main reasons for their hunting: getting out into nature, and bringing back food for the table. Marilyn Stone emphasizes the entire process: "I love being out in nature, the constant challenge of getting close to game and the feeling of self-sufficiency. I know I can take an animal from the shot to the table myself." Carolee Boyles, an entrepreneur in Florida who arranges all-women hunting expeditions in North America and Africa, says the main satisfaction for her is "knowing I can do those things, and am competent at them. That includes taking apart an animal and processing it for consumption." But her reasons for hunting run deeper than that, as well:

I certainly enjoy being out in the woods. No, enjoy is the wrong word. I crave it. I see myself as being part of the process of living when I hunt. I don't mean the day-to-day stuff that we do, but the connections of life and death that are a part of our biological and spiritual selves. It's probably about half and half between those two things. The person that is "me" just isn't complete without both of these experiences.

Diane Lueck is a hunter education instructor in Wisconsin and stresses that when she is teaching ethics to her students, generally adolescent boys and girls though some adults also take these courses, she always emphasizes that it is "*never* wrong not to shoot. In hunting, as opposed to recreational shooting, you are making a decision that is far greater" than whether or not to pull the trigger. "One thing that I experience as a hunter," Lueck says, "is the humbling knowledge that I alone can decide whether to shoot. I define myself as a hunter, not as 'someone who hunts.' All the processes—scouting, learning about the animals, honing skills, living where we do, butchering our own animals—are part of that definition. . . . I am truly fortunate to live where I can learn from the animals and be part of their cycle/our cycle of life."

This sense of process, of participation in the life cycle, seems for the women who hunt to amount less to the kind of recreation that restores one's energy than to the fundamental re-creation that restores one's self, or soul. It can, as a result, be tough to pin hunting down to one meaning, or motivation. "My reasons for hunting?" responds Montanan Judy Cornell:

Oh, so complex. My second strongest reason for hunting is the food value. I love game meat and knowing that it is lean and less exposed to chemicals than commercial meat. I know the land the animal lived on, what weather it endured, and I become part of that place. I could not hunt without intending for the animal to become food. But foremost, hunting is a wonderful excuse to spend an inordinate amount of time walking uphill and down. If it weren't so primal, if it didn't provide food, this expenditure of resources in pursuit of recreation would be suspect.

Speaking, perhaps, with the wisdom of youth, thirteen-year-old Katherine from Wisconsin states it more succinctly: "I hunt mainly for food, but since I get a rush sitting out there waiting for the kill, I also hunt for fun."

Colorado college student Tabitha ("Tabby") Zokaitis grew up around guns; her father taught her to shoot and, when he died, left her a lifetime membership at a shooting range. Tabby started hunting in 1999, at the age of twenty-two. Her reason?

. . . to gain a respect for the animals I eat. I am a vegetarian because of the way food is processed and I began thinking about killing my own meat. So far I have not killed anything but I intend to go back out until I do. When I finally kill an animal I want to use all of its parts. My dad had a really neat elk-skin coat and I would like one of my own. Even though I don't think it is the fashion statement I want to make, I know someone who will wear it often.

Sandra Froman began hunting after years of firearms experience in other contexts because "I was curious about how I would feel about killing an animal, if it would upset me or excite me. Although I love animals, and enjoy watching them in the wild, hunting has given me a new appreciation of my own connection to nature, and the fact that as human beings, we are not separate from the earth and the animals we share it with." In addition, Froman, NRA board member and sec-

ond vice president, reflects: "Hunting teaches me to be 'in the moment,' what Buddhists call being 'mindful' about where you are and
what you are doing at that very moment, not thinking about the past
or worrying about the future. Mindfulness is a form of meditation;
being mindful heightens your awareness of the experience and en-
hances your enjoyment of life."

Frequently for hunters, male and female, being "in the moment"—whether stalking or still-hunting, sitting in a duck blind or
tree stand—does not involve the choice of whether or not to pull the
trigger. One need not kill to have had a good day's hunt. Jodi Bishop
remarks that she doesn't care if she comes home empty-handed. "I always see something amazing while I'm hunting. I love to watch the
birds and chipmunks, trees and sky." New Jersey hunter Cathy Blumig
emphasizes how hunting connects her to the ecosystem:

*I would feel very distant from the wildlife and the habitats those animals live
in if I didn't hunt. It would be as if nature was something "over there" and I
would have to travel to it, to experience like Disneyland. Being an active participant in an ecosystem gives my experiences in the outdoors more meaning
and changes my relationship with the outdoors. . . . I have a direct and more
honest association with the things that sustain my life.*

Asked what she ultimately derives from hunting, Diane Lueck tells
a story about a recent afternoon, during whitetail rutting (mating)
season:

*I was down in the swamp, hunting. Or maybe just observing. And that's the
part of hunting that is really special—we get to see what other people don't. I
wanted to check if a second buck was in this area; I had seen a small one. I
was hunkered down in a brush blind, and saw a doe a good ways to my west.
Then, in just a few minutes, I heard slow stomping, and a nice-sized buck
emerged into my vision from the east. He walked the whole length of the*

swamp, until he came across her trail. Slowly still, he switch-backed around until he found her. He gave her a little "goose" that made her jump, and just as slowly he herded her back east. This whole process was about sixty yards from me and took about twenty-five minutes. What a show!

The best nature shows, hunters seem to agree, are not the ones on PBS. They are the ones a person sees when, in the moment, one sees, as Maggie Hachmeister puts it, "like a predator . . . and that feels good."

Hunting with a Difference

Whether female hunters experience being predators in the same ways, or to the same extent, as males do is an open question. Women have a reputation in the hunting community for taking fewer high-risk, low-percentage shots than men—that is, for deciding, more often than do men, against taking a tricky or an overly difficult shot, and against shooting at or near the close of hunting hours, when a wounded animal might escape into darkness and be difficult to track until the next morning. Ironically, this makes women somewhat "better" shots than men statistically, because they fire, overall, fewer shots with a greater success rate.

Does it make women better hunters, in the ethical sense, as well? To some extent, it might. Men's more pronounced tendency to take high-risk, long or "fancy" shots surely correlates with their inclination to cite demonstrating marksmanship and doing better than their hunting companions as prime motivations for hunting. Although, as Susan Ewing has remarked, there are surely some "Bub-ettes" out there, most women aren't trying to live up (or down) to the "macho factors" that drive many men's hunting.[34] In *The Hunt*, John Mitchell bemoans the fact that something about hunting seems to bring out the boy in full-grown men.[35] This might just be because most male hunters learned to hunt when they were boys, and too many carry into adulthood the adolescent view that rules articulated by inscrutable father figures (whether they be parents or state wildlife agencies) are made to be broken, or at least bent.

Women, most of whom learn hunting as adults, seem to approach gun use and safety with somewhat more maturity. As we have already observed, firearms safety instructors universally affirm that women and girls make better pupils than males do. They are less inclined to see guns as symbolic extensions of themselves or to regard them as something they should "naturally" know how to use. They are more likely to ask questions not simply about how something should be done, but about why it should be done in a certain way. This concern for process, coupled with the fact that they are most often incorporating hunting into an already formed adult moral perspective, may carry over into women's approach to hunter ethics. It certainly helps to explain why game wardens generally report an improvement in overall hunter behavior when women hunters are present, and perhaps accounts for the fact that proportionally fewer women than men are cited for hunting violations.

Of course, this is at best speculative. What we do know is that women hunt for approximately the same reasons as men, having chiefly to do with getting "away from it all," getting down to something primal and real, getting in touch with the sources of their sustenance—physically, with the animals that become their food, spiritually with the earth both they and these animals walk on. Women derive approximately the same levels of satisfaction from hunting as men do. They express these satisfactions in terms of the gratification of putting food on one's own table and knowing where it came from, the growth in self-esteem that comes from learning a difficult skill and doing it well, testing one's endurance and abilities, feeling more confident and more capable, more at one with nature. The reasons women hunt may be best summed up by Sandra Froman. "It makes me happy," she says, "to be alive."

Snapshot

Abigail Kohn, *Cowboy Dreaming: Guns in Fantasy and Role-Playing*

"This is truly Halloween for adults."

—Cowboy action shooter, discussing the appeal of the sport

I had my first experience with guns when I was an anthropology graduate student at the University of California. I had been studying culture-specific psychiatric syndromes in American society, but my former interests were starting to lose their appeal. While casting about for a dissertation topic, and hoping to engage my interests in criminology, I met another graduate student, Michael,[1] a cultural anthropologist who was in the process of writing his dissertation on tourism in Morocco.

Michael and I hit it off immediately, and we began working and spending time together. We had a lot of common interests, one of them being the study of conspiracy theories in the militia groups that were so high profile in the mid-1990s. We decided that one way we

Abigail Kohn is a medical anthropologist at the University of California, Berkeley and San Francisco.

could learn more about them was to do some observation in places where we assumed militia groups gathered. From several newspaper articles and television news programs, we gleaned that shooting ranges and gun shops might be good places to start. Knowing little about shooting as a sport or a phenomenon, we assumed (rather naively) that local shooting ranges would naturally be hotbeds of radical political activity. We thus decided to pursue this line of interest by visiting several ranges.

Looking back, our naiveté was obvious. Shooting ranges are used by a wide variety of people who are ostensibly there for one thing: shooting. We had no idea if we were meeting anyone who belonged to a militia group, and we were very aware of the potentially rude and prying nature of questions designed to find out. Obviously, but unfortunately for us, militia members don't usually wear signs or badges. But we did meet a number of gun enthusiasts, men and women who were quite open and willing to discuss their interest in, and enjoyment of, guns. We quickly realized that reorienting our research interests to gun enthusiasm would be easier socially and politically, not only in terms of meeting people to interview, but also conducting the participant observation that would be necessary for us to do anthropological research. I eventually took on gun enthusiasm as the topic of my dissertation, and I became an active "cowboy action shooter," participating in the competitive sport of cowboy action shooting, which entails dressing in Old West style clothing and shooting replicas of nineteenth-century revolvers, rifles, and shotguns.

Like many of the women I met during my fieldwork, I was first introduced to guns by a male intimate, in my case Michael. Though I grew up in a family that wasn't overtly opposed to gun ownership, we did not keep guns in our home. My cousins and uncles on my mother's

side hunted in their home state of Wisconsin, but no one in my im-
mediate family was interested in guns. Though my father is a military
historian, he has never been particularly interested in firearms or ar-
mories, except as accessories to the broader issues of war, and military
policy and strategy, in American history. My mother, a psychothera-
pist and former nurse who disliked discussions of guns and violence
in general, probably had something to do with his lack of interest.

Michael, on the other hand, did grow up with guns. When
younger, he hunted with his father and brother in New England. As
an adult, he had a small gun collection consisting of a rifle, a shotgun, and a starter pistol, which he used to train his dog to hunt. His
regard for guns went hand-in-hand with his other traditionally
masculine interests: motorcycles, single malt Scotch, and the hunting itself. He was full of seeming contradictions: highly educated, a
secular Jew, an anthropologist, pro-feminism and pro-choice, and
yet very interested in guns. Strange combinations indeed for a graduate student at Berkeley.

In the early preparation for our research into militia groups, I
asked him if he had ever used a semi-automatic handgun. He said no,
so I asked if he was interested in learning to shoot them. Despite what
I knew of him, I was still somewhat hesitant about this line of questioning: after all, we were at "Cal" (U.C., Berkeley), and I had learned
never to make assumptions about what is or is not acceptable in these
politically correct times. He said that he had always been interested
in trying a semi-auto, and so we made plans to learn together.
Michael found an indoor range that rented handguns, and we
planned what I later conceptualized as our first date together.

When our mutual friends learned of our upcoming visit to a
shooting range, some were appalled, others simply amused.

"What are you going to wear?" asked several, clearly trying to
imagine what a "first date/first handgun" scenario might entail.

"You should dress up like Bonnie and Clyde," said one. Apparently gun-related fantasies are not restricted only to those who shoot.

"No, wear flannel. Everyone else will be in flannel," said another (who was not coincidentally from Seattle).

"I know," said Michael, after several more comments from the peanut gallery. "We should get really dressed up."

I was immediately excited by this idea. "Like James Bond! We could wear evening clothes."

I was eager to wear the slinkiest, blackest dress I could find. I envisioned myself in an elegant number with high heels and long black satin gloves, holding a shiny silver pistol, head tilted in profile. And plenty of red lipstick.

When we finally drove off to the range, Michael in his hand-tailored Moroccan black silk suit and me in my new long black gown, I was deep into my fantasy. After a twenty-minute lesson from a bemused if slightly suspicious rangemaster, we had our rented Glock 9mm in hand. As Michael and I approached the crowded firing line (a busy range for 7:30 P.M. on a Tuesday), reality hit me. What the hell was I doing?

The gun had looked huge when the rangemaster introduced it to us. It was heavier than I thought it would be (despite the fact that everyone says Glocks are so lightweight), and definitely looked quite deadly. Despite my earlier fascination, I found it rather frightening. The eye protection was old and slightly cloudy, and the ear protection was already making my head ache. The suspicions of the rangemaster had made me feel foolish, and the stares of the other shooters made me feel self-conscious. Everyone was going to bear witness to our incompetence, and we had purposefully drawn attention to ourselves because of our clothing. This was not so fun.

Michael set the gun down, pointing downrange per instructions, and loaded one of the clips as the rangemaster had shown us. He then politely turned to me and said, "After you, Abby."

"No, you first." I was genuinely nervous now. I was worried not only about looking foolish but also hurting myself.

"No, please, you first." He was somewhat insistent (covering his own nervousness, he later admitted), and he gestured toward the gun.

I swallowed my fear and walked up to the line. I slowly loaded the other clip with ammunition, and after glancing back at him for encouragement, I picked up the Glock. My only thought was that I would prove to him how ballsy I was. I inserted the clip, and carefully pointed downrange. My eyes blurred from concentrating so hard on the front site. The trigger squeeze was smooth and quick. The recoil after firing the first round was intense, and I was startled by the bucking of the gun in my hand. But I clamped down my anxiety and fired again, and again and again. By the fifth shot, I felt my confidence returning. I was even managing to hit the paper target. By the eighth or ninth shot, I turned my ankle just so (and missed the target, of course). But when I turned back to Michael and caught the admiring look in his eyes, it was all worth it.

After we had packed it in and were driving home, I could still feel the adrenaline pumping through my system.

"That was great," I said to Michael, implicitly checking for his reaction.

"It was great," he nodded. "I need a drink."

This first experience shooting has given me a window into how and why shooting guns recreationally can be so appealing, even sexy. One of the first and primary reasons, and the one I will focus on specifically, is the role of guns in fantasy, role-playing, and the creation of a persona, or identity. Recognizing and wrestling with these issues were important parts of my fieldwork experience with shooters, and with cowboy action shooters in particular. This was primarily true because I was and still am somewhat ambivalent about guns and their role in American society. Though I purchased several guns and learned to shoot during my fieldwork, and in fact enjoyed these activities, I was not and am not a "tried and true" gun enthusiast. Occasionally, when I think about guns, I still make a strong symbolic association between these guns and the acts of violence committed with them. This is a visceral reaction for me, knee-jerk and emotional, not one that is necessarily founded on intellectual knowledge or rational thought. I recognize that this association is a part of my own symbolic beliefs and is not necessarily shared by most of the gun enthusiasts I know. For them, guns symbolize a variety of things, in particular the core American values of individualism, freedom, liberty, and responsibility. But because of my association, I cannot always take a straightforward pleasure in guns, in the same way that my good friends who are shooters can. We sometimes argue about these issues, and I respect their views as different from my own. Our different stances are reinforced by the variety of different and even opposing cultural messages about guns in America, which is one of the reasons that gun ownership is so controversial in American society. But my own ambivalence made my attraction to guns, and men who use them (Michael in particular), complicated and even troubling to me. Enter the role of guns in fantasy and role-playing.

In order to most effectively learn about gun enthusiasm, and even allow myself to enjoy the arduous process of doing the fieldwork itself, I developed several personae, or identities in more anthropological terms. The personae I cultivated to become a shooter, as well as a cowboy shooter in particular, were quite different from my usual persona, that of a somewhat bookish, politically liberal graduate student. When I went shooting, I became "Bonnie" to Michael's

"Clyde," a brazen woman who wore red lipstick and shot semi-automatic handguns. I took perverse pleasure in consciously appropriating a traditional symbol of masculinity (the gun) and combining it with symbols of almost hyperfemininity: a slinky black dress, heels, and red lipstick. This was a version of "dangerous femininity" that felt very different from my usual presentation of self, and I had found a safe, legitimate place in which to explore it. I also took an unfamiliar pride in the ways that men seemed to respond to it. Later, when I met and began working with cowboy action shooters, I became "Abby Oakley, Annie Oakley's citified cousin," dressing in nineteenth-century ball gowns and lacy petticoats, but managing a 12-gauge shotgun "just like one of the boys." The fact that I played these roles to engage in my work allowed me to express aspects of my self that would make me uncomfortable in my day-to-day life. I could revel in these different identities and explore the different expressions of power, and even sexuality, that each different role seemed to engender.

In this space of fantasy, I could put my ambivalence about guns and their associations with violence to rest for a time. In American popular culture, guns symbolize a variety of potent and attractive things. Any number of films and television programs will educate the consumer to the power of guns, their ability to command respect and even fear, the necessity of their use for the rugged American individual, who might take on the form of the loner cop, the independent cowboy, and even the dangerous secret agent/femme fatale. During cowboy shooting, or simply on the range with Michael, I could imagine myself as these characters, play them for all they were worth, and enjoy myself being people I would probably not really relate to in "real life." And I could take pleasure watching the men who engaged in cowboy action shooting, with their unabashed displays of masculinity and sexuality, which I am wary of in real life, but find powerfully sexy and appealing in that fantasy world. Guns are an essential part of the fantasy roles in these spaces of play: guns are indicators of power and *control*.

The question of whether or not guns are used as actual means of controlling situations, or of preventing criminal victimization, is an issue that is hotly debated in academic circles.[2] But in fantasy worlds, guns can clearly and unequivocally represent power and control. Because fantasy zones are "safe" zones, unencumbered by the complicated realities of politics or social taboo, I could enjoy this fantasy space relatively free of guilt. I took great pleasure in watching the more talented cowboy shooters draw and shoot during competitions, or simply amble by in full cowboy regalia, complete with leather chaps and boots, cigars and Stetsons, six-shooters strapped to their sides. And I was told by several male friends that female cowboy shooters were enormously appealing in their long dresses and white gloves, handling shotguns and pistols with equal ease.

When I first started cowboy shooting, I joined shooters for a dinner after an afternoon shoot. I sat across from a man in his late sixties who'd been cowboy shooting for some time. He asked me if I was a shooter, and I answered that I was. He said, "That's great. I think its great that you shoot. I like a woman who can *do* something. I have a wife and two daughters—a house full of house cats." This last was said with some disgust, and gave rise to a good deal of sympathetic head shaking from others at the table. I'm not blind to the wealth of sexism in this backhanded compliment, but this shooter was getting at something that makes the sport so appealing for shooters who partake. This is not simply a fantasy of lonely cow*boys* mixing it up on a modern-day range—this is a collective fantasy, a shared vision of "tough" men *and* women engaging in a sport that they can enjoy together. In the words of another shooter, "This is fun because everybody is in tune with the fantasy." Cowboy action shooting harks to a familiar world: from the "frontier thesis" of nineteenth-century historian Frederick Jackson Turner to the classic Hollywood Westerns, Americans, particularly the middle class, have been generating and consuming images of the frontier and the Wild West for generations. On the modern-day cowboy range, men and woman alike can revel in the most politically incorrect of masculine or feminine traits, all finding expression in this made-up world of gunslingers and dance-hall girls, everybody toting a 12-gauge and a .45.

And women are encouraged to be as masculine (or ballsy, in other words) with their guns as they desire. I sincerely enjoyed the fact that, eventually, shooters expected me to push myself, to oper-ate high-caliber, heavy long guns and powerful handguns. My fem-ininity was not in question, despite the fact that I was more than competent in this stereotypical male arena. The fact that several of the top female cowboy action shooters in the country regularly at-tended the same shoots as I did undoubtedly paved the way for such unconscious acceptance of cowgirls on the range. But even with this caveat, I was impressed by the gender egalitarianism on the range, and it helped to fuel my pleasure in the sport. This mod-ern reconfiguration of the nineteenth-century frontier was fascinat-ing, if only fanciful. And it also fueled the appeal (and I would add somewhat cynically, the fantasy); instead of finding my more manly aspects threatening or distasteful, these cowboys seemed to enjoy them all the more. I am unsure of whether this regard would have carried over into real life, but it was never an issue.

There are a host of reasons why men and women enjoy shooting sports: I have discussed only one of them. But I believe it is an im-portant one, not simply because I experienced it myself, but because it helps to understand the ubiquity of guns in American popular cul-ture. Guns play a long-standing and increasingly contested role in American history and society. They are associated not only with our greatest heroes and their actions, but also with our most detestable criminals and villains. Guns in films and on television have come to symbolize the traits of these heroes and villains themselves. Guns now stand on their own as signifiers of power, danger, control, and competence, as well as the more obviously negative qualities of dangerousness, savagery, and senseless violence. All of these traits, positive and negative, have been and continue to be recognized and even valorized in the American psyche. Guns have thus become a natural on the landscape of the American imagination, and strapping on a pair of six-shooters can thus give free rise to a host of cowboy dreams.

5 Sometimes Girls Just Want to Have Fun

Recreational and Competitive Shooting

Shooting for fun: to the anti-gun activist, this is probably the ultimate oxymoron. How can a deadly weapon be an instrument of enjoyment? It's one thing to confront the social realities that drive some women to opt for armed self-defense; one might not agree with their decision, but only the most vehement gun prohibitionist will refuse to appreciate their reasoning. And one might feel women have no place in combat, or in the tough arena of law enforcement, yet acknowledge that thanks to the women's movement, some women are free to make that choice. One may find hunting distasteful, or wonder why any woman in her right mind would want to spend hours sitting in a cold, soggy swamp waiting for a deer to wander into her rifle's sights, but admit that so long as she's going to use the meat, then it's ethically defensible, anyway.

But should guns be fun? What pleasure can people derive from playing with firearms? And at what social cost? With gun-related gang

violence in poor neighborhoods, and school shootings in more affluent ones; with violence-saturated programming on television and in
blood-soaked action movies; what sort of role models are adults providing, when they use guns as playthings?

Of course, the dire warnings of Handgun Control, Inc., and kindred groups notwithstanding, no one actually familiar with firearms
would ever confuse a gun with a toy. The experiences of handling a
gun, feeling its heft, and firing it, feeling its explosive power and recoil, make it literally impossible to know a gun as anything other
than a deadly serious piece of machinery. However, gun enthusiasts
universally affirm that these same experiences make shooting great
recreation. Sport shooting is, quite literally, a blast. And a growing
number of female shooters are saying it just isn't fair to let men have
all that fun to themselves.

Gunfighter Nation?

The centerfold wears gingham. Her name is Diamond Rose, and she
is "Miz August/September 1999" in *Trail's End* magazine, a publication dedicated to "Rediscovering the Old West." Like any other centerfold, she has a resumé:

*Diamond Rose is a lady that has an impressive set of credentials when it
comes to shooting sports. She is a life member of the NRA, member of the
Shartlesville Fish and Game Association, safety officer for the Hamburg Rifle
and Pistol Club, member and range officer for the Lost Posse of the Topton
Fish and Game Association, NRA certified instructor in pistol, rifle, and shotgun and, finally, a rifle instructor for the Boy Scouts of America.*[1]

In real life, she is a self-employed beautician in Berks County, Pennsylvania, a wife and grandmother, a gourmet baker, a collector of
John Wayne memorabilia, and a gun collector with such an extensive

arsenal that her friends jokingly refer to her as "President of the Berks County Gun-of-the-Month Club." Her name is Rose Loose; "Diamond Rose" is her Cowboy Action Shooting alias.

Cowboy Action Shooting (CAS) is perhaps the fastest-growing recreational shooting activity around. Partly competition, partly historical reenactment, and largely an excuse for grown-ups to act rowdy and play out all their cowboy fantasies, CAS brings together women and men from all walks of life who share a common interest in preserving the history and traditions of the Old West. The Single-Action Shooting Society (SASS) is the largest CAS membership organization, with nearly thirty thousand members nationwide. Each has a registered "alias," which is unique. Some shooters opt for historical identities (Bat Masterson, Judge Roy Bean, General U.S. Grant); others play on their real-life occupations (Lady Doc is a Ph.D. biochemist; Lilly Lawless is an attorney); most go with more whimsical alter egos like Aimless Annie, Wildcat Kate, Buck Roo, Lottie Dah, Naughty Pines. CAS clubs bear names which may or may not relate to their geographical location—the Everglades Rifle and Pistol Club is in Florida and the Alamo Moderators in Texas, while the Hole in the Wall Gang is in New York, the Cheyenne Social Club is in Pennsylvania, and the Doc Holliday's Immortals ride the range in Georgia. Club presidents are called Territorial Governors; at shooting matches, groups of contestants are organized into posses. Major CAS shooting events have evocative names like Helldorado, Range War, Mule Camp, and the world championship CAS event, End of Trail.

CAS requires shooters to dress the part. Specialty "mercantile" catalogues sell authentic reproductions of Old West attire in natural fabrics like wool, cotton, and corduroy. A few female shooters wear trousers, but really serious ones generally shun pants for more historically accurate skirts, bustles, and petticoats. Some wear vintage clothes. And some shoot vintage guns as well, though most of the firearms CAS shooters use are reproductions of the guns that won the West: single-action revolvers, black-powder rifles, and shotguns.[2] The only anachronism allowed at CAS matches comes in the form of eye and ear protection, required of all shooters for safety reasons.

A typical CAS shooting match spans a weekend and involves a series of target shooting situations with Wild West themes ranging from fending off bandits attacking a stagecoach to shooting at stationary targets from a (mechanical) bucking horse. There are men's, women's, and junior events. In between heats, shooters socialize, trade stories and shooting advice, and browse vendors' stands selling everything from buffalo jerky to hand-crafted powder horns to Western artwork to reloading equipment. In the evening, the saloon opens, and there's more socializing and singing around the campfire. At the close of a match, the best shooters in different events and shooting categories receive prizes, as do the wearers of the best costumes. (In order to be eligible in the costume category, one must be a shooter; indeed, Powder Bern, now one of the top women CAS shooters in the country, began shooting because she couldn't compete in costume otherwise.) At the close of the weekend, participants break camp and head back home to their day jobs; participants at the fall 1999 Range War outside of Oakland, California, included a dentist, an engineer, an elevator repair man, a computer specialist, a biochemist, a realtor, a manicurist, a corrections officer, an artist/musician, a gunsmith, and a police officer, among other occupations. Most of the participants were married couples, in which both partners were shooters.

What is going on here? It's a little bit historical reenactment, a little bit role playing; it's also serious shooting. Unlike Revolutionary or Civil War reenactors on the one hand and tactical shooters on the other, CAS shooters use live ammunition, and lots of it. They see firearms—real guns with real ammo—as an essential part of a larger picture, what SASS publications refer to as "the Spirit of the Game":

It is a code by which we live. Competing in "The Spirit of the Game" means you fully participate in what the competition asks. You try your best to dress the part, use the appropriate competition tools, and respect the traditions of the Old West. Some folks would call it nothing more than good sportsmanship. We call it the "Spirit of the Game."[3]

CAS shooting events are characterized by the participants' sense of community and camaraderie. Scoring points matters, but maintaining a spirit of mutual support and a shared vision of a lost, though arguably better world obviously matters more. *Trail's End* magazine and *The Cowboy Chronicle*, SASS's monthly newspaper, are filled with historical lore as well as current events, with a focus on creating a living connection between urban present and frontier past. The imagination of the typical CAS participant may be fueled as much by Hollywood as by history, but what seems to drive it is a self-conscious blend of bodacious playfulness with a rock-solid value system. CAS is a family-oriented activity, and proud to be so.

1999 CAS Junior Girl's world Champion Randi Rogers (a.k.a. Holy Terror) is a good walking example of the kind of values CAS promotes. The twelve-year-old is not only already an expert shooter; she is also a straight-A student and active in her church. Susan Laws, who writes about CAS for *Women & Guns* magazine, says "Randi's 'Holy Terror' nickname is all in fun as the quiet little cowgirl is also a talented piano player and spends many hours playing for appreciative audiences at a local Nursing Home." Laws concludes in an article about Randi and other junior female shooters: "Shepherding a teen into adulthood doesn't take an entire village, but sometimes a good posse can help!"[4]

Laws and other CAS enthusiasts are sensitive to the fact that many people, when they first hear of CAS, are appalled to learn that not only are grown-ups play acting Wild West fantasies with real bullets, they are intentionally bringing children into their fantasy.

201

"Anti-gunners, who see neither the forest nor the trees, wring their hands and ask with honest ignorance, 'What kind of kids like shooting guns?' If they would take time out from self-inflicted hysteria to look around, they would see wonderful young people." They would also see adults who are in most respects very much like themselves. Except for the fact that they like having fun with guns.

These same "anti-gunners" would also be impressed by the large number of women who are drawn to CAS. Competitive shooting is a genuinely equal-opportunity pastime. In that regard, CAS has a lot in common with other, perhaps more conventional, shooting sports. And here we come to one of the thorniest topics for opponents of women's gun use: the question of competition as, shall we say, serious fun. The serious competitive aspects of cowboy action events can be downplayed or ignored by shifting the focus to peripheral issues, such as the costuming of participants or the antique nature of the firearms involved. Hoopskirts, bonnets, lace gloves, and parasols emphasize the femininity of the shooters. Single-shot rifles and classic revolvers can be intellectually separated from so-called assault rifles, or other more modern, more menacing guns. The elaborate scenarios sometimes used in CAS events can be appreciated as theater. And the events often represent shooting situations that symbolize legitimate situations of self-defense or protection of others. But when all is said and done, what attracts some women and girls to Cowboy Action Shooting is what attracts others to other forms of target shooting. Skeet enthusiast Diane Weber sums up the appeal: "I love seeing targets shatter against the sky."

Competitive shooting ranges from a few casual rounds of trap at the local shooting range, to shooting competitions such as those sponsored by the NRA and the National Police Shooting Championship, to the various Olympic shooting sports. They cannot be disguised or dismissed as anything but exactly what they are: women using firearms not only in competition against other women, but frequently against men. This forces critics to face directly any prejudices or preconceived notions they have about the noncompetitive nature of women or about women's relative abilities as shooters. In no other sphere is the gun so clearly a "great equalizer."

Stepping Up to the Firing Line

Girls and women represent a steadily increasing segment of the target shooting population. Indeed, in 1994 the National Sporting Goods Association reported that more women purchased long guns for hunting or target shooting between 1989 and 1992 than purchased handguns during the same period.[5] The trend appears to have continued throughout the nineties. The Women's Shooting Sports Foundation (WSSF) reports that between 1989 and 1997 (the last year for which figures were available), in shotgun target sports—that is, trap, skeet, and sporting clays, the various sports involving shooting clay targets—women's participation increased 23 percent, to almost 1,200,000 female shotgunners. By 1997 the number of female rifle target shooters was 1,842,000 (down slightly from 1989), and handgun target shooters held steady during the period at over 2,600,000. Factoring in increasingly popular specialized categories like muzzle-loading and airgun shooting, and recognizing that there is some overlap because many women participate in several shooting sports, the WSSF estimates that by 1997 approximately four million American women were target shooters.[6] Some of these women shoot competitively; the majority shoot purely for recreation.

One of the things that seems to draw women to the shooting sports is that this is one area in which not only can women compete with men, but being female may actually be an advantage. Shotgun instructor Michael McIntosh remarks, "I have taught several women to shoot, both formally and informally, and I believe I've learned more from them about the nature of shooting than they ever learned from me." Based on his experience, McIntosh argues that women not only can shoot as well as men, but they frequently stand a better chance of becoming adept at shooting. Why? Attitude is the key:

I have yet to meet a woman who believes that being born female implies an innate ability to handle a gun. The converse is not true for a lot of men. . . . The fact is, ability to shoot isn't part of anyone's sexual identity, male or female, but men, especially young ones, seem to have a hard time learning that. Some never do. None of the women I've taught were defensive about being a novice, and that gave them an important advantage: They could concentrate on learning to hit a target without fretting over what it meant to their egos if they missed. Eye-hand coordination, the crux of shooting, works best when the conscious mind is undistracted—and stuffing pieces of your ego into a gun along with the shells is a major-league distraction.[7]

Like women hunters, women sport shooters do not have any macho point to make. That seems to make it easier for them to get down to the basics of good shooting. Alaskan biathlete and NRA firearms safety instructor Faith Nava agrees that women are easier to teach:

They have greater concentration and discipline . . . and little or no preconceived ideas of shooting. They listen to the coach/instructor better than men. . . . And they get more excited about it! It's something they never thought they could do and here they are, doing it well. Their confidence levels shoot up (pardon the pun), and they carry their newfound self-confidence into other areas of their lives, such as refusing to be a victim.

Former National shooting champion Mary Godlove adds: "Given a quantitatively and qualitatively equal group of nonshooting men and women, the women will learn to shoot better, faster than the men.

. . . I've done a whale of a lot of coaching at all levels, and I've almost always found females to be 'quicker' at picking up the sport."

The Women's Shooting Sports Foundation has been the major force working to popularize shooting sports among women nationally. In 1988, a group of women in Houston, Texas—all of them competitive shooters and hunters—held a "women only" sporting clays event, to benefit a local shelter for abused women and children. They figured they'd be lucky if twenty women showed up for their advertised "charity shoot"; in fact, ninety-seven did. This was more than had entered that year's Texas state championship. The Ladies Charity Classic became an annual event; in 1993, 250 women came from seventeen states to participate in what had come to be called the Mother Shoot. Favorable media coverage, including a feature on ESPN, led the National Shooting Sports Foundation (NSSF) to provide funding, and WSSF was born, with the dual purpose of promoting shooting sports among women, and representing the needs and interests of women to the hunting and shooting industry. With a current membership of five thousand (95 percent of them women) in forty-eight states, WSSF sponsors shooting clinics and hunts throughout the country, as well as disseminating information about female-friendly gun clubs and instructors. However, by far its most popular, and highest-profile, events are the now dozens of Ladies Charity Classic Events held annually. Each event brings together novice and seasoned shooters, and begins with free expert instruction for women new to shooting. The proceeds from entry fees go to women-centered causes like breast cancer awareness, rape crisis and domestic violence programs, Big Brother/Big Sister programs, children's hospitals, and the Special Olympics. By the close of 1999, WSSF had raised over a million dollars for these charities.[8]

Were any other organization raising funds for such worthy causes, it would no doubt be applauded as representing the best that feminism has to offer. But because guns are involved, perhaps predictably, the WSSF Charity Classics came under fire early on. *New York Times* columnist Bob Herbert noted in 1994 that "with so many men already armed, new markets must be found. . . . Most of us see homicide as a huge problem, but the blood is not flowing fast enough to suit the firearms industry. It is going after women big time." Working from the Violence Policy Center report, *Female Persuasion—A Study of How the Firearms Industry Markets to Women and the Reality of Guns,*[9] Herbert specifically cited the Ladies Charity Classic Events, as ways the shooting industry tries to "entice" women into gun use: "It is just about impossible to overstate the insidiousness of seeking out women concerned with issues like domestic violence and breast cancer for the sole purpose of putting guns into their hands. But nothing is beneath the gun merchants, who have yet to find a sewer too slimy to swim in."[10] Herbert went on to castigate gun merchants for propagating the "fraudulent myth" of armed self-protection.

Sue King, then WSSF executive director and one of the original organizers of the Ladies Charity Classics, took exception to Herbert's characterization of WSSF. "Our programs," she said in a press release, "provide women with a safe, fun shooting opportunity which also teaches firearms safety and responsible ownership." In fact, the release also pointed out, "None of the programs of the Women's Shooting Sports Foundation address or promote the use of guns for personal protection. Recreational shooting, such as skeet or sporting clays, involves the use of inanimate targets and is an entire spectrum apart from the use of firearms for personal protection."[11] WSSF may have been giving too much argumentative ground to their opponents here, since most women who possess firearms for sporting purposes also cite self-protection as an additional advantage of being armed. Diane Weber, a writer/editor in Virginia who has been sport shooting since 1991, says about her shooting:

Shooting improves my mind. It brings me into contact with the opposite sex on an equal, and respectful, basis. It gives me enormous confidence. I was once followed up to my apartment by a thug and nearly missed a horrible incident. I could never sleep after that—until I learned to shoot. It is probably not politically correct to say this, but owning a gun and knowing how to use it gives me a personal sense of power over my life and over my destiny. It has made me feel stronger and more in control over my fate than anything ever has.

Linda Washburn, a management consultant in Michigan who has been shooting recreationally for fifteen years, also links sport to self-protection:

[Shooting] also has a more practical side, in that my .380 is for personal defense. I feel a lot more comfortable when Robert is away knowing that I have the ability to defend myself should the need arise. In fact, my first shooting was for that reason (self-defense), and I have moved into the recreational shooting for the enjoyment and challenge.

Many, probably most, female gun owners draw similar connections between the recreational and self-protective uses of their firearms.

As for the question of "political correctness": a little hands-on knowledge can indeed lead a woman to change her mind about guns. Riva Freifeld, for example, a New York–based film and television editor, used to be vigorously anti-handgun. She had reason to be: a child in her family had been injured by a friend playing with his father's gun. In 1995, she began research for an anti-gun documentary, and although she had never touched a gun ("I was horrified by them"), she was persuaded to try shooting. To her surprise, she "loved it."[12] Freifeld subsequently found Herbert's editorial not only offensive, but illogical. In an article in *Human Events,* pointing out that Herbert makes generalizations about women as a group that he would never tolerate about, say, African Americans as a group, she continued:

Herbert seems to be obsessed with a non-problem: law-abiding women taking up weekend target shooting, which, in his opinion, is a significant factor in the "gun violence" of today's America. . . . Perhaps Herbert should take a closer look at these women who take up target shooting. They are learning how to properly and safely use a gun, and thus lessening the chances of having that gun used against them. . . . What Herbert doesn't recognize is that a large number of American women quietly own guns, and that virtually none have ever misused the gun.[13]

That the pleasure of target shooting can be so strong as to convert an "anti-gunner" into a "gun nut" would indeed be reason for alarm, were it not for the fact that women have such a good overall track record when it comes to firearms safety. However, anti-gun activists are far more comfortable with the image, however much it conflicts with reality, of women who will become dangerous to themselves and others as soon as a gun is placed in their hands.

Guns in Schools

The same assumption applies, of course, to young people. In the wake of the killings at Columbine and other high schools in the late 1990s, critics called for the abolition of shooting sports at summer camps, and the abolition of high school shooting teams. Guns, they argued, are just too seductive for impressionable teenagers to handle.

These critics were obviously on to something. Ninth-grader Leslie Lotspeich, a member of the Tieton Junior Rifle Club in Yakima, Washington, recalls about her introduction to shooting: "At first I didn't want to do it. It looked really scary. I thought you weren't supposed to shoot guns, that they were bad. . . . It took me about a month to get over that." Her sister-shooter in the club, eighteen-year-old Kelly Brown, is one of the coed club's best shots; she bought her own gun with money she saved up from babysitting. Young women like these take to shooting with passion—but not without a sense of the responsibility that goes with handling guns. Ninth-grader Lisa Last, a founding member of the rifle team at Great Neck South High School in New York, wrote in an essay on riflery as a good sport for teenagers: "When properly instructed, the seductive nature of a gun's dark side becomes non-existent. A firearm is regarded as a piece of precision equipment, worthy of respect for the power it yields but never is it regarded as a weapon." Last also wrote about how one observing a rifle match "might, in all honesty, claim the athletes to be more civilized than the general population," exhibiting camaraderie and generosity not only to one another, but to members of the opposing team. "A mental sport, target shooting consists of aiming at a bullseye a certain distance away, and a shooter is really only competing with himself [*sic*]. The competition breeds no aggression."[14]

Colorado college student Cathy Winstead, who started shooting at the age of seven and at eighteen was the first woman ever to win the national championship in smallbore hunting rifle silhouette shooting, strikes a similar note regarding the positive impact of shooting on teenagers: "Shooting most of my life was a way for me to stay out of trouble. I knew that drugs and other bad habits would get in the way of my shooting so I never touched the stuff. Everyone tends to see the bad aspects of guns, but my life would not be the same without them."

The experience and insight of young women like Last and Winstead might have come in handy for the Chicago school board as it deliberated its 1999 decision to eliminate riflery from Junior Reserve Officer Training (JROTC) programs in the city's public school system. The decision affected nine thousand cadets. Until the media focused attention on these programs in the wake of the massacre at Columbine High in Colorado, they were considered safe and appropriate—even by firearms opponents. A member of the Illinois Council Against Handgun Violence visited a shooting class at Lake Forest High School and was quoted as saying, "I don't see how shooting in Olympic-style competition within the school creates a problem of gun violence. It's under strict supervision."[15] It should be pointed out that the riflery training these cadets were receiving involved high-performance air rifles that simulated the conditions of actual riflery; neither high-powered rifles nor live ammunition were used.

Responding to the school board's decision, Richard Pearson of the Illinois State Rifle Association cited a four-year study funded by the U.S. Justice Department's Office of Juvenile Justice and Delinquency. The study, conducted between 1995 and 1999, tracked the behavior of four thousand children between the ages of six and fifteen in Denver, Pittsburgh, and Rochester, New York. It found that children who came from homes where firearms were lawfully owned and handled by youths under adult supervision were "markedly less likely to use illegal drugs or commit crimes than were their counterparts who obtained guns illegally." Miriam Ortiz, a sixteen-year-old JROTC staff sergeant, told the *Chicago Tribune*: "You get a feeling in the pit of your stomach. I really got upset when they told us they were going to cancel it. It's not fair to take away something that kids love and that has no harm to it."[16] School shooting programs at all levels boast extraordinary safety records. Protesting the abolition of riflery in the Chicago schools, the coach of the Waukegan High School rifle club, retired Army Major William Kelo, reported only one accident in twenty-eight years of coaching the team. That accident involved the team's equipment manager falling down a flight of stairs and breaking her leg.[17]

But something approaching hysteria has characterized most press reports about Columbine and other school shootings, and their after-math. This perhaps makes it more difficult for many people to even entertain the idea that recreational or competitive shooting could possibly be appropriate activities for teenagers. Ohio teenager Laura Kuntz reflects, "It used to be hard for me to tell my other friends that I like to shoot guns. Sometimes it is hard still. People's opinions of you can really change when they find out you shoot, but a lot of the time I wish that they wouldn't. This is something that I wish could change." What would it take to effect this change—to overcome what Susan Laws called the "honest ignorance" of those averse to using guns for serious fun? Some knowledge of the history of women's competitive shooting might be a good place to start.

A Brief Overview of Women in Competitive Shooting

It is difficult to identify with any certainty when women began to enter formal shooting competition. Descriptions of women competitors from the past refer to their participation on college teams or in state or local matches. These college teams represent very real opportunities for scholarships for women shooters, as well as experience invaluable in later national or international competitions.

The National Rifle Association began holding National Matches in 1873.[18] Elizabeth Servaty "Plinky" Topperwein was the first woman to compete in an NRA National event, in 1906 at Sea Girt, New Jersey.[19] Men and women shot in the same matches at first; eventually separate women's competitions were added. National matches are now held at Camp Perry, Ohio. In 1955, Viola E. Pollum was the first woman to win the overall National shooting title, besting 488 other men and women competitors.[20] Her victory was all the more impressive because the event involved 640 shots, double the number in the event in previous years.

Shooting events had been added to the summer Olympic games in 1896. The actual events included in the Olympic competitions have been changed over time, as have the scoring methods.[21] Women's competition in sport pistol, air pistol, smallbore rifle (three position), and air rifle were all added to the 1984 Los Angeles Olympics; however, women had been competing in mixed events since 1968. In fact, the first woman to win an Olympic shooting medal was an American, Margaret Murdock, who won a silver medal in 1976 in the coed smallbore rifle three-position event.[22]

The rules and format for the women's events differ from those in the men's events. For example, in the air pistol competition, men have an hour and forty-five minutes to attempt sixty shots, while women are given an hour and fifteen minutes for forty shots. In these initially segregated events, American women showed well, with Ruby Fox capturing a silver medal in the sport pistol competition, Wanda Jewell taking a silver in the smallbore rifle competition, and eighteen-year-old Pat Spurgin taking the initial gold medal in the air rifle competition.[23] In 1992, American Launi Meili established new Olympic records in both the smallbore rifle and the three-position rifle events.[24] Women continue to compete in mixed teams with the men in the trap shooting and skeet shooting events. In 1996, American Kim Rhode celebrated her seventeenth birthday by taking the gold medal in trap.

What makes a woman a competitive shooter? In 1956 the NRA conducted a survey of forty-one of the foremost women in American shooting sports. Each woman was asked how she had become involved in shooting and the reasons she enjoyed shooting. Their responses to these questions revisit some of the themes we have encountered previously. Over half of the women had learned to shoot from either their husbands or other male family members, often their fathers. Like some women hunters in midcentury, these women felt they had a choice of either learning to shoot or becoming "shooting widows." Adelaide McCord reported, "When I married, my husband was a shooter and it was either shoot or be a sports widow, and at twenty-one no one likes to be left to that."[25] Few of the women reported being recruited. Instead, they had watched from the sidelines and curiosity or boredom had intervened, as described by Gladys Rising: "I took up shooting after occasionally accompanying my husband to the rifle range and sitting in the car and crocheting." But however demure these women may have been about stating their reasons for becoming shooters, they took to shooting with a vengeance. McCord had been National Woman's Smallbore Rifle Champion four times when she responded to the questionnaire, as well as having been a four-time member of the U.S. Dewar Trophy International Smallbore Rifle Team. Rising had coached the NRA women's smallbore rifle team in 1955 and established a "number of National women's records."[26]

The women's stated reasons for enjoying shooting included the enjoyment of meeting people with common interests, satisfaction at being able to develop expertise at a task generally perceived as male, and sharing a family activity. Several of the women spoke of having taught their children to shoot. For many, competitive shooting events were also cherished social events. McCord, for example, who had learned to shoot to avoid being a sports widow, continued with her competitive shooting after the death of her husband left her an actual widow. She reported that the shooting events kept her in touch with her friends.

The NRA continued to report on champion women competitive shooters in their magazine *American Rifleman*, in its "Shooting Champions" column. A sample of these women through the years illustrates their diversity. Gail N. Liberty appeared on the cover of the magazine in May 1964. At the time, Liberty was a nurse in the Air

Force and a two-time winner of the National Women's Pistol Championship.[27] Liberty's military training had not included any firearms instruction; she learned to shoot when she decided to purchase a handgun for self-protection. Liberty began shooting in February of 1961. By June of that year she was a regular member of the Sheppard Air Force base pistol team, and in July—after having shot for only five months—won the National Women's .22 Championship. Liberty continued with her winning ways in 1962 when she was selected as one of two women to represent the United States at the World Shooting Championship in Cairo, Egypt. She tied for first place with a Russian competitor, but lost in a shoot-off by two points, capturing the silver medal. In 1963 she set records for Women's Service Pistol competition for slow fire at 50 yards, timed-fire, rapid-fire, National Match Course, and aggregate fire. She capped the year by winning the U.S. International Women's Center-Fire and Rapid-Fire titles at Fort Benning, Georgia, setting records for rapid-fire and rapid-fire aggregate shooting, and equaling the record for center-fire shooting.

Lucile W. Chambliss appeared in the 1960 "Shooting Champions" column[28] and again in *American Rifleman* in April 1970.[29] The first column chronicles Chambliss's career as a competitive shooter. By 1960 she had taken the women's title at the Mid-Winter Pistol Championships eight out of nine times; had placed six times in the top three in the National Women's Pistol Championship at the Camp Perry matches; and had been the first woman in American shooting history to earn a place on the U.S. Mayleigh Cup Pistol team, an international competition team. At that time she held two incongruous professional roles. She was employed by the Winter Haven, Florida, Police Department as both a secretary and a pistol instructor. It was the second role that was the topic of the 1970 column. Chambliss had appeared as a guest on the television program *What's My Line?* on which a panel of celebrities attempted to identify the profession of guests. Chambliss stumped the panel, and went on to demonstrate her shooting expertise for the panel and studio audience.

The sport of competitive shooting has even spawned dynasties of female champions. Marianne Jensen Driver was featured in the original 1956 sample of champions; she was the 1953 Ohio State Woman Smallbore Rifle Champion and coached the Women's International Smallbore Rifle Team in 1954. In 1961, *American Rifleman*'s shooting champions column featured her older daughter, Lenore M. Jensen, who at that time was a student at Central Michigan University and had won four national smallbore rifle titles in a two-year period.[30] Her major competitor for the 1960 title was her younger sister, Marianne "Candy" Jensen. Lenore's mother, the elder Marianne, was credited with teaching and encouraging Lenore's competitive shooting career. The article was careful, however, to mention that shooting was not her only activity of note. Ms. Jensen was reported as having appeared on the President's Honor List every semester of her college career, and was the 1959 campus homecoming queen.

Lenore's sister Candy was featured in the July 1963 column.[31] She was the youngest shooter to earn a place on the 38th World Shooting Championship team representing the United States, placing fifth of sixteen international women shooters. Jensen began to shoot when she was twelve years old and was taught primarily by her mother, with help from her sister Lenore. Interestingly, it was also noted that while Candy loved competitive shooting, she withstood the pressures of competition by viewing the sport as "only fun. . . . She does not practice, dryfire, or have any of the regular training habits."[32]

The personal information that was included in the columns about these three champions reveals gender biases of the time. Clearly, these women were expert shooters. Each profile, however, took pains to include some traditionally, and nonthreateningly, feminine characteristics. The matriarch emphasized the social aspects of shooting competitions. The older daughter was also the homecoming queen. And the younger daughter didn't practice; the girl just wanted to have fun. In each case the subtext proclaimed: Yes, they're shooting champions, but they're *also* feminine women.

Recent Champions

Launi Meili competed in both the 1988 and the 1992 Olympic games, in smallbore and air rifle competitions. Meili came from a family of hunters. As a child she accompanied the hunters but did not, and does not now, participate in the shooting aspects of the hunt. Her family's concern that she learn appropriate gun safety led them to enroll her in a class when she was eleven years old. Meili went on to compete on the rifle team at Eastern Washington University. Though she was no stranger to competitive shooting, the Olympic games represented a unique challenge.

In the 1988 Olympics, Meili broke the Olympic record in the preliminary round. Since women's smallbore and air rifle shooting events were new to the Olympics, Meili's accomplishment was surrounded by more than the usual uproar and hype. During the finals, Meili reports that her concentration was broken and she dropped to sixth place. Learning from this experience, in the 1992 games Meili again broke the Olympic record in the preliminary round but was able to maintain her poise and to win the gold medal in both smallbore and air rifle competitions.

Recently, other women have also been winning their fair share of important shooting competitions. Nancy Tomkins-Gallagher, winner of the 1998 NRA National High Power Championship at Camp Perry, was introduced to shooting at the age of ten or eleven by her father, a former Arizona Highway Patrol officer and hunter education instructor, and sharpened her skills, which she has subsequently applied to high-power rifle competitions and to hunting, in NRA-supported junior programs. Married to a former six-time NRA High Power Champion shooter, Tomkins-Gallagher has taught her daughters to shoot, and now that they are in their teens, the family vacations consist of making the rounds of the various shooting matches, ending each tour with the Camp Perry matches. As one of the top women competitors in her field, Tomkins-Gallagher does her best to promote shooting sports to other women.[33]

Shooting through the center of a Life Saver candy (which she still has) was one of the early shooting feats of U.S. Marine Corps staff sergeant Julia Watson, winner of the 1998 National Trophy Individual (NTI) Rifle Match, and the first woman ever to be awarded the "Mountain Man" trophy—awarded on the aggregate scores from the NTI, the President's Rifle Match, and the National Trophy Team Rifle Match. To accomplish this feat, she outshot a field of 1,353 female and male competitors.[34] Watson shot and hunted with her father as a child and first became aware of the Marine Corps shooting team at her first National match in 1992. It was also the first match at which she competed with high-power rifles. She joined the Marine Corps upon her graduation from high school, and within two years was chosen for the elite Marine Corps Shooting Team. While Watson's primary service role is as a heavy-equipment mechanic, she is quick to point out that every marine is a rifleman.

Shooting the heavy M-1, M-14, and M-16 rifles has "spoiled" Watson for Olympic shooting. She is no longer interested in shooting the lighter smallbore .22 caliber rifles used in Olympic competition. And with the Marine Corps dropping their shotgun competition team, Watson could only compete at the Olympic level if she switched branches of the service to the Army, something she is unwilling to do. "I have too much pride in the tradition of the Corps," she states. Watson has been awarded two noncombat meritorious promotions based on both her shooting and her regular duties.[35] Watson cites not only her father as a mentor, but also other shooters such as Nancy Tompkins-Gallagher as providing her with support and coaching. "If we help each other and teach each other what we know and give each other new ideas," she remarks, "then we'll all become better—together."

Women acquitted themselves well at the NRA sponsored 1999 National Police Shooting Championships.[36] Three women took top honors; all attributed their success to men. FBI special agent Cathy D. Schroeder, a firearms instructor for the Bureau, was Service Revolver Woman Champion. She was introduced to the sport of competitive shooting by her husband and gave him the credit for her win. Schroeder also earned the title of Service Revolver Woman Champion in 1991, 1992, and 1999.

Los Angeles Count deputy sheriff Patricia Fant was the 1999 Semi-Automatic Women's Champion. She stated that she noticed that in sex-integrated competitions she found, "I sometimes still have to prove myself."[37] Fant's male mentor was identified as a fellow instructor. She credits him for training her ability to focus: "Women are taught to pay attention to many things at an early age. Men can block things out."

The third police champion, Diana Dunigan, won the Overall National Police Woman Champion title. Dunigan is also a firearms instructor, at the Federal Law Enforcement Training Center in Glynco, Georgia. She took the title competing with a broken arm, having had the cast removed two days before the competition. The stress injury resulting from the competition required subsequent reconstructive surgery. Dunigan also cites male mentors as the source of her discipline and focus.

A pattern emerges from popular press accounts of women's shooting prowess. These women have attained a skill level at the very top of their sport, and they are all deservedly proud of their accomplishments. Yet the point is almost invariably made that they haven't learned to shoot at the expense of their femininity. When it comes to the earlier champions, this is not especially surprising. Women shooting champions in the fifties and even the sixties were clearly violating sex-role stereotypes with their choice of a nontraditional, aggressive sport. So, for the married champions their marital status was highlighted, and for the other champions social and friendship aspects of their participation were highlighted. For later champions, however, even including the 1999 police shooters, the NRA magazines continued to find a need to emphasize the shooters' feminine side. They were homecoming queens, or only shot "for fun," that is, not really to be aggressively competitive. And they generally had men to thank for their skills. This was true even for women who instruct police officers in firearms skills. Perhaps we haven't come as far as we thought. Where, one might reasonably ask, are the shooting champions who beat men "fair and square" and can step forward and take the credit for their accomplishments without the need to worry that winning in competitive shooting somehow equates with a loss of their worth as women?

"It's All a Mental Game"

The answer to this question may be that the problem lies more in the eye of the beholder than in the eye of the woman who is lining up her sights on the shooting range. As in so many other gender-coded arenas in American social life, women who shoot competitively seem to appreciate the value of compromise. If men need to see them as non-threateningly feminine, what's the harm? Annie Oakley, the first high-profile markswoman in American history, always dressed demurely in skirts and corsets; indeed, one of the most amazing things about her shooting was that she was able to overcome the limitations the Victorian toilette placed on her freedom of movement. (See illustration no. 1.) Throughout her public life, Oakley took pains to demonstrate what she referred to as her "ladyhood." And while she vigorously urged women to learn how to shoot, not only for recreational enjoyment but also for the self-protective advantages shooting afforded them, she steered clear of political issues like women's suffrage and the emergent feminist movement.

Many contemporary female shooters adopt a similar stance. Within the shooting world, "ladies" is generally the preferred term when referring to women. While female shooters, like males, embrace political perspectives across the spectrum from liberal to conservative, there are many who deliberately shy away from the term "feminist." For some, this is because the word represents being anti-male. But for a larger number, it is more likely due to the fact that, conventionally, "feminist" equates with "anti-gun." And because these women are involved in the original equal-opportunity activity, they may honestly feel less discriminated against than women involved in other activities that place them in competition with men. Indeed, some female shooters self-consciously play with gender categories, as if to say, "I enjoy being a girl—*and* a world-class markswoman!"

Mary Godlove, a middle-school agriculture teacher in Georgia, won her first shooting championship at the age of thirteen. She no longer shoots competitively, but still enjoys getting out to the range at every opportunity:

I usually shoot with men who expect to be better than me. Sometimes they are, but usually they are not. It adds a dimension of respect. Most don't really like being "shown up" with a firearm, but then again, they don't really mind. The ones who'll gripe loudest to my face are the first to tell all their buddies how good I am. Usually, they want the buddies to shoot against me so I can beat them too. It's all in good fun. The camaraderie among shooters is the most attractive aspect of the sport.

Regarding competition itself, Godlove comments: "Women are great competitors. Shooting is one of the few gender-indifferent sports. Anyone with a bit of natural ability, a lot of learned skill, and boundless determination can realize success in shooting."

Of course, competition means different things to different people. Pam Voss, a "full-time mom" in Colorado who was for ten years a member of the U.S. National Rifle Team and winner of numerous national and international medals, says, regarding women as competitors: "Women on the firing line are the best of friends, but when it comes to the sport, we are fiercely competitive. No one 'lets' someone else win a match. Women really could compete equally with men in shooting." As we've seen, whether or not women compete against men depends on the shooting event. Marcia Davis, a communications specialist in Michigan who was introduced to shooting four years ago through a self-defense course and now hopes to make the Olympic pistol team, explains:

For women, there are two events in international pistol (in addition to rifle, shotgun, and running target): sport pistol (.22 caliber) and air pistol. We never compete against men and some men joke about this fact, claiming that the men are afraid the women will beat them! Seriously, it's all a mental game and that's the beauty of it. Once you get past the fundamentals, it's all in your head and the challenge is to not be psyched out during a match. The other thing about international pistol in this country that can be perceived as a benefit to a new competitor like myself is that there aren't many women who do it so it's easy to participate in matches and advance. Also, it's a sport that can be done well into "older" age.

Sixteen-year-old Emily Kuntz, who shoots a .22 caliber rifle with the Vienna Cougars Junior Rifle Team in Ohio, says: "I think women have an excellent role as competitors in shooting. We know how to go out there and show those men what we're made of!" Linda Ritchie Oliver, an eighth-grade history teacher in Tennessee, remembers winning her first shooting championship when she was even younger than Emily Kuntz: "When I was thirteen years old, I could beat the best shooters in the country. As a woman, being able to beat the best men and women in the USA was a very empowering thing." Oliver, now in her forties, no longer shoots competitively, but still spends a lot of time on the range. Echoing Davis's comment about how there are really no age limitations in shooting, she remarks that "shooters can be on top of the game at thirteen years of age and expect to improve as they age. Some of my shooting buddies are over eighty and I don't always beat them!"

The gun has been referred to as the "great equalizer." In competitive shooting, at least when it comes to differences of gender and age, that certainly seems to be the case.

Happiness Is a Warm Gun

Like hunters, female competitive shooters often develop special, even intimate relationships with their guns. And, maybe because camouflage isn't an issue, they are more liable than hunters to "feminize" their favorite firearms in one way or another. Smallbore rifle champion Cathy Winstead describes her favorite gun: "It is a pink smallbore silhouette rifle. My dad and I worked on it and painted it when I was about eleven. When it is in my hands I feel as if I am with an old friend and we can do anything together." Corinne Flask, a collegiate competitive shooter and future law enforcement officer, talks about her Anschutz 2002 air rifle:

I love my air rifle. I wouldn't give it up for anything. I have one of the first ones and it has a laminated color stock of purple, pink, blue, and black. It gives me the attitude I need. I can trust my gun to do what I want it to. And it's pretty!

Pam Voss recalls her own Anschutz 2002 fondly: "I didn't own it very long, but it was good to me. She was like my baby and it was very hard to part with her when I retired."

Those who find Voss's likening of a gun to a baby surprising might be even more stunned by Zeni Thakkar's comments about her rifle, a .22 sport rifle. Thakkar grew up in India where her mother and older sister, quite unconventionally, taught her to shoot. She represented India in international shooting events, before relocating to the United States, where she is a senior accounts manager in an Illinois information technology firm. About her relationship with her gun, Thakkar says:

My favorite gun has been my Anschutz, which I have had for seven years. It has brought me a lot of medals. We have an age-old tradition in India when we worship our machinery/tools/weapons, no matter if they are nonliving, but which have brought us our food and means for living. I worship my Anschutz the same way. In my opinion a favorite "anything" would be one with which you have spent limitless time. I am sentimental about my gun.

The relationships women forge with their competition guns clearly relate directly to what those guns do for them, and not only as shooters, but as individuals. Olympic hopeful Marcia Davis explains:

Shooting is fun because it's a game against yourself. You don't need anyone else to participate, although shooting with others makes it fun as well. More importantly, what shooting does for me is allow me to use the mental focus I have and funnel it into something challenging and athletic. I was never athletic in school except for playing volleyball, and for some reason it's important

223

to me to develop that aspect of myself, to be more well rounded. It gives me a sense of power as well, to know that I'm good at it, especially because the main reason I bought a handgun in the first place was for self-defense. People who know I'm a target competition shooter jokingly say "don't get on her bad side" but that still helps to reinforce my confidence in aiming. Also, improving my performance/scores does wonders for my shooting confidence as well as self-esteem.

Female shooters constantly emphasize the mental and emotional benefits of shooting, and the way these benefits connect to the fact that in shooting, your primary competitor is yourself. Pam Voss reflects:

Shooting is a great individual sport. It allowed me to be completely focused and use a great deal of mental concentration. I was also able to judge my personal potential knowing it was just me, my gun, and the target, and perfection was the goal.

Shooters sometimes talk about the "Zenlike" experience of competitive shooting. Linda Ritchie Oliver, for example, explains:

Shooting is fun because it is mostly a mental sport. You do not have to be Godzilla to win. What I most enjoy about shooting targets is the Zen experience of centering my sights on the target, waiting for the right conditions, and squeezing the trigger. . . . Initially, shooting gave me the confidence I needed to become self-actualized.

Diane Weber, a Virginia writer/editor, is involved in several competitive shooting sports and derives different satisfactions from each:

I like skeet shooting for its conviviality . . . I shoot pistol because it is useful, and I rely on a pistol for self-protection. I shoot rifle because it is an exercise in focus, concentration, perfection of movement, and a little personal exercise in Zen. I have tried the Aikido "unbendable arm" exercise with pistol shoot-

ing and gotten some wonderful targets. I have talked to a lot of Gold Medal shooters . . . who have described Zenlike experiences in shooting.

Many shooters cite self-improvement as their goal. Smallbore shooter Valerie Boothe observes:

Shooting is fun because it provides ways of challenging myself. I shoot to see how I can better myself and my shooting. Shooting makes me more aware of my inner self. . . . I think shooting is the best sport. It provides an avenue to release frustration, teaches self-discipline, and is the only true co-ed sport I know of and doesn't have an age limit.

Boothe, a collegiate rifle instructor in Mississippi, remarks about the women she works with: "Women are fierce competitors. I feel they are more serious about their shooting. I think women still feel as though they have something to prove." Zeni Thakkar's experience is similar:

Shooting has always given me motivation and solace, out of my hectic life with studies when I was young, and work, now. Shooting has helped me develop patience, concentration, confidence, determination, devotion, and dedication, and all these have helped me with all aspects of my life. . . . This has been one sport where size and strength really don't matter and women can compete equally with men. . . . I would think women make better shooters, because we have better mind control and stability, and as shooting is more a mental game than physical—I think women make better shooters.

For girls and women who grew up in a context where women aren't supposed to want or like to compete, time on the firing line teaches extraordinarily valuable lessons. Faith Nava, a restaurant server in Homer, Alaska, grew up in a shooting family; her father started the College Cubs Junior Shooting Club in Fairbanks when she was a child, and she spent most of her time on the shooting range at the University of Alaska. It seemed natural for her to become both a hunter and a competitive shooter. But she was sensitive, nevertheless, to the fact that her gender kept her from being "one of the boys":

Being a woman competitor all my life I feel I had to do better because basically guns were a man's world. I was continually having to "prove myself." Luckily I was a damn good shot and could! Lately I've been into trap shooting and enjoy the challenge. I continually see more women in the shooting sports than I used to. I love that.

Lenore Jensen, one of the collegiate shooters profiled in *American Rifleman* in 1961 (she was the Dean's List student and homecoming queen), is today Lenore Lemanski and works as a school counselor in Michigan. She still shoots competitively. She reflects on what forty-five years of riflery have done for her:

Shooting has been very good to me. As a shy and awkward teenager, shooting was my first significant accomplishment—especially winning the national women's smallbore championship in 1959 and 1960. I also won in 1963, two years after I was married, and again in 1994, just to show that you're never too old for this game! My greatest thrill was winning the National Iron Sight Championship in 1986. I had not been shooting well that year, but at Camp Perry I had two good days and beat the whole field, including the top male shooters in the country. I felt good about it, but my almost sixteen-year-old daughter felt even better. Jana always understood power, and grasped how much respect and credibility a woman who could shoot well received.

Lemanski cites an additional benefit of shooting, for her personally: "In the summer of 1998 I went through breast cancer—mastectomy, chemotherapy, the whole nine yards—and was amazed at how non-traumatic the whole episode was for me." In addition to her religious faith, she credits "the training/discipline of my years of shooting" for getting her through the trauma. For Lemanski, and thousands of women like her, shooting clearly affords a way to achieve self-knowledge and personal empowerment.

Trouble in Paradise?

Many of the most successful competitive women shooters began their experiences on high school or college rifle or pistol teams. Currently over forty colleges sponsor National Collegiate Athletic Association (NCAA) rifle competitions. Teams are generally co-ed, in part because of the excellence of the women shooters, but also because including women helps colleges meet the requirements established by Title IX of the Civil Rights Act, which requires gender equity in the support provided by colleges and universities to their athletic programs.

The 1999 National Collegiate Rifle Championships were won by the largely female team from the University of Alaska—Fairbanks. In winning its second championship, the Alaska team established a new NCAA record. In air rifle, Melissa Mulloy and teammate Dan Jordan shot identical scores of 392 (of 400 possible); their teammate Kelly Mansfield shot a score of 391. The same three shooters recorded the top three scores in the smallbore competition. Mansfield won both the individual smallbore and air rifle competitions.[38] This is a good example of the significant role women play in this sport at the collegiate level.

Many of the college shooters cut their teeth in competitions on their high school rifle teams, often as a part of a Junior Reserve Officers Training Program (JROTC). As we saw earlier, however, media-induced near-hysteria over the rash of school shootings in the late 1990s has led some school districts—most notably the Chicago city school system—to limit, or even prohibit, firearms programs in schools. Such moves raise the real possibility that shooters, female and male, who might have honed their skills and qualified for the

National team may in future not have the chance. The United States Olympic shooting teams have won more medals than any other country, due in no small part to their female members.[39] It would be ironic, to say the least, were Olympic athletes to suffer as a result of shortsighted policy decisions based more upon political cant than solid information.

But then again, when it comes to sport and competitive shooting, as in the cases of self-defense and hunting, sisters are doing more and more of it for themselves. Faith Nava, who grew up shooting in Alaska, has taught her daughter and her husband's two sons to shoot:

It is so rewarding to see their excitement when the pop can falls off the saw-horse or the holes in the target are in the 10 ring. Passing on the love of shoot-ing to the next generation is very important. It's where my education began, with the College Cubs Junior Shooting Club, and though we don't have that opportunity here in Homer, I can at least teach the young people around me.

Many shooters share Nava's commitment to working with novice shooters, sharing the joy and personal rewards of shooting. Across the country, instructors volunteer their time and energy in BOW work-shops, introducing women to large and smallbore riflery, shotgun-ning, and handgun shooting. The WSSF provides free instruction for beginners at all of its shooting events. With people and programs like these passing on their skills and enthusiasm, the future of women's recreational and competitive shooting looks reasonably bright.

Postscript

For too long now, firearms enthusiasts and firearms opponents have talked at each other, around each other, about each other, and against each other. What has been missing is any sense of a real conversation—perhaps because, as generally happens in such polarized situations, no one has really been listening. One of the key premises of feminist theory is that polarization is a major tool that male-dominant culture uses to silence and marginalize women. If for no other reason than this, anti-gun feminists should reevaluate their facile assumption that guns and women don't mix. Those women who have crossed the gender divide—pistol, shotgun, or rifle in hand—are blazing a trail toward a richer, if decidedly more complex, understanding of what genuine equality between the sexes is all about. We respectfully disagree with the appropriators of Audre Lorde's sentiment, though not with the spirit of Lorde's own feminism, which was all about celebrating diversity among women: the Master's house *can* be dismantled using his tools. Or, better yet, those tools in the hands of women and men working, and playing, together can build a much better house.

Of course, there must be room in this new dwelling for radical differences of opinion, and different choices arising from varying needs, life circumstances, and personal tastes. Most of the gun women we know understand where their anti-gun sisters are coming from, even if they don't agree with them. They might argue that the woman who eschews a gun for personal protection and relies upon the man in the house, or the authorities, to take care of her is the one who is really deluded into a false sense of security. They might suggest that to depend upon men to maintain the peace and to go off to war, while women keep the home fires burning, amounts to hypocrisy. They might argue that, unlike the hunter who understands the processes of nature and participates in getting her food to the table, the woman who gets her meat in the market is buying a reality as shrink-wrapped as her steaks, and as devoid of flavor. And they might say to the woman who doesn't understand how shooting a gun skillfully can be not only fun, but deeply empowering—well, you just don't know what you're missing. But that's your choice.

Choice, of course, is another watchword for feminism. We could hardly end this book by urging all women to take up arms. Many women choose not to involve themselves with firearms, for very good reasons. Gun ownership is not only a deeply personal choice, founded in self-knowledge, it is also a life-or-death decision in a way few others are. It carries with it a host of responsibilities. But, as the words of the gun women in the preceding chapters amply demonstrate, it can also bring security, satisfaction, a sense of empowerment, confidence, independence, a sense of accomplishment, happiness. These are all things, not to overwork a gun metaphor, worth aiming for. For many women, making the informed choice to be or become a gun woman is a vital step in taking aim.

As we remarked at the outset, one of the frustrations we encountered in researching this book had to do with the invisibility of gun women, not only in public discourse about guns and gun control, but also in the academic and popular literature relating to firearms and their use. Even within the pro-firearms literature, the numbers of women who own firearms for self-protection or other reasons could generally be discerned only by reading between the lines. Despite the prominent mention of women in the heated debate over the effect of right-to-carry legislation, gun-owning women themselves have been either silent or, apparently, silenced. And in outdoor publications and those relating to competitive shooting, beyond the occasional token article, women who find enjoyment and fulfillment in firearms have been virtually invisible. We, and our sister gun women, hope to see all this change.

The academic literature on guns needs to incorporate the experiences and perspectives of the women who own and use them, to more adequately reflect the demographics of America's "gun culture." And if the contemporary debate over gun control is ever to get beyond the name-calling phase it seems to be stuck in, not only anti-gun feminists but political and cultural conservatives as well need to rethink their biases about the sorts of women who might own guns, and their reasons for being gun women.

Popular sporting and gun publications can play a role here, in educating the nonhunting, nonshooting public about the realities of women's gun use. Since the male gun owners, writers and editors we know tend as a group to be supportive of gun women, we suspect our near-invisibility owes less to antipathy than to a kind of paternalistic hangover, the habit of thinking of guns as a "guy thing," even when they know better. But we believe their hearts are in the right place.

As to the news media, we're not so sure. But we do know that, again, if our vitally important public conversation about firearms and their role in American society is to progress beyond the stereotyping and scapegoating that presently characterizes it, then news men and women must recall those lessons they learned in journalism school, about fairness and accuracy in reporting. America's gun women have a voice—no, actually, many voices. And many stories to tell. To deny them their place in the conversation, or in any other way to demean or trivialize or oversimplify their experience as women, as gun owners, and as citizens of a free society is explicitly anti-female, and implicitly anti-feminist.

As we remarked in the beginning, this book in no way claims to be the last word on its subject. To the contrary, we trust it will generate many more words, some of them heated and some, we hope, reflective, toward building a truly inclusive conversation. Gun women need to have their say in the multifarious debate about guns, violence, and feminism in contemporary America. We are happy to have done our part to bring some of these women to light. Soldiers and survivors, students and stay-at-home moms, homecoming queens and radical feminists, fierce competitors and solitary still-hunters, professionals from all walks of life and regions of the country, some politically conservative, some progressive, some self-declared feminists, some not, and many probably falling into that familiar gray area of "I'm not a feminist, but . . ."—all these women have important things to say about what being a gun woman means to and for them. Can we afford not to listen?

More simply, can we talk?

Notes

Notes to the Introduction

1. According to Peggy Tartaro, editor of *Women & Guns* magazine, the precise number of female gun owners in America is impossible to determine. Eleven million is the lowest figure generally cited, 17 million the highest.

2. One of us is a member of the NRA, the other is not. One of us has written about the women's market for firearms industry trade publications, the other has not. Both of us hunt, although for one of us it figures as a far larger motivation for gun ownership than for the other. We both own handguns, which one of us loves shooting recreationally while the other keeps hers solely for self-protection and much prefers her long guns. One of us, who demands that her guns be as beautiful as they are functional, has over the years developed brand loyalty to particular lines of rifles and shotguns; the other, equally fussy about handgun actions and calibers, is hard-pressed in a pinch to remember the make of her hunting rifle. Both of us are feminists but come at it from different directions: one is a social scientist who studies gender stereotypes, the other a humanist who specializes in feminist theory and method.

3. Don B. Kates, Jr., in Don B. Kates, Jr., and Gary Kleck, *The Great American Gun Debate: Essays on Firearms and Violence* (San Francisco: Pacific Research Institute for Public Policy, 1991), 9. Kates documents all of these phrases, which are direct quotations, with citations to the *Miami Herald*, *Atlanta Constitution*, *Washington Post*, columnist Garry Wills, the *Albany* [NY] *Times Union*, *Detroit Free Press*, *Philadelphia Inquirer*, *Washington Star*, *Chicago Sun-Times*, *San Jose Mercury-Times*, *Arizona Republic*, *Los Angeles Herald Examiner,* and *Los Angeles Times,* and cartoonist Herblock.

4. Geoffrey Dickens, "Outgunned: How the Network News Media Are Spinning the Gun Control Debate," January 5, 2000. The report can be accessed on the World Wide Web at www.mrc.org.

5. See Jeff Jacoby, "The Media's Anti-Gun Animus," *Boston Globe,* January 17, 2000.

6. These studies, of most of which Arthur Kellermann was the primary author, are discussed in chapters 1 and 2 below.

7. In 1988, *Library Journal* reported that, according to "a highly placed source in Washington, D.C. . . . the American Library Association lobby and the National Rifle Association lobby are the only ones whose information was considered truthful and reliable by legislators." *Library Journal,* September 15, 1988.

8. Don B. Kates, Jr., points out that in the public-health literature relating to guns, "firearms and their ownership are invariably discussed as social pathology rather than as a value-neutral phenomenon." See Kates, "A Controlled Look at Gun Control: A White Paper on Firearms and Crime in Connection with the Author's Oral Presentation before the Select Committee of the Pennsylvania Legislature to Investigate the Use of Automatic and Semiautomatic Firearms," Harrisburg, September 20, 1994, 21.

9. Edgar A. Suter, neurosurgeon and chair of Doctors for Integrity in Research and Public Policy, notes, regarding the *New England Journal of Medicine*'s no-data-are-needed policy: "For matters of 'fact,' it is not unusual to find third-hand citations of editorials rather than citations of primary data." Suter, "Guns in the Medical Literature A Failure of Peer Review," *Journal of the Medical Association of Georgia* 83 (March 1994): 133. Most of Kellermann's articles appeared in the *New England Journal of Medicine.*

Notes to Chapter 1

1. The terms were coined, respectively, by historians Richard Hofstadter in "America as a Gun Culture," *American Heritage* 21 (1970), 4–7, 26–34, and Richard Slotkin in *Gunfighter Nation: The Myth of the Frontier in Twentieth Century America* (New York: Atheneum, 1992).

2. Under Fire, *Business Week,* August 16, 1999, 65.

3. Associated Press report, "Support Grows for Plugging Handgun Sales," *Billings* [Montana] *Gazette,* June 4, 1993, 1.

4. "Should You Own a Gun?" *Glamour,* January, 1994, 44.

5. Steve Fishman, "What You Know about Guns Can Kill You," *Vogue,* October 1993, 142.

6. "Targeting Women," *USA Today,* May 24, 1994, 12A.

7. Quoted by Melinda Hennenberger, "The Small Arms Industry Comes On to Women," *New York Times,* October 24, 1993.

8. "Arming Women Won't Protect Them," *Chicago Tribune,* January 17, 1993.

9. "Boy Toys," *New Republic,* March 30, 1992, 45.

10. Chief among them: A. Kellermann et al., "Gun Ownership as a Risk Factor for Homicide in the Home," *New England Journal of Medicine* 329 (1993): 1084–91; A. Kellermann and D. Reay, "Protection or Peril? An Analysis of Firearms-Related Deaths in the Home," *New England Journal of Medicine* 314 (1986): 1557–60; A. Kellermann et al., "Suicide in the Home in Relationship to Gun Ownership," *New England Journal of Medicine* 327 (1992): 467–72; A. Kellermann and J. Mercy, "Men, Women and Murder: Gender-Specific Differences in Rates of Fatal Violence and Victimization," *Journal of Trauma* 33 (1992): 1–5; J. Sloan, A. Kellermann, et al., "Handgun Regulations, Crime, Assaults and Homicide: A Tale of Two Cities," *New England Journal of Medicine* 319 (1988): 1256–62. For critiques, by medical professionals, of the methodological problems raised by these and other patently anti-gun articles in the medical literature, see Edgar A. Suter, M.D., "Guns in the Medical Literature—A Failure of Peer Review," *Journal of the Medical Association of Georgia* (March 1994): 133–48; and Miguel A. Faria, M.D., "Second Opinion: Women, Guns and the Medical Literature—A Raging Debate," *Women & Guns*, October 1994, 14–17, 52–53. See also Don K. Kates, Jr., and Gary Kleck, *The Great American Gun Debate: Essays on Firearms and Violence* (San Francisco: Pacific Research institute for Public Policy, 1997), chapter 5.

11. See Margaret Gordon and Stephanie Riger, *The Female Fear: The Social Cost of Rape* (Chicago: University of Illinois Press, 1989).

12. Tom W. Smith and Robert J. Smith, "Changes in Firearms Ownership among Women, 1980–1994," *Journal of Criminal Law and Criminology* 86 (1995): 133–49.

13. Gary Kleck, *Targeting Guns: Firearms and Their Control* (New York: Aldine DeGruyter, 1997), 78.

14. Susie McKellar, "Guns: The last frontier on the road to equality?" in Pat Kirkham, ed., *The Gendered Object* (Manchester and New York: Manchester University Press, 1996), 75.

15. Elizabeth M. Blair and Eva M. Hyatt, "The Marketing of Guns to Women: Factors Influencing Gun-Related Attitudes and Gun-Ownership by Women," *Journal of Public Policy and Marketing* 14:1 (Spring 1995).

16. Coalition to Stop Gun Violence, packet of promotional materials with the cover, "America Is Bleeding to Death from Gun Violence," mailed to one of the authors in the spring of 1993.

17. Bob Herbert, "The 'Elegant' Handgun," *New York Times,* December 4, 1994, sec. 4, p. 19.

18. *Female Persuasion: A Study of How the Firearms Industry Markets to Women and the Reality of Women and Guns* (Washington, D.C.: Violence Policy Center, 1994).

19. Debra Dobray and Arthur J. Waldrop, "Regulating Handgun Advertising Directed at Women," *Constitutional Law* 12 (1991): 113–29. This article also relies heavily upon Kellermann's studies to argue that gun ownership is chiefly dangerous to the female gun owner.

20. Alana Bassin, "Why Packing a Pistol Perpetuates Patriarchy," *Hastings Women's Law Journal* 8:2 (Fall 1997): 351–63. Not all feminist legal scholars have taken so reductive a view of women's relationship to firearms, of course. For articles arguing in favor of women's armed self-defense, see especially Inge Anna Larish, "Why Annie Can't Get Her Gun: A Feminist Perspective on the Second Amendment," *University of Illinois Law Review* (1996): 467–508; and Sayoko Blodgett-Ford, "Do Battered Women Have a Right to Bear Arms?" *Yale Law and Policy Review* 11 (1993): 509–57.

21. Naomi Wolf, *Fire with Fire: The New Female Power and How It Will Change the 21st Century* (New York: Random House, 1993), 216.

22. Laura Shapiro, "She Enjoys Being a Girl," *Newsweek,* November 15, 1993, 82. It is worth noting that Wolf's discussion of women and guns occupies a total of six pages in a 353-page book, infinitesimal in comparison to the page-space Shapiro devoted to critiquing it.

23. Ann Jones, "Living with Guns, Playing with Fire," *Ms.,* May/June 1994, 44.

24. "No, Feminists *Don't* All Think Alike (Who Says We Have To?)," *Ms.,* September/October 1993. The other analysts featured in the round-table discussion were Gloria Steinem, bell hooks, and Urvashi Vaid; see pages 34–43.

25. See Audre Lorde, "The Master's Tools Will Never Dismantle the Master's House," in Cherríe Moraga and Gloria Anzaldua, eds., *This Bridge Called My Back: Writings of Radical Women of Color* (Latham, N.Y.: Kitchen Table Press, 1983), 98–101. It bears noting that the article itself is actually about issues of exclusivity in feminist theory and practice, and has nothing remotely to do with firearms.

26. "Women as Action Heroes," *Glamour,* March 1994, 153. Italics in original.

27. "Neither Pink Nor Cute: Pistols for the Women of America," *The Nation,* May 15, 1989.

28. Wendy Brown, "Guns, Cowboys, Philadelphia Mayors, and Civic Republicanism: On Sanford Levinson's *The Embarrassing Second Amendment,*" *Yale Law Journal,* December 1989, 661–67.

29. See Douglas Laycock, "Vicious Stereotypes in Polite Society," *Constitutional Commentary,* Summer 1991, 399, 406; italics in original. For another critique of Brown's response to Levinson, see Mary Zeiss Stange, "Feminism and the Second Amendment," *Guns & Ammo Annual* (1992): 6–9.

30. Laycock, "Vicious Stereotypes in Polite Society," 401.

31. Natalie Angier, *Woman: An Intimate Geography* (Boston and New York: Houghton Mifflin Company, 1999), 265, 267.

32. Anne Campbell, *Men, Women, and Aggression* (New York: Basic Books, 1993), 37–38.

33. Jones, "Living with Guns, Playing with Fire," 43.

34. "Where Do We Go from Here? A Interview with Ann Jones," *Ms.,* (September/October 1994), 60.

35. Carol Silver and Don Kates, "Self-Defense, Handgun Ownership, and the

Independence of Women in a Violent, Sexist Society," in Don Kates, ed., *Restricting Handguns: The Liberal Skeptics Speak Out* (Croton-on-Hudson, N.Y.: North River Press, 1979), 139.

36. Wolf, *Fire with Fire*, 315.

37. Tara Baxter with Nikki Craft, "There Are Better Ways of Taking Care of Bret Easton Ellis than Just Censoring Him," in Diana E. H. Russell, ed., *Making Violence Sexy: Feminist Views on Pornography* (Buckingham, U.K.: Open University Press, 1993), 253.

38. See remarks by De Clarke in Russell, *Making Violence Sexy,* 245–46.

39. D. A. Clarke, "A Woman with a Sword: Some Thoughts on Women, Feminism, and Violence," in Emilie Buchwald, Paula R. Fletcher, and Martha Ross, eds., *Transforming a Rape Culture* (New York: Milkweed Editions, 1993), 396.

40. See Paola Tabet, "Hands, Tools, Weapons," *Feminist Issues,* Fall 1982, 3–62.

41. Diana E. H. Russell, "From Witches to Bitches: Sexual Terrorism Begets Thelma and Louise," in *Making Violence Sexy*, 267.

42. Clarke, "A Woman with a Sword," 401.

43. See chapter 2 below.

44. Cited and quoted in Blodgett-Ford, "Do Battered Women Have a Right to Bear Arms?" 553.

45. Nyla R. Branscombe and Susan Owen, "Influence of Gun Ownership on Social Inferences about Women and Men," *Journal of Applied Social Psychology* 21 (1991): 1567–89.

46. Frances O. F. Haga, "Images of Fear," paper presented at the 1992 American Society of Criminology meetings in New Orleans, Louisiana.

47. Frances O. F. Haga, Michael L. Vasu, and William V. Pelfrey, "Domestic Violence versus Predatory Assault," paper presented in the Division on Family Violence, 1993 Annual Meetings of the American Society of Criminology, Phoenix, Arizona. All subsequent citations are to this study, the copy of which the author received from Professor Haga via electronic transmission was not paginated.

48. Ann Japenga, "Would I Be Safer with a Gun?" *Health,* March/April 1994, 61.

49. Linda Hasselstrom, "A Peaceful Woman Explains Why She Carries a Gun," *High Country News,* December 31, 1990, 15.

50. Leslie Marmon Silko, "In the Combat Zone," *Hungry Mind Review,* Fall 1995, 44, 46.

51. Maureen Dowd, "Guns and Poses," *New York Times,* May 9, 1999, Op-Ed section, 17.

52. Quoted in an Associated Press report, *Minneapolis Star-Tribune,* May 22, 1999.

53. *Today Show*, NBC, August 25, 1999.

Notes to Chapter 2

1. Betty Friedan in interview with Ann Japenga, *Health* magazine, March/April 1994, 54.

2. *New Yorker,* July 1976, 58.

3. "Suicide Deaths and Rates per 100,000," www.cdc.gov/ncipc/data/us9794/Sui.htm.

4. John L. McIntosh, "1996 Official Final Statistics—U.S.A. Suicide: Prepared for the American Association of Suicidology." www.iusb.edu/~jmcintos/SuicideStats.html.

5. David B. Kopel, "Children and Guns," in David B. Kopel, ed., *Guns: Who Should Have Them? (*Amherst, N.Y.: Prometheus Books, 1995), 309.

6. See Arthur Kellermann and D. Reay, "Protection or Peril? An Analysis of Firearms-Related Deaths in the Home," *New England Journal of Medicine* 314 (1986): 1557–60.

7. See J. Sloan, Arthur Kellermann, et al., "Handgun Regulations, Crime, Assaults and Homicide: A Tale of Two Cities," *New England Journal of Medicine* 319 (1988): 1256–62; Kellermann and J. Mercy, "Men, Women and Murder: Gender-Specific Differences in Rates of Fatal Violence and Victimization," *Journal of Trauma* 33 (1993): 1–5; and Arthur Kellermann et al., "Gun

Ownership as a Risk Factor for Homicide in the Home," *New England Journal of Medicine* 329, no. 15 (1993): 1084–91.

8. Ann Japenga, "Would I Be Safer with a Gun?" *Health,* March/April 1994, 61.

9. See, for example, Don B. Kates et al., "Bad Medicine: Doctors and Guns," in Kopel, *Guns: Who Should Have Them,* 233–308; Edgar A. Suter, "Guns in the Medical Literature—Failure of Peer Review," *Journal of the Medical Association of Georgia* 83 (March 1994): 133–48; Miguel A Faria, "Second Opinion: Women, Guns and the Medical Literature—A Raging Debate," *Women & Guns,* October 1994, 14–17, 52–53; Don B. Kates et al., "Sagecraft: Bias and Mendacity in the Public Health Literature on Gun Usage," in Don B. Kates and Gary Kleck, *The Great American Gun Debate* (San Francisco: Pacific Research Institute for Public Policy, 1997), chapter 5.

10. Gary Kleck, "Can Owning a Gun Really Triple the Owner's Chances of Being Murdered?" Annual meeting of the American Society of Criminology, Toronto, November 1999.

11. See Gary Kleck, *Targeting Guns: Firearms and Their Control* (New York: Aldine de Gruyter, 1997), chapter 7; Kates and Kleck, eds., *The Great American Gun Debate,* chapters 1 and 2; Don B. Kates, Jr., *Policy Briefing. Guns, Murders and the Constitution: A Realistic Assessment of Gun Control* (San Francisco: Pacific Research Institute for Public Policy, February 1990), 45–57; David B. Kopel, "Peril or Protection? The Risks and Benefits of Handgun Prohibition," *Saint Louis University Law Review* 12 (1993):285.

12. James D. Wright, "Ten Essential Observations on Guns in America," in Jan E. Dizard et al., *Guns in America: A Reader* (New York and London: New York University Press, 1999), 501.

13. C. Ringel, "Criminal Victimization 1996: Changes 1995–96 with Trends 1993–96." (Washington, D.C.: Bureau of Justice Statistics National Criminal Victimization Survey, 1997).

14. See D. E. H. Russel, *Sexual Exploitation: Rape, Child Sexual Abuse, and Workplace Harassment* (Beverly Hills, Calif.: Sage, 1984); and National Victim Center, *Rape in America* (Arlington, Va., 1992).

15. See K. F. Ferraro, *Fear of Crime: Interpreting Victimization Risk* (Albany,

N.Y.: State University of New York Press, 1995); P. W. Rountree, "A Reexamination of the Crime-Fear Linkage," *Journal of Research in Crime and Delinquency* 35(3) (1998): 341–72; R. B. Taylor and J. Covington, "Community Structural Change and Fear of Crime," *Social Problems* 40(3) (1993): 374–94; and J. A. Will and J. H. McGrath III, "Crime, Neighborhood Perceptions, and the Underclass: The Relationship between Fear of Crime and Class Position," *Journal of Criminal Justice* 23(2) (1995): 163–76.

16. David C. May, "The Effect of Fear of Sexual Victimization on Adolescent Fear of Crime," Ph.D. diss., Mississippi State University, 1997, 2.

17. Joanne Belknap, *The Invisible Woman* (Boston: Wadsworth, 1996).

18. Rape Statistics, National Victim Center, April 23, 1992.

19. Belknap, *The Invisible Woman*, 144.

20. C. Hale, "Fear of Crime: A Review of the Literature," *International Review of Victimology* 4 (1996): 79–150; see also Gordon and Riger, *The Female Fear.*

21. R. Warshaw, *I Never Called It Rape* (New York: Harper and Row, 1988).

22. H. S. Field, "Attitudes toward Rape: A Comparative Analysis of Police, Rapists, Crisis Counselors, and Citizens," *Journal of Personality* 36 (1978): 156–79.

23. J. E. Krulewitz and J. E. Nash, "Effects of Rape Victim Resistance, Assault Outcome, and Sex of Observer on Attributions about Rape," *Journal of Personality* 47 (1979): 557–74, 558.

24. L. Williams, "Violence against Women," *Black Scholar,* January/February 1981, 18–24.

25. See D. A. Smith and C. D. Uchida, "The Social Organization of Self-Help: A Study of Defensive Weapon Ownership," *American Sociological Review* 53 (1988): 94–102; and K. F. Ferraro, "Fear of Crime: Interpreting Victimization Risk."

26. Ferraro, "Fear of Crime."

27. Carol K. Oyster, "Firearms Related Attitudes and Behaviors of Female and Male Firearms Owners: Shattering the Stereotypes," American Society of Criminology, annual meeting, Toronto, 1999.

28. Susan Laws, "Heidi Smith, New Age Cowgirl: 'Pioneer Spirit for the Next Millennium,'" *Women & Guns*, January/February 2000, 26–29.

29. Ibid., 27.

30. E. A. Stanko, *Intimate Intrusions* (London: Routledge and Kegan Paul, 1985).

31. Murray A. Straus, Richard J. Gelles, and Suzanne Steinmetz, *Behind Closed Doors: Violence in the American Family* (New York: Anchor Books, 1980).

32. Ibid.

33. Murray A. Straus and Richard J. Gelles, "Societal Change and Change in Family Violence from 1975 to 1985 as Revealed by Two Surveys," *Journal of Marriage and the Family* 48 (1986): 465–79.

34. Richard J. Gelles and Murray A. Straus, *Intimate Violence* (New York: Simon and Schuster 1998).

35. Pat Tjaden and N. Thoennes, "Prevalence, Incidence, and Consequences of Violence against Women: Findings from the National Violence Against Women Survey," Research Brief, National Institute of Justice Centers for Disease Control and Prevention, 1998.

36. Angela Browne, *When Battered Women Kill* (New York: Free Press, 1987). Browne is also the source of information for the next paragraph.

37. See Don B. Kates, "The Value of Civilian Handgun Possession as a Deterrent to Crime or a Defense against Crime," *American Journal of Criminal Law* 18 (Winter 1991).

38. Richard W. Stevens, *Dial 911 and Die* (Hartford, Wis.: Mazel Freedom Press, 1999).

39. Paxton Quigley, *Armed and Female* (New York: Dutton, 1989).

40. Recounted in Japenga, "Would You be Safer."

41. Martha McCaughey, *Real Knockouts* (New York and London: New York University Press, 1997).

42. Ibid., 156.

43. Ibid., 8.

44. Ibid., 17.

45. Ellen Snortland, *Beauty Bites Beast: Awakening the Warrior in Women and Girls* (Pasadena, Calif.: Trilogy Press, 1998), 186.

46. See Sarah E. Ullmann and Raymond A. Knight, "Fighting Back: Women's

Resistance to Rape," *Journal of Interpersonal Violence* 7 (March 1992); Sarah E. Ullmann and Raymond A. Knight, "The Efficacy of Women's Resistance Strategies in Rape Situations," *Psychology of Women Quarterly* 17 (1993): 23–38; P. B. Bart and P. B. O'Brien, *Stopping Rape: Successful Strategies* (Elmsford, N.Y.: Pergamon Press, 1985).

47. Robert J. Cottrol, Op-Ed piece in the *Los Angeles Times,* November 7, 1999.

48. James D. Wright and Peter H. Rossi, *Armed and Considered Dangerous: A Survey of Felons and Their Firearms* (New York: Aldine de Gruyter, 1986).

49. Gary Kleck and Marc Gertz, "Armed Resistance to Crime: The Prevalence and Nature of Self-Defense with a Gun," *Journal of Criminal Law & Criminology* 86 (1995): 150–87.

50. Kleck, "The Frequency of Defensive Gun Use."

51. Kleck and Gertz. "Armed Resistance to Crime."

52. Gary Kleck, personal communication, October 12, 1999.

53. Kleck, "The Frequency of Defensive Gun Use," 160.

54. Carol K. Oyster, "An Updated Snapshot of Gunowners," *Women & Guns,* May/June 1999.

55. Oyster, "Firearms Related Attitudes and Behaviors of Female and Male Firearms Owners."

56. See Quigley, *Armed and Female.*

57. Don B. Kates, Jr., "Introduction," in Kates and Kleck, *The Great American Gun Debate.*

58. Reported on ABC, *World News Tonight,* April 6, 1998.

59. Stephen Teret and Garet Wintemute, "Handgun Injuries: The Epidemiologic Evidence for Assessing Legal Responsibility," *Hamline Law Review* 6 (1983): 341–46.

60. Garet J. Wintemute, "Childhood Drowning and Near-drowning in the United States," *American Journal of Diseases of Children* 144 (1990): 663–69.

61. J. A. Davis and T. W. Smith, *General Social Surveys, 1972–1993* (Chicago: National Opinion Research Center; Ann Arbor, Mich.: Inter-university Consortium for Political and Social Research, 1993).

62. Davis and Smith, *General Social Surveys, 1972–1993.*

63. Sloan, Kellermann, et al., "Handgun Regulations, Crime, Assaults, and Homicide."

64. R. H. Seiden, "Suicide Prevention: A Public Health/Public Policy Approach," *Omega* 8 (1977): 267–76.

65. John R. Lott, Jr., and David B. Mustard, "Crime, Deterrence and Right-to-Carry Concealed Handguns," *Journal of Legal Studies* 26 (1997): 1–68.

66. John R. Lott, Jr., *More Guns, Less Crime: Understanding Crime and Gun-Control Laws* (Chicago: University of Chicago Press, 1998).

67. Ibid., 160.

68. Gary Kleck, *Point Blank: Guns and Violence in America* (New York: Aldine de Gruyter, 1991).

69. Don B. Kates, Jr., "Firearms and Violence: Old Premises and Current Evidence," in T. R. Gurr, ed., *Violence in America,* vol. 1, *The History of Crime* (Thousand Oaks, Calif.: Sage, 1989).

Notes to Chapter 3

1. Lois Joy Brady, "Vows: Arlene Beckles, Steve Imparato," *New York Times,* Sunday Style Section, February 27, 1994.

2. Rhoda Unger and Mary Crawford, *Women and Gender: A Feminist Psychology,* 2d ed. (New York: McGraw-Hill, 1996).

3. Frances Elaine Donelson, *Women's Experiences: A Psychological Perspective,* (Mountain View, Calif.: Mayfield, 1999).

4. See Rosabeth Moss Kanter, *Men and Women of the Organization* (New York: Basic Books, 1977); Barbara Gutek, *Sex and the Workplace: The Impact of Sexual Behavior and Harassment on Women and Organizations* (San Francisco: Jossey-Bass, 1985); and C. L. Williams, *Gender Differences at Work: Women and Men in Nontraditional Occupations* (Berkeley: University of California Press, 1989).

5. Kanter, *Men and Women of the Organization.*

6. Frances Heidensohn, *Women in Control? The Role of Women in Law Enforcement* (Oxford, U.K.: Clarendon Press, 1992).

7. Dorothy Moses Schulz, "Invisible No More: A Social History of Women in

U.S. Policing," in Barbara Raffell Price and Natalie J. Sokoloff, eds., *The Criminal Justice System and Women: Offenders, Victims, and Workers,* 2d ed. (New York: McGraw-Hill, 1995), 372–82.

8. Ibid., 376.

9. Ibid., 378.

10. Ibid., 379–80.

11. Many thanks go to Agent Roger Trotter, one of the Academy instructors, for assisting in recruitment of interviewees, to the Academy for allowing permission to conduct the interviews, and to the women who shared their time and experiences.

12. C. West and D. H. Zimmerman, "Doing Gender," *Gender and Society* 1 (1987): 125–51.

13. James W. Messerschmidt, *Masculinities and Crime: Critique and Reconceptualization of Theory* (Lanham, Md.: Rowman and Littlefield, 1993), 125.

14. Connie Fletcher, *Breaking and Entering: Women Cops Talk about Life in the Ultimate Men's Club* (New York: HarperCollins, 1995).

15. Ibid., 16

16. Susan E. Martin, "The Interactive Effects of Race and Sex on Women Police Officers," in Price and Sokoloff, eds., *The Criminal Justice System and Women,* 383–97.

17. A. Smith and A. J. Stewart, "Approaches to Studying Racism and Sexism in Black Women's Lives," *Journal of Social Issues* 39 (1983): 1–13.

18. Susan E. Martin, *Breaking and Entering: Policewomen on Patrol* (Berkeley: University of California Press, 1980).

19. Fletcher, *Breaking and Entering,* 5.

20. Susan L. Miller, *Gender and Community Policing: Walking the Talk* (Boston: Northeastern University Press, 1999).

21. Ibid., 24.

22. Ibid., 5.

23. Ibid., 3.

24. Heidensohn, *Women in Control?* 159.

25. James Stinchcomb, *Opportunities in Law Enforcement and Criminal Justice Careers* (Lincolnwood, Ill.: VGM Career Horizons, 1996).

26. Robin Finn, "Tough Truant Officer Is True Romantic," *New York Times,* January 28, 2000, Metro Section, B2.

27. Judith Hicks Stiehm, "Women, Men and Military Service: Is Protection Necessarily a Racket?" in Ellen Boneparth, ed., *Women, Power and Policy* (New York: Pergamon Press, 1982), 282.

28. Sheila Tobias, *Faces of Feminism: An Activist's Reflections on the Women's Movement* (Boulder, Colo.: Westview Press, 1997), 171.

29. Ellen Goodman, "Drafting Daughters," in Angela G. Dorenkamp et al., eds., *Images of Women in American Popular Culture* (San Diego and New York: Harcourt Brace Jovanovich, 1985), 282.

30. Stiehm, "Women, Men and Military Service," 282.

31. Ibid., 289–290. The Camus reference is to Albert Camus's essay, "Neither Victims nor Executioners," reprinted in *Liberation,* February 1960.

32. David E. Jones, *Women Warriors: A History* (McLean, Va.: Brassey's, 1997).

33. Sue Heinemann, *Timelines of American Women's History* (New York: Roundtable Press, 1996). Except where otherwise noted, Heinemann's *Timelines* is the source for information about women's wartime experiences in the paragraphs that follow.

34. The NRA recently instituted the Sybil Ludington Award, annually presented in recognition of a woman's contribution to public education about responsible firearms use.

35. Stiehm, "Women, Men and Military Service," 284.

36. Ibid., 285.

37. Jones, *Women Warriors,* 242.

38. Heinemann, *Timelines of American Women's History,* 242.

39. Jean Ebbert and Marie-Beth Hall, *Crossed Currents* (McLean, Va.: Brassey's, 1993). 264. Quoted in Jones, *Women Warriors,* 243.

40. Carol Burke, "Military Folk Culture," in Mary Fainsod Katzenstein and Judith Reppy, eds., *Beyond Zero Tolerance: Discrimination in Military Culture* (Lanham, Md.: Rowman and Littlefield, 1999), 53.

41. Ibid., 53.

42. Katzenstein and Reppy, *Beyond Zero Tolerance,* 6.

43. See, for example, R. W. Scofield, "Task Productivity of Groups of Friends and NonFriends," *Psychological Reports* 6, no. 3 (June 1960): 459–60; J. E. McGrath, "The Influence of Positive Interpersonal Relations on Adjustment and Effectiveness in Rifle Teams," *Journal of Abnormal and Social Psychology* 65, no. 6 (1962): 365–75; and Stephen J. Zaccaro, "Nonequivalent Associations between Forms of Cohesiveness and Group-Related Outcomes: Evidence for Multidimensionality," *Journal of Social Psychology* 131, no. 3 (1991): 387–99.

44. Elizabeth Kier, "Discrimination and Military Cohesion: An Organizational Perspective," in Katzenstein and Reppy, eds. *Beyond Zero Tolerance,* 46.

45. Carol K. Oyster, *Groups: A User's Guide* (Des Moines, Iowa: McGraw-Hill, 2000).

46. Kier, "Discrimination and Military Cohesion."

47. Rhonda Cornum (as told to Peter Copeland), *She Went to War* (Novato, Calif.: Presidio Press, 1992), 27–28.

48. Sue Guenter-Schlesinger, "Persistence of Sexual Harassment: The Impact of Military Culture on Policy Implementation," in Katzenstein and Reppy, eds., *Beyond Zero Tolerance,* 195–212.

49. Ibid., 197.

50. Ibid., 202.

51. Kier, "Discrimination and Military Cohesion," 37.

52. Erving Goffman, *Asylums: Essays on the Social Situation of Mental Patients and Other Inmates* (Garden City, N.Y.: Doubleday, 1961).

53. Kier, "Discrimination and Military Cohesion."

54. Burke, "Military Folk Culture." On the misogyny endemic to military combat-oriented culture, see also Joan Smith's essay, "Crawling from the Wreckage," in Smith, *Misogynies: Reflections on Myths and Malice* (New York: Fawcett Columbine, 1989, 1992), 141–56.

55. Kier, "Discrimination and Military Cohesion."

56. Stiehm, "Women, Men and Military Service," 288.

57. Paul E. Roush, "A Tangled Webb the Navy Can't Afford," in Katzenstein and Reppy, eds. *Beyond Zero Tolerance.*

58. Burke, "Military Folk Culture."

59. Elizabeth L. Hillman, "Dressed to Kill?" In Katzenstein and Reppy, eds., *Beyond Zero Tolerance,* 68.

60. Marjorie B. Garber quoted in Hillman, "Dressed to Kill?" 73.

61. "Women's Midshipmen Shoes, 1976," quoted in Hillman, "Dressed to Kill?" 72.

62. Jones, *Women Warriors,* 247.

63. Katzenstein and Reppy, *Beyond Zero Tolerance,* 5.

64. Ibid., 265–66.

65. Ibid., 266.

66. Cornum, *She Went to War.*

67. Oyster, *Groups: A User's Guide.*

68. Katzenstein and Reppy, eds., *Beyond Zero Tolerance,* 3.

69. Ibid., 16.

70. Barbara Ehrenreich, *Blood Rites: Origins and History of the Passions of War* (New York: Metropolitan Books, 1997), 230.

Notes to Chapter 4

1. The literature relating to the hunting hypothesis is extensive. See especially Richard B. Lee and Irven DeVore, eds., *Man the Hunter* (Chicago: Aldine, 1968); Robert Ardrey, *The Hunting Hypothesis: A Personal Conclusion Concerning the Evolutionary Nature of Man* (New York: Atheneum, 1976); and Lionel Tiger, *Men in Groups* (New York: Random House, 1971). For a review of the literature, and of the various feminist responses to it, see Mary Zeiss Stange, *Woman the Hunter* (Boston: Beacon Press, 1997), chapters 1 and 2.

2. See Desmond Morris, *The Naked Ape* (New York: McGraw-Hill, 1967), 53.

3. See Donna Haraway, *Primate Visions: Gender, Race and Nature in the World of Modern Science* (New York: Routledge, 1989), chapter 8. On the feminist critique of the hunting hypothesis, see Frances Dahlberg, ed., *Woman the Gatherer* (New Haven: Yale University Press, 1981); Michelle Rosaldo and Louise Lamphere, eds., *Women, Culture, and Society* (Palo Alto: Stanford University Press, 1974); Peggy Reeves Sanday, *Female Power and Male Dominance: On the Origins of Sexual Inequality* (Cambridge and New York: Cambridge

University Press, 1981); Nancy Tanner and Adrienne Zihlman, "Women in Evolution. Part I: Innovation and Selection in Human Origins," *Signs: Journal of Women in Culture and Society* 1:3 (1976): 585–608; and Adrienne Zihlman, "Women in Evolution. Part II: Subsistence and Social Organizations among Early Hominids," *Signs: Journal of Women in Culture and Society* 4:1 (1978): 4–20.

4. On the theoretical problems with the gathering hypothesis, and for a much more detailed discussion of the entire debate over the role hunting may have played in human evolution, see Stange, *Woman the Hunter;* on the complex relationship between women and warfare, see Barbara Ehrenreich, *Blood Rites: Origins and History of the Passions of War* (New York: Metropolitan Books, 1997).

5. See especially Susan Griffin, *Woman and Nature: The Roaring Inside Her* (New York: Harper Colophon, 1978); Andree Collard with Joyce Contrucci, *Rape of the Wild: Man's Violence against Animals and the Earth* (Bloomington and Indianapolis: Indiana University Press, 1988); Carol Adams, *Neither Man nor Beast: Feminism and the Defense of Animals* (New York: Continuum, 1990); Maria Comninou, "Speech, Pornography and Hunting," in Carol Adams and Josephine Donovan, eds., *Animals and Women: Feminist Theoretical Explorations* (Durham and London: Duke University Press, 1995).

6. Collard, *Rape of the Wild*, 1–2.

7. Paola Tabet, "Hands, Tools, Weapons," *Feminist Issues,* Fall 1982, 3–62.

8. Linda Ritchie Oliver. A former shooting champion, Oliver shoots rifles competitively. She describes her rifle as "a piece of sports equipment," distinguishing it from her handgun.

9. Sherwood Washburn and C. S. Lancaster, "The Evolution of Hunting," in Lee and DeVore, eds., *Man the Hunter*, 299.

10. Steve Grooms, "Upland Women," *Gray's Sporting Journal,* August 1997, 36–41.

11. William Rae, "Long Live Outdoor Life," *Outdoor Life,* June 1968, 6.

12. John G. Mitchell, *The Hunt* (New York: Alfred Knopf, 1980), 5.

13. Margaret G. Nichols, The Proper Perspective, *Field & Stream,* March 1973, 179, 264.

14. See Mark Damian Duda, Steven J. Bissell, and Kira C. Young, "Factors Related to Hunting and Fishing Participation in the United States, Phase V: Final Report." (Responsive Management, P.O. Box 389, Harrisonburg, VA 22801.)

15. See John F. Reiger, *American Sportsmen and the Origins of Conservation* (New York: Winchester Press, 1975); and Thomas R. Dunlap, *Saving America's Wildlife* (Princeton: Princeton University Press, 1988).

16. See David C. Itzkowitz, *Peculiar Privilege: Social History of English Fox-hunting 1753–1885* (Sussex, England: Harvester Press), 1977.

17. See Merle Hoffman, "Do Feminists Need to Liberate Animals, Too?" *On the Issues,* Spring 1995, 18–21, 54–56.

18. Personal communication, December 1999.

19. Letter dated December 22, 1995.

20. Heidi Prescott, "How Hunters Make My Job Easy," Fourth Annual Governor's Symposium on North America's Hunting Heritage, August 28–31, 1995, Green Bay, Wisconsin, *Proceedings*, 108–12. (Available from Wildlife Forever, 12301 Whitewater Drive, P.O. Box 3401, Minnetonka, MN 55343.)

21. All quotations which follow are from the report as it was downloaded from the Fund for Animals website; the report was not paginated. Nor was its authorship specified. According to a Fund staff member reached by telephone in December 1999, the report was a collaborative effort "by the staff in general, probably about ten people." The woman at Fund named Norman Phelps, but emphasized that he was not the sole author.

22. Quoted in Mary Zeiss Stange, "Women in the Woods," *Sports Afield,* June 1995, 102.

23. Haraway, *Primate Visions*, 49.

24. Vera Norwood, *Made from This Earth: American Women and Nature* (Chapel Hill and London: University of North Carolina Press, 1993), 218. The following references to Norwood's book are all to chapter 7, "Women and Wildlife."

25. Norwood, *Made from This Earth*, 226.

26. Glenda Riley, *The Life and Legacy of Annie Oakley* (Norman: University of Oklahoma Press, 1994).

27. Glenda Riley, *Women and Nature: Saving the "Wild" West* (Lincoln and London: University of Nebraska Press, 1999), 129.

28. Alan Farnham, "A Bang That's Worth Ten Billion Bucks," *Fortune* (March 9, 1992): 81.

29. "Women's Participation in the Shooting Sports: Upward Trend Continues," NSSF Information Service, February 1995.

30. Farnham, "A Bang That's Worth Ten Billion Bucks," 81.

31. "Breaking Down the Barriers to the Participation of Women in Angling and Hunting," proceedings of the conference held at Treehaven Field Station on August 25, 1990, 15.

32. Robert M. Jackson, "The Characteristics and Formative Experiences of Female Deer Hunters," *Women in Natural Resources* 9, no. 3: 20.

33. Jose Ortega y Gasset, *Meditations on Hunting*, trans. Howard B. Wescott (New York: Charles Scribner's Sons, 1972), 110–11.

34. See Mary Zeiss Stange, "Hunting with a Difference: Do Women Make Better Hunters than Men?" *Bugle* 17:1 (January/February 2000): 69–75.

35. Mitchell, *The Hunt*, 67.

Notes and References to Abigail Kohn's *Cowboy Dreaming*

Acknowledgements. I would like to thank the following people for their assistance in lending ideas and reading drafts: Judith Barker, Jesse Dizard, Lynne Kohn, Carol Oyster, and Mary Zeiss Stange. I alone am responsible for any errors in this text.

Notes

1. Michael is a pseudonym.

2. Mary Zeiss Stange (1995) succinctly summarizes and challenges the literature that suggests women cannot effectively prevent their own victimization through gun use. Her position, which is also clearly articulated in the works of Kates (1997) and Kleck (1997), suggests that guns can be and are used to minimize and even prevent criminal victimization.

References

Kates, Don B., Jr. "Introduction, " in D. B. Kates, Jr., and G. Kleck, *The Great American Gun Debate: Essays on Firearms and Violence* (San Francisco: Pacific Research Institute for Public Policy, 1997).

Kleck, Gary. *Targeting Guns: Firearms and Their Control* (Hawthorne, N.Y.: Aldine de Gruyter, 1997).

Stange, Mary Zeiss. "Arms and the Woman: A Feminist Reappraisal," in David B. Kopel, ed., *Guns: Who Should Have Them?* (Amherst, N.Y.: Prometheus Books, 1995).

Notes to Chapter 5

1. Tom S. Nickas, "Miz August/September 1999 'Diamond Rose,'" *Trail's End Magazine,* August/September 1999, 34–35.

2. Indeed, in the face of potentially ruining handgun-related litigation, Colt Inc. announced in 1999 that they would cease production of most of their handguns, but would continue to produce firearms for single-action shooters. "The Gun That Won the West" in the nineteenth century may, ironically, be the same gun that saves the company in the twenty-first.

3. Single Action Shooting Society membership brochure. (Published by SASS, 1938 North Batavia Street, Suite M, Orange, CA 92865.)

4. Susan Laws, "Teens on Target in the New Old West," *Women & Guns,* September/October 1999, 34–35.

5. See Grits Gresham, "Women Take the Field," *Sports Afield,* May 1994, 50.

6. "Women's Participation in the Shooting Sports," National Shooting Sports Foundation Information Service, September 1998. Citing the NSSF as its source, an article in *Business Week* (June 2, 1997) placed the total of women sports shooters at 7.5 million, with an additional 2.5 million women hunting.

7. Michael McIntosh, "Women and Shooting," www.alloutdoors.com February 26, 1999.

8. Shari LeGate, WSSF executive director, telephone conversation, January 26, 2000.

9. On this report, see chapter 1.

10. Bob Herbert, "Targeting Women for Guns," *New York Times,* December 7, 1994, Op-Ed page.

11. WSSF press release, dated December 9, 1994.

12. Quoted in Resa King and Sandra Dallas, "What Do Women Want? Guns, Actually," *Business Week,* June 2, 1997, 91.

13. Riva Freifeld, "In Defense of Self and Family: Most Women Use Guns for Legitimate Reasons," *Human Events* 51:6 (February 17, 1995): 13–14.

14. See "Despite Reported Concerns, Junior Rifle Teams Thriving," *New Gun Week,* August 10, 1999, 15.

15. Megan O Matz, "Schools' Rifle Teams Come under Scrutiny," *Chicago Tribune,* Internet Edition, November 5, 1999.

16. "Chicago Schools Kill JROTC Riflery Program," *New Gun Week,* December 1, 1999, 1.

17. *Chicago Tribune,* November 5, 1999.

18. "Women Can Shoot," *American Rifleman,* June 1956.

19. Personal communication from J. B. Roberts, Jr., Community Service Programs Division of the NRA, December 16, 1999.

20. *American Rifleman,* June 1956.

21. Many Americans are unaware that shooting competitions are included in the Olympic games. As with all Olympic events, there are very specific requirements as to the acceptable equipment and the rules and regulations of the events. Safety is emphasized in all events—competitors are encouraged to wear ear protectors and shatterproof shooting glasses. The clothing allowed in rifle events is governed by a series of rules.

The three main types of shooting events are rifle, pistol, and shotgun. The rifle events include both smallbore rifle (using .22 caliber rifles) and 4.5mm air rifles. The air rifle competitions were introduced in 1984 because of extensive use of air rifles in training, low expense of ammunition, and ease of creating facilities. Men and women compete separately in smallbore events, which involve shooting from three positions: prone, standing, and kneeling. The 50-meter smallbore rifle targets consist of concentric rings (the largest of which is 6 inches in diameter) with a bullseye 4.1 inch in diameter. For the 10-meter smallbore event, the largest ring is 1.8 inches in diameter with a bulls-eye of only .01 inch across. The women competitors fire twenty shots in each of the positions in a time limit of an hour and a half. The eight top-scoring competitors from the preliminary round advance to a shoot-out final. In the air rifle competition, women shoot a preliminary round of forty shots in an hour and fifteen minutes at a target 10 meters away. The final consists of ten shots with a time limit of seventy-five seconds per shot in a standing position.

The women's air pistol competition uses 4.5mm pistols and allows an hour and fifteen minutes to complete forty shots. The women's rapid-fire sport pistol event involves a first round of thirty shots that must be fired within a time limit of six minutes per five-shot series. The rapid-fire series involves thirty shots with a time allowance of three seconds per shot. The targets are placed at a distance of 50 meters for free pistol and 25 meters for the rapid-fire competitions.

The trap and skeet events allow all types of smooth-bore shotguns that do not exceed 12 gauge. The targets for both events are saucer-shaped clay disks that are 4.3 inches in diameter (the use of live pigeons was discontinued early in the 1900s). The clays are launched from a pit for trap events at predetermined trajectories. They must fly 75 meters from the pit. For the skeet events, the clays are launched from two towers (the low and high houses). The shooting stations are set in a semicircle between the two houses. The preliminary round of the trap event involves shooting 125 targets in five series of 25 each. In the double-trap event (in which two clays are launched simultaneously), women shoot at 120 targets. In trap, double trap, and skeet, the top six shooters in the preliminary round advance to the finals.

For all events, the scores from the final shoot-out are added to the total from the preliminary, and the winner is determined by the highest point (number of clays hit) total. In the case of ties, a sudden-death, shot-by-shot tie-breaker is held. (*Source:* C. Searle and B. Vaile, eds., *The IOC Official Olympic Companion.* [London: Brassey's Sports & the International Olympic Committee, 1996].)

22. Ibid.

23. David Wallechinsky, *The Complete Book of the Olympics* (New York: Little, Brown, 1992).

24. Searle and Vaile, *The IOC Official Olympic Companion,* 343.

25. "Women Can Shoot," *American Rifleman*, June 1956, 20.

26. Ibid., 22.

27. "Shooting Champions. Lt. Gail N. Liberty," *American Rifleman,* May 1964, 12.

28. "Shooting Champions. Lucile W. Chambliss," *American Rifleman,* July 1960, 12.

29. "Lady Pistol Champ Baffles TV Panel," *American Rifleman*, April 1970, 12.

30. "Shooting Champions. Miss Lenore M. Jensen," *American Rifleman*, June 1961, 54.

31. "Shooting Champions. Marianne Jensen," *American Rifleman,* July 1963, 12.

32. Ibid.

33. Brian C. Sheetz, "High Power's Top Guns," *American Rifleman,* May 1999, 30–33, 65–66.

34. Ibid.

35. Nancy Norell, "Father-Daughter Hunting Helps Put Julia Watson in the Record Books at National Matches," *Women & Guns,* March–April, 1999, 30–33.

36. Melinda G. Bridges, "Behind These Women Champions . . . Are Men?" *American Guardian,* January 2000, 50.

37. Ibid.

38. NCAA Championships website: www.ncaachampionships.com/sports/rifle/99champ_results.html.

39. L. Meili, personal communication, January 11, 2000.

Suggestions for Further Reading

Cornum, Rhonda, as told to Peter Copeland. *She Went to War*. Novato, Calif.: Presidio Press, 1992.

Cottrol, Robert J., ed. *Gun Control and the Constitution: Sources and Explorations on the Second Amendment*. New York and London: Garland Publishing, 1994.

D'Amico, Francine, and Laurie Weinstein, eds. *Gender Camouflage: Women and the U.S. Military*. New York and London: New York University Press, 1999.

Dizard, Jan E., Robert Merrill Muth, and Stephen P. Andrews, Jr., eds. *Guns in America: A Reader*. New York and London: New York University Press, 1999.

Ehrenreich, Barbara. *Blood Rites: Origins and History of the Passions of War*. New York: Metropolitan Books, 1997.

Gordon, Margaret F., and Stephanie Riger. *The Female Fear: The Social Cost of Rape*. Urbana and Chicago: University of Illinois Press, 1991.

Heidensohn, Frances. *Women in Control? The Role of Women in Law Enforcement*. Oxford: Clarendon Press, 1992.

Jones, Ann. *Next Time, She'll Be Dead: Battering & How to Stop It*. Boston: Beacon Press, 1994.

Kates, Don B., Jr., ed. *Restricting Handguns: The Liberal Skeptics Speak Out*. Croton-on-Hudson, N.Y.: North River Press, 1979.

Kates, Don B., Jr., and Gary Kleck. *The Great American Gun Debate: Essays on Firearms and Violence*. San Francisco: Pacific Research Institute for Public Policy, 1997.

Kleck, Gary. *Targeting Guns: Firearms and Their Control*. New York: Aldine de Gruyter, 1997.

Kopel, David, ed. *Guns: Who Should Have Them?* Amherst, N.Y.: Prometheus Books, 1995.

Kopel, David, ed. *The Samurai, the Mountie and the Cowboy: Should America Adopt the Gun Controls of Other Democracies?* Amherst, N.Y.: Prometheus Books, 1992.

Lott, John R., Jr. *More Guns Less Crime: Understanding Crime and Gun Control Laws.* Chicago and London: University of Chicago Press, 1998.

McCaughey, Martha. *Real Knockouts: The Physical Feminism of Women's Self-Defense.* New York and London: New York University Press, 1997.

Metaksa, Tanya K. *Safe, Not Sorry: Keeping Yourself and Your Family Safe in a Violent Age.* New York: Regan Books/HarperCollins, 1997.

Morrow, Laurie, and Steve Smith. *Shooting Sports for Women.* New York: St. Martin's Press, 1996.

Nisbet, Lee, ed. *The Gun Control Debate: You Decide.* Amherst, N.Y.: Prometheus Books, 1990.

Price, Barbara Raffell, and Natalie Sokoloff, eds. *The Criminal Justice System and Women: Offenders, Victims and Workers.* New York: McGraw-Hill, 1995.

Quigley, Paxton. *Armed and Female: Twelve Million American Women Own Guns, Should You?* New York: St. Martin's Press, 1993.

Stange, Mary Zeiss. *Woman the Hunter.* Boston: Beacon Press, 1997.

Taffin, John. *Action Shooting: Cowboy Style.* Iola: Krause Publications, 1999.

Wright, James D., and Peter H. Rossi. *Armed and Considered Dangerous: A Survey of Felons and Their Firearms.* New York: Aldine de Gruyter, 1994.

Index

LadySmith revolver. *See* Smith &
Wesson
La Femme Nikita, 21, 23
Law enforcement. *See* Community
policing; Police protection; Women
in law enforcement
Lehrman, Karen, 26
Lorde, Audre, 34, 81, 229
Lott, John, 45, 96–97
Low-income women: at increased risk
for assault, 70, 86
Ludington, Sybil, 125, 246n. 34
Lueck, Diane, 161

Man the Hunter, 148–50, 153. *See
also* Hunting hypothesis of human
origins
Marine corps, 135, 217
Marinettes, 127
Martial arts training, 49, 82
McCarthy, Carolyn, 24
McCaughey, Martha, 82–83
McKellar, Susie, 28–29
Meili, Launi, 212, 216
Metaksa, Tanya, 3
Methodology in statistical report-
ing, 70
Military culture, 130–37
Mitchell, John, 156–57, 184–85
"Model Mugging" courses, 82
Mother Shoot (WSSF), 205
Ms., 33, 35, 39, 41
Murders, gun-related, 65
Mustard, David, 96

National Collegiate Athletic Association (NCAA) rifle competitions, 227
National Crime Survey, 68, 69, 70

National Crime Victimization Survey,
68, 69, 70, 71, 76
National Opinion Research Center, 28
National Organization for Women
(NOW), 123, 124
National Rifle Association, 3, 4–6, 23,
25, 30, 32, 33, 39, 64, 182, 198,
202, 211, 212, 213, 218, 246n. 34;
"Refuse to Be a Victim" program,
23, 25, 29, 39; Women's Issues and
Information Office, 23
National Shooting Sports Foundation,
23, 173, 205
*National Survey of Fishing, Hunting and
Wildlife-Associated Recreation,* 172
National Violence Against Women
Survey, 68, 69, 71, 76
National Women's Survey, 68, 69,
70, 71
NCS. *See* National Crime Survey
NCVS. *See* National Crime Victimiza-
tion Survey
New England Journal of Medicine, 24
News media, 3–6, 27, 54, 75, 209–10,
232; anti-gun bias, 3–6, 25–26,
210–11
Nichols, Margaret G., 157
Norwood, Vera, 168–69, 171
NOW. *See* National Organization for
Women
NRA. *See* National Rifle Association
NRA National matches. *See* Camp
Perry
NSSF. *See* National Shooting Sports
Foundation
NVAW. *See* National Violence Against
Women Survey
NWS. *See* National Women's Survey

Oakley, Annie, 22, 155, 170, 171,
219–20; her "ladyhood," 170, 220.
See also illustration 1
Olympic Games, 202, 212, 216, 217,
228, 253n. 21
Outdoors for Women, 158

Pacifism, 43, 50–51, 81, 124–25
Patrick, Brian, 4
People for the Ethical Treatment of
Animals (PETA), 160
Permits to carry, 40, 96–97. *See also*
Concealed-carry
Pitcher, Molly, 126
Pogrebin, Letty Cottin, 34–36, 41, 55
Police protection, 40–41, 52, 72,
78–80, 123, 125
Policewomen, 105–10, 115–122. *See
also* Women in law enforcement
Police work, firearms proficiency in,
110, 111
Predatory crime, 46–47, 51–52
Prescott, Heidi, 162, 163
Protective orders, 79
"Pseudopacifism," 124–25
Public health literature on guns,
66–67, 93

Quigley, Paxton, 3

Rape and sexual assault, 45, 47,
68–72; underreporting of, 69, 71;
women's fear of, 27, 37, 71–73
Rawlings, Marjorie Kinnan, 155
Recreational shooting, 24
"Refuse to be a Victim" program
(NRA), 23, 25, 29, 39
Rhode, Kim, 212

Rifles, 89, 173, 203
Riger, Stephanie, 27
Riley, Glenda, 170–71
Rocky Mountain Elk Foundation, 157,
161
ROTC, 131
Ruby Ridge, 24
Rural women, 70

SASS. *See* Single-Action Shooting
Society
"Saturday night specials," 86
School shooting programs, 208–11,
227–28
School shootings, 24, 198, 208, 211,
227
Second Amendment Foundation, 64
Second Wave feminism. *See* Feminism
Self-defense: armed, 33–36, 39–47,
62–63, 80–92, 96–98, 197, 206–7;
lethal-force, 24, 44–45, 81–84; un-
armed, 37, 83–84
Service academies. *See* Training acade-
mies, military
Seton-Thompson, Grace Gallatin,
155, 170
Sex-role stereotypes: female, 107–8,
123, 147, 215–16, 219; male, 107–8,
115, 119, 122–23, 147. *See also* Gen-
der stereotypes
Sexual harassment, in the military,
133–34, 138
Shields, Nelson, 64
Shotguns, 89, 110, 173, 203
Silko, Leslie Marmon, 48, 51–52, 54
Silver, Carol, 41
Single-Action Shooting Society (SASS),
199–201, illustration 11

About the Authors

Born and raised in suburban New Jersey, Mary Zeiss Stange had never been camping or fired a gun until she was over thirty. In college, at Syracuse University, she majored in English Literature, graduating Phi Beta Kappa in 1972; she subsequently earned master's and doctoral degrees in Religion and Culture Studies. She has taught English, Religion, and Women's Studies at several public and private colleges and universities. Since 1990, she has been an associate professor of women's studies and religion at Skidmore College, where for eight years she served as director of the Women's Studies Program. The author of *Woman the Hunter* (1997), as well as numerous scholarly and popular articles on topics ranging from women, hunting, and environmental ethics to issues like gun control and animal rights, Stange divides her time between teaching in upstate New York and ranching in Montana, where she and her husband Doug operate the Crazy Woman Bison Ranch.

Carol K. Oyster was raised primarily in Southern California and received her degree in Psychology from UCLA in 1970. After almost a decade moving through a progression of interesting employment situations, she returned to school at night to complete a master's degree in Counseling Psychology from Loyola-Marymount University in Los Angeles. Her final pre-academic job was as secretary to the Social Psychology division of the Psychology Department at UCLA, and her decision to pursue a doctorate in that area was based partly on encouragement from her supervisors. She received another master's degree and doctorate in Social Psychology from the University of Delaware.

She is currently employed as a Professor of Psychology and Women's Studies at the University of Wisconsin at La Crosse. Her expertise in research design and statistics has resulted in numerous publications and presentations in diverse areas of psychology. Her two textbooks, *Introduction to Research* (1987) and *Groups: A User's Guide* (2000), were written out of frustration with the existing materials available for students. She was recently appointed Research Director for *Women & Guns* magazine, which has allowed her research to move in the new direction exemplified in this book.